No Time to Cry

Vera Leinvebers

iUniverse, Inc.
Bloomington

No Time to Cry

iUniverse books may be ordered through booksellers or by contacting:

iUniverse
1663 Liberty Drive
Bloomington, IN 47403
www.iuniverse.com
1-800-Authors (1-800-288-4677)

ISBN: 978-1-4620-5844-0 (sc)
ISBN: 978-1-4620-5845-7 (hc)
ISBN: 978-1-4620-5846-4 (e)

Library of Congress Control Number: 2011919456

Printed in the United States of America

iUniverse rev. date: 10/24/2011

No Time to Cry

In loving memory of my late
MOTHER, FATHER, AND BROTHER.

Me after a recital

Astrological philosophy proclaims that
if you exist in this world among us,
it is because the world needs you.

*My family in happier times: Father, me ("Lara"),
"Lars" (my brother), Mother**

* *Please see note to readers and preface for an explanation of the
names "Lara" and "Lars," as used throughout this book.*

Contents

Me

Note to Readers

In order to remain true to the sensibility of my recollections, I have chosen to write this memoir by relating the significant events that I remember about my war-ravaged childhood, describing the ways these events would intrude, unbidden, upon my consciousness throughout the rest of my life.

My story begins in 1944, when I was a very young child—that was when my parents and I had to flee our beloved homeland, Latvia. At the end of the war I was only seven. I provide the time frame to give you some sense of chronology before you begin reading, but please understand that because of the extreme horror and trauma that I endured, I do not recall my childhood in terms of my age or specific years but, rather, in terms of the indelible images which those events etched into my memory.

As you read, please realise that the story may "jump" in time; this is because when I think back on those years, even now, my sense of time is inevitably fragmented—yet it is only by preserving that fractured sense of time in my narrative that I am able to honestly and authentically share my story. I ask you to keep in mind that the entire time of the war as I experienced it transpired in a very short span of time, chronologically—but it felt endless to me as a young child living through it. I recount that time in the same way that I recall it, and I also have tried to capture the way in which my memories literally burst into my consciousness, triggered by some ordinary happenstance like a thunderstorm. Similarly, the dialogue and interior monologue and thoughts that you read all reflect the language skills and thought processes that I possessed at the time when they occurred. I trust that your emotional intelligence will enable you to follow me as I retrace my journey, re-creating the semblance of a unified whole from the fragments of my memories and my fractured sense of time.

Finally, as further explained in the preface, I have chosen to call myself "Lara" for the purpose of telling my story, which I thank you for reading.

−VL

Preface

This is a story that I have wanted to share for some time, but finding a way to put it in words took tremendous effort. I owe my humble thanks to the people who helped me to survive the exodus from my homeland, as well as to those friends who gave me the encouragement and moral support to "walk" again through the sorrowful past by putting it on paper. It took a lot of courage and faith to survive those difficult wartime years, but it also took much love from those who reached out to me with that most sterling faculty: their emotional intelligence. This same faculty gave birth to this book. Just as I accepted their reaching out to me, now I hope that you—my readers—will accept my reaching out to you by sharing my experiences. I believe that emotional intelligence must be shared, so that we all can reach our full potential—as individuals and as humankind. Because you have chosen to read my story, I suspect that you share this belief ... by the time you finish reading, I trust that you shall.

From the cover and title page of this book, you already know that my name is Vera. I was a child in Latvia during World War II. Because returning to those devastating years of my war-torn childhood has been very difficult for me, I have chosen to call myself "Lara" and to call my brother "Lars" when telling my story. Every word, thought, and feeling that I relate in this memoir is true; I changed the names in order to give myself the separation I needed so that I could travel back in time, mentally and emotionally, and tell my story from the perspective I'd had as a little girl caught in the middle of the turmoil of the war. As I wrote—and as I remembered—it was almost as if I were holding the hand of that little girl, and helping her through it all. Thus, Lara and my childhood self, as well as the woman I was to become, all are one and the same; likewise for my recollections of my brother Lars.

Before I began the writing process of creating this memoir, all my memories of that abhorrent war coalesced into the nightmarish image of attackers abducting me from my own life and throwing me into a nest of the "living dead," by which I mean people who have followed a corrupting influence to destroy. The beautiful images of my idyllic early childhood turned to horrific ones in the passage of a seemingly single moment in time. Horror and trauma have the power to warp time in that way.

As a small child, I had never known that life could be ugly. I had only seen people working hard and earning the deserved rewards of their labours; they did not need, or choose, to waste time on self-deception, because they held the gift of life in far too high a regard. In that momentary shift from happiness to horror, I watched the trapped, the small, and the feeble suffer at the hands of their vicious attackers. I watched not as an observer, but as a witness—by that I mean that I felt compelled to react and, ultimately, to relate what I saw, as I do now in the pages of this memoir. Far too few of the victims of those attackers survived. As a witness, even though a child I intuitively knew that that would be the case. I came to think of the attackers not only as assassins but also as "living dead": they had allowed evil to corrupt them and destroy their sense of humanity, and that was what enabled them to murder the innocent. Thinking of the attackers in that way somehow helped me to survive. The theory was my own childhood invention—the attackers had deprived themselves of life by following the corrupting influence of evil, dying inside instead of heeding the prophecy of life and valuing its gifts. Although it was a childhood invention, as an adult, I marvel at both its wisdom and its resonance throughout the decades since.

Time has passed, and the wounds have healed, leaving scars that nothing can ever erase, not even time. Nevertheless, I now have a vision that I, in a small way, can encourage others to realise how fortunate we all are—and that we should count our blessings even on days when all is not the way we wish it might be. Because of my childhood experiences, I recognise that the world is full of other Laras who could use the helping hand of caring adults, and I hope that these youngsters find that caring and wisdom—and that those who can provide them will do so.

★ ★ ★ ★ ★

I'm sure you can recall the children's song about the tiny spider in the waterspout: that simple tune sends the timeless message that the sun always comes out again after the rain. The sun has always been there for me, but I did have to work hard to push the clouds away and to help the less fortunate do the same.

I believe that enduring challenging times causes our dispositions to change, enabling us to more effectively compare the outcomes of both malevolence and benevolence. Furthermore, I believe that such endurance, when successful, makes us stronger, wiser, and kinder. During my wartime childhood, when I suffered extreme physical and mental abuse at the hands of the attackers, I hid my tears from those assassins. I believe that, even in their moral stupor, realising how powerless they really were dismayed the living dead: they were not able to break the spirit of a little girl. Even if they did not recognise that, they did not break my spirit—and that was a victory, not just for me, but also for those who perished ... and, most of all, for humanity, which lives on.

As you will learn from my story, I am a concert pianist. My music has always sustained me, and I cherish that gift. In turn, I have devoted my time to share the treasure of music with those in need: I play for the terminally ill, and I taught myself music notation in Braille so that I can teach those who cannot see how to play music, not just listen to it.

The definition of happiness was difficult for me to understand when I was young, as that word had found no place during my journey, other than in my earliest memories, which the need to survive in the midst of daily chaos and horror had pushed to the very back of my mind. I have always believed that I am the luckiest person in the world because I survived such extreme trauma, misery, and turmoil. The assassins stole everything from me, including my emotions, but my courage and faith sustained me—and these will always strengthen me and help me work toward creating a better tomorrow. Now I believe that I will be content anywhere, even standing on a dime, because I put it there.

I invite you to join me as a traveller on the path of my war-ravaged childhood, a path that clearly proves that no matter how much one might suffer, when the goal is to survive there is simply "no time to cry."

—*VL*

1
Fallen Edifice

As I have described, I was a very young child ruthlessly thrown into the midst of a war that brought utter destruction and the gravest horror throughout Europe: this came to be known as World War II. Throughout my war-torn childhood, I frequently became so distraught with deep grief that my heart almost burst. Anyone observing me would have described me as a desolate-looking little girl who had to bear on my own the burden of keeping myself alive.

The attackers had stolen my childhood from me, as with other children in that time and place. Many times during those dreadful days, I would suddenly find myself identifying with others forced to share the same cruel fate; together, we walked the same ragged road of refugees. But those I found myself walking that road with were far older than I; though they certainly were no more deserving of the horror than I, they at least might have had some carefree and joyful years when they were young. Robbed of my childhood and thrown into cruel misery without their many years of experience and the wisdom it brings, I could not comprehend the chaos that swirled around me. All I could do was stand in the midst of it all, dazed and dumbstruck, as the same three questions echoed through my child's mind: *Why? Who? Where?* Now, as an adult, I wonder if those older people had any clearer understanding than I did at that time. Perhaps the enormity of such evil is beyond comprehension, and no wisdom exists that can make sense of it.

Regardless, I learned to deeply trust and believe in the goodness of my own heart, even while caught up in turmoil so great that I had to struggle constantly to keep my hope for better days alive. My hope and faith collided with harsh reality at every moment of every day, but I forced myself to hold onto my fast-fading memories of how my life had been before the nightmare began. ...

★ ★ ★ ★ ★

I was brought up in a home of abundance, where basic values and respect governed. My parents had acquired the means to maintain our standard of living, and they never doubted that as a result of their arduous efforts they would succeed. They taught me to respect hard work and integrity, and to value the gift of life above all else.

Images of my idyllic early childhood faded fast in the wake of horror, but I clung to them. They filtered across the screen of my mind's eye in wisps, like the threads of a gossamer web. Frequently I felt confused and frustrated to the point of righteous anger—although I didn't think of it that way as a child, of course—when I observed how easily malice could prevail in the midst of adversity. Again, I did not understand or even realise this, so much as I simply witnessed it and could not deny what I saw. I suppose the soul within me was vastly older than my chronological age at that time. Often I was so overwhelmed by my grief that I felt as if I should apologise for existing. In those moments, I struggled to value the gift of life, but my parents had instilled it so deeply within me that it prevailed in spite of everything around me—even in spite of my physical and emotional exhaustion. In the midst of such extreme havoc, it was the only way that I could deal with my circumstances. I was too young to contemplate the loss and evaluate the impact of the "fallen edifice" of society—the shock of the way in which social mores, standards, and behaviour had tumbled into the dust, leaving a trail of death and destruction.

The harsh winds of tyranny had swept across 1930s Europe, eventually closing in on the Baltic countries, tearing our flags to shreds, destroying our culture, scorching our land, and killing our people. As I struggled to survive in my native Latvia, the only thing that kept me alive was my love of life and my instinct for survival.

Most of the time, I had to be alone, pushed away and ignored, because the adults were so consumed by the attackers' invasion that they had no time to pay attention to my childish needs. I understand now that they did the best they could. As they fought for all of us to stay alive, keeping me physically safe was the best they could manage. Still, to me, the innocent child, it felt like physical pain had settled in every cell of my body. Sometimes I wondered what it would be like to dream again. I had dim memories of having dreamt once upon a time, but I had neither the will nor the time to dream during that horror. All I had left was the faith that I would survive the abuse we suffered at the hands of our attackers.

★ ★ ★ ★ ★

Gradually, I began to recognise the trees by their sounds—I had already completed intense instruction at the piano, and my acoustic ability was quite keen. These sounds often guided me through the darkness when I had no other means of finding my way. The cascading willow that reached down to the creek was the best hiding place; its soft sound caressed my ears like the most delicate harp. The stately pine, with its intoxicating fragrance, resisted the forceful wind, and its branches resonated like a cello or an oboe. The spruce whispered daintily like a flute, and the huge oak stood strong like a warrior, never submitting to any storm, its creaking like that of the bassoon. The chestnut tree was the tallest of them all, with clusters of blooms trying to reach the heavens; its sound alone reminded me of my beloved piano. The trees became my friends: I listened to them, and they helped me decide which direction would best enable my safe escape.

All those trees were destroyed by fire. Barren and scorched, they would never again sway in the breeze or invite the birds to perch and sing. The luxuriant vegetation that had once reached toward the sun was now gone, diminished to blackened sticks and stumps, and even ashes. The snow that used to sparkle was now covered with the footprints of an angry mob, and the birds' very shadows were afraid of themselves. The fragrance of the trees had been extinguished, and the magical sounds of their music had been silenced— forever, it seemed to me.

The fire was an act of brutality that had ravaged both my homeland and me. The dark clouds seemed to weep for me because I had witnessed such sorrow—and because my tears had run dry and I had no time to cry. I also felt, even then, that my life was like a beautiful song interrupted by brutality: a sharp and vicious staccato that had pierced a melody that, otherwise, would have been smooth and serene.

Throughout the hardships I had to endure, I cannot recall anybody trying to comfort me. I was completely on my own, pushed away and overlooked, even though, looking back, I recognise my parents did the best they could to ensure that we all stayed alive. In order to survive, I stayed in my own comfort zone of shadow and solitude, seeking refuge there by closing my eyes and covering my ears to escape from all the ugliness.

Vera Leinvebers

★ ★ ★ ★ ★

It was difficult not to find any answers to my endless questions; it would be many years before I understood that the adults were as unable to comprehend our situation as I was. How could a child whose only experiences up to that point had been of love and honesty and respect for all life come to terms with an enemy so insidious—with an evil so seductive that it warped those who formerly had seemed to be good people—that she could never be certain whom it was safe to trust? I learned that the only way to get through the day was by not asking any questions. Instead, I remained in my self-imposed seclusion—my refuge of solitude and silence—intuitively knowing, as only a child forced to grow up too soon can know, that nothing would ever be the same again.

With the grief born of that intuitive knowledge, I began to consider what I already had learned about my country and our people, realising that, strategically, the Baltic countries were geographically situated in a most favourable location for planning the operations of war both on land and sea. I knew that many invading forces had tested my native Latvia and our neighbouring countries many times throughout the centuries. The strength of the hardy people who dwelt along the Baltic Sea—who had never given up, and who had worked so hard, despite many risks and much abuse at the hands of conquering forces—had brought these countries onto the map of the world. Baltic resources, so rich culturally, historically, geographically, and agriculturally, kept these lands endlessly inviting to aggressors. As a result of such aggression, the history and literature of this region reflect suffering and strength, the combination of which leads to the ability to survive—as countries and as human beings. The folklore strongly states and reflects the abundance of the land and the people, in all forms of art; the creators of such art continued to express this, even as they struggled to survive during the wartime occupation.

Because I was but a child during the war, although I already had learned about some of my heritage, I did not—could not—know of the wealth of historical, cultural, and natural treasures awaiting my appreciation. Nevertheless, the attacking forces either stole or destroyed it all before my uncomprehending eyes. The Baltic countries were stripped of the bare necessities of life, yet the spirit of the people could never be broken. Even though I witnessed my beloved Latvia being turned into a wasteland, I simultaneously drew strength from the same land that had sustained my people for centuries. I bore witness, and now I write with that same strength, in tribute to my country—and to those who found the courage to fight, even if they perished in the process.

The tyranny, which had acquired its power through merciless force and used that acquired power so unjustly on the innocent, swept through the Baltic countries in the same way that it had swept through the rest of Europe. Throughout that fateful time, I had no idea it was to be the last summer I would spend in the country of my childhood, so cruelly stolen from me and so viciously destroyed, as the land itself was. Before long, fate would remove me to faraway places where only the screams of that sweeping tyranny remained, leaving in the wake of its brutal devastation nothing but scars.

I spent countless hours hiding where the shadows and silence gave me time to think about the turmoil—even after the war, I would think about it—and the only conclusion I could reach, the only sense I could make of all that senselessness, was that tyranny has no virtue. It cannot possibly have any virtue or any goodness. It does not have the courage or rightful means to build on the genuine values of hard work and justice and respect for life; it only has the means to destroy. It operates by the sheer dint of its power, accumulated by force—by brutality—not by right. The power acquired by war machines can only lead to ignominious defeat, as neither effort nor the ability to think is required to devastate the land or its people. Nothing daunts such an unthinking and thereby merciless juggernaut in its quest to convert culture and beauty—and life!—into rubble, ashes, and dust.

I witnessed the result of the actions of tyranny and its turbulent mob. I was too young to express myself in words—and who was there for me to talk to, anyway? How could I, a mere child, find words to describe what I felt and what I witnessed? The music of my childhood swirled in a deafening cacophony, and I wondered if I would ever hear beautiful sounds again.

As I explained, my intuition enabled me to sense the gravity of the situation, and so I realised that tyranny never has any creative ideas or plans for development of higher standards of living, because tyranny does not value life. On the contrary, I saw that tyrannical actions not only proved costly for the victims but also worked to the detriment of that tyranny's own long-term existence. Again, I cannot really describe how I knew this, other than to say that, somehow, I just knew. With disgust, I saw the tyranny in my child's mind as a mammoth monster, and I imagined that monster's brain devouring itself through its own insatiable greed. This vision helped me to survive, because I knew that evil would not prevail.

Unfortunately, tyranny, on its journey to power, which destruction and terror facilitate, manufactures malice and feeds on fear and prejudice, to the detriment of many innocent people. The fallacies that it promulgates eventually result in its digging its own grave, but not before the innocent suffer catastrophically—the horror inherent in the system of tyranny inevitably does collapse, but never without devastation.

Those who suffer such circumstances, in whatever capacity and to whatever degree, cannot escape without the deepest scars. Even now, after a lifetime spent living in Canada, far from the war in both distance and time, I still struggle to find the answers and reasons for my past experiences. It has been endlessly painful to remember the days of torment. Many times I wondered why I was chosen to live. Was it to relive every painful moment? Was it to capture and record my memories, so that I could share them with others—so that the world will never forget, and never repeat, such evil? Perhaps I will never know; but, by telling and sharing my story, perhaps I will come closer to knowing.

I have since met others who have endured similar brutalities of war; their scars, like my own, are so deeply embedded in their souls that we do not need words to recognise one another. Our silence, our discreetly uttered sighs, and our facial expressions all speak volumes; we communicate more meaningfully than mere words could ever allow us to, whether with one another or with others whom we encounter.

Let me elaborate on this before you read the rest of my story. As an adult, I could find contentment just by looking at a panorama of healthy trees, finding such peace and serenity—and, yes, quiet joy—in watching those trees as they swayed in the breeze, kissing the sun and welcoming the birds, as trees are intended to do, not marred and scorched by the scourge of war. I was able to hear the natural music again. I often thought about people who have not had to experience the cruelties and demoralisation of war and conquest; always I wondered if they took the time to notice the infinite beauty of nature and freedom and to recognise the sensitivity of their balance—and also whether they realised the responsibility we all have for ensuring their continuing existence.

I wondered—and still do—if they taste a piece of bread the same way I do, and if they marvel at the potato the way I still do. I remember the one I dug up in the field. Ravenous, I ate it raw, grateful for the sustenance. That potato was of inestimable value to me in my hunger— it held the power of life for me—yet I shared it with my beloved mare, Lolo, so that we both might live, even if only for one more day. Every day is precious, especially when you know it might be your last. No matter how difficult, vicious, cruel, or violent the times were, I always shared—simply because I knew all too well how it felt to be hungry to the point of true starvation. And, yes, I still find bread and potatoes every bit as magical as they were all those years ago; and I still share whenever I see the need.

In the midst of that horror, I could recall glimmers of my early childhood, and I remembered my parents' generosity to others, which left an indelible mark on my character. I have never strived to accumulate possessions for my own comfort; instead, I have always believed that it is more important to help and give to others, especially those closest to me. I can still feel the shock and horror of watching my brother and many other young men forced to sacrifice their lives in the combat that brought such destruction and devastation across all of Europe.

I took refuge in solitude and silence, wondering what it would be like to dream. I had dreams as a very young child, of course, but in the midst of horror, I could no longer dream. I wondered, but I found no answer—all I could do was long for the chance to dream again and to experience the outcome of but one dream. Once I emerged from the nightmare of war, I was free again—to speak, to plan, to hope, and even to dream—but my only wish was that, somehow, all wars could be erased, as if they had never happened ... and would never happen again.

2
Knock On the Door

The typical city noises of Toronto had faded, and daylight would soon follow suit. I was looking forward to the weekend, because it meant I would be free of all responsibilities. Having finished my usual weekly workload, I was now free to do as I liked; I could spend some time in the garden, read the books that I had set aside, or simply enjoy the quiet.

While it was still light enough to read, I decided to do all three things I anticipated enjoying: spend some time in the garden, read one of the books I'd set aside, *and* enjoy the quiet, all at once. I picked up a book that had lately kept me in great suspense, determined to read as much as I could before dusk.

The misty twilight wrapped me in a blanket of tranquillity. All was quiet. The magic of the twilight hour took hold of me as it always did, and I let myself sink into its soothing embrace. With each passing minute, the shadows grew longer. The twilight deepened to dusk, and the garden appeared to have dozed off, yet it still dispersed its fragrance all around me.

I placed my book on the small table beside me and closed my eyes in order to better soak up the tranquillity. I was alone, and in that precious moment the glory of nature made me feel almost dizzy. Breathing in the intoxicating scent of nature, I wondered if I was to remain by myself to enjoy it all. My hand rested on a page of the last chapter; my arm was extended but not strained. The air moved above it pleasantly—just a flutter, but enough for me to feel the change. My sensitivity to nature's nuances had not abated in the years since my childhood. Because of all the years I had spent as a pianist, my hands and fingers were particularly sensitive. As I felt the air lightly brush over my hand and arm, I opened my eyes just in time to see a bird fly over the treetops back to its nest. Next to the book, a small snail had started to emerge from its shell and move toward my hand. Nature had answered my wondering: I was not to remain alone this evening, as little *Helix aspersa* had chosen to be with me.

My wondering continued. Did the little garden snail want to tell me its story? Was it a metaphor for my own story? Could I share my story with this tiny creature? After all, we each stayed inside our shells, seeking to protect the tender parts of ourselves, the parts we sought to nurture and guard from pain.

As I watched the little marvel near the edge of my hand, I empathised with its trepidation and its courage. After all the years of hiding many dark feelings so deeply in my heart, had the time come to share them? Would they cease to surface, unannounced and unbidden, if I shared them? If I gave voice to my feelings about those gruesome days of my childhood, would I be able to emerge from the dark abyss of my past? Would I be free of it at last? Looking at the hard shell protecting the snail's delicate body, I felt as if I finally had a kindred spirit who would be able to endure listening to my painful story. I'd always been reluctant to burden anybody; it took so much strength and compassion to share the deep grief of another person. Little *Helix aspersa* however, had a shell into which it could retreat if need be. I had my own shell for exactly the same purpose; mine was invisible but every bit as strong.

It turned quite dark as I pondered, and the damp air brought me back to the days I had faced during my escape. I had been a young child— merely six years old—but those days were still very much alive in my memory, etched so sharply that memories were frequently more vivid than the present moment. The emotional and psychological wounds that I had sustained as a result of those traumatic events were deep enough that I could still feel them still bleeding deep inside me—deeper than the deepest part of my body. They bled in my soul.

Maybe that was the reason why I felt best in solitude, where I did not have to show how torn apart I really was or how I had learned to piece myself together and go through life as a sort of "patched" person. My heart and soul had been shattered, but I had managed to reassemble them. Still, I was not completely whole; the delicate seams of my repairs were always in danger of coming apart again. It took great daily effort to appear whole when the core of me was a mass of shreds that I kept together through sheer will. People who have not endured deep trauma do not, and cannot, understand what it is like to bear this burden or how much energy it takes to hold oneself together; doing so doesn't just "happen" as it should, and does, for most people.

Maybe I felt best in solitude simply because I did not want to burden others with the pain of my story. I had often told myself that I would never recover if I kept reliving the story by retelling it—even though I could not possibly forget. Ever. More to the point, I had never felt it necessary to analyse my own feelings—I had never had the luxury of time that required, either. All I could do was just keep going, doing the best I could every day, hoping that my efforts and good intensions would change the lives of others in a constructive and positive fashion, especially if any of them would have to face hardships. I prayed that no matter what hardships others might have to face, they would not be as horrific as the ones that I had faced so many years ago during my war-torn childhood.

I took comfort that, despite having been such a young child during the war, my reminiscences were not entirely about the awful things I'd had to endure. All those wonderful and carefree days before the darkness enveloped us also came to mind: the times when I could remember the adults around me facing life with strength and gladness. Every moment had not been happy or pleasant, of course—having been so very young, I could not remember every single detail of day-to-day life—but I could remember how people had faced life's surprises and challenges and the amusements they had employed in order to do so. I smiled, recalling harmless, pleasant mischief, but even the rogues in our midst had never visited actual cruelties upon their neighbours.

As the evening wore on the dampness deepened. I shivered, more from my memories than any chill in the air. It was still summer in Canada, where the climate was similar to that of my native Latvia. My recollections began to drift back to the winters of my childhood, happy reminiscences of that golden time before the nightmare began.

★ ★ ★ ★ ★

Baltic winters could be very demanding, to say the least. The temperature would drop mercilessly, and heavy snowfall was typical. Even on the days when all that was visible were rooftops and smoking chimneys, the daily rituals of life went on as usual. Life could be very challenging, but the people did not think much of it. They kept performing their daily duties, as everybody was used to the winter climate. The predictable extreme cold and abundant snow were normal conditions of our lives, and we accepted them as such, adjusting to them without undue effort as autumn turned to winter each year. This ability was a part of me, and I suppose it later helped me find a way to somehow endure the unendurable. I breathed deeply as I sat in my garden, wishing to focus on the happier times.

On those wintry days when the roads seemed to disappear beneath the deep blanket of white snow, horse-drawn sleighs replaced cars. Children would ski to school. Some days were so cold that the very words we spoke seemed to freeze in the air. Horses, bells on their harnesses, were covered with colourful blankets that kept the animals warm. People would bundle up in their warmest coats for sleigh riding. The bells on the horses' harnesses would ring through the crisp, cold air. During blizzards and snowstorms those same bells served as warnings to the other travellers. Many times it became a challenge to reach one's destination, but that was just the way of life for people in the Baltic countries.

I continued to derive comfort from thinking of those cold, snowy days, which were always warmed by the people's goodwill toward one another. My fond recollections drifted to my school days. I'd never missed a day of school, in sunshine or storm. We girls always received refreshments upon our arrival, regardless of the weather, six days a week. Morning prayers followed refreshment time. One hundred girls would gather in the large assembly room, with me at the piano.

I'd never had a chance to take part in either gymnastics or plays, because I had to play the piano for all the activities at school. That was all right, though—I so loved my music! Besides, my parents enrolled me in ballet, which I also loved.

I could still recall with great joy the day that I first wore a white tutu. I was playing a cygnet in *Swan Lake,* and I absolutely adored my role. In later years, I came to understand the reason why it was such an engaging experience: it merged my deep loves of nature and music. I would actually imagine that I *was* a little cygnet, right down to the flying. While attempting the *grand battement,* convinced that I was a little cygnet, I suddenly discovered that I couldn't really fly after all. On the stage floor, I ended up more of a gosling, but the entire experience was a positive one, and I always remembered it with sheer delight.

The Baltic winters were harsh indeed, but even that harshness held the kind of raw beauty that one can always find in nature. The beauty of summer was every bit as natural, of course, but softer. The heady fragrance from the luscious gardens and orchards filled the summertime air. The warm, soft breezes always seemed to carry laughter and songs over the whole countryside. As summer gave way to fall, the fields would turn into a golden sea, farmhands harvesting the crops while singing joyous songs that echoed through the valleys.

In the fall the brook near my childhood home would overflow. In the winter it all would freeze, turning the meadow into a spacious, crystalline sea that shimmered on sunny days. It was there that I learned to ice skate. My father had been a figure and speed skater, and he started to teach me some basic skating skills. There were plenty of slopes nearby, motivating me to learn to ski also, which was good, as this would become the necessary mode of transportation to school on days when the snowstorms swirled around us.

My beloved Latvia was a land of hard work and cherished dreams, which, all too soon, an invasion of brutality would shatter.

My happy recollections ended with that thought, which then focused on one long-ago winter's night that I remember too well—the fateful night when my life changed forever, when everything turned dark and horrible.

It was a very cold and snowy Christmas Eve. The snow had already fallen for many hours, with no end in sight. A thick blanket of white covered the ground, and all the trees were encrusted with snow. The trees appeared to be in deep slumber, as if waiting for spring to come. The first burst of warm air would rouse the still-sleepy trees, which would not awaken fully until the birds began to sing, building their nests once again in the trees' branches.

What a joyous time spring will be! I pressed my eyes shut, filled with happiness at the mere thought of it. Opening my eyes, I looked out the window to see that we were snowed in. *Only Santa will be able to get through, but that's all right.*

The sun was gently setting, caressing our town in its glow and leaving a golden trail all along the blanket of deep snow. My young eyes filled with tears, and I wished I could follow the magical trail of fading sunshine—perhaps I might find a land of peace and happiness at the end of it. Even at such a tender age, my visions of Santa began to vanish. I could not understand why so many of my friends had to leave their homes, never to return. They were lost forever, I knew. I missed them so much. Maybe there was a place where there were no tears and no loud screams. As the last of the sun disappeared and the trail of gold faded into the descending darkness, I knew that if there was such a place, it was far, far away.

Night fell with a quiet sigh from the snow-laden trees. The first stars began to wink, and I strained to see them twinkle amidst the falling snow. I wished with all my might that one of those stars was mine. Yes, my very own little star that would look for my brother, Lars. My star would help me find the beautiful, peaceful place—Lars and I could go there, and we would be allowed to laugh and sing and be happy, and nobody would come and hurt us. Ever. I thought of my missing friends, pressed my eyes shut again, and whispered, "There is a star for each one of you! Just reach for it, wherever you are." I opened my eyes and scanned the sky, choosing the smallest, most well-hidden star for my own. It was so small that only happiness could fit on it, and no bad people could ever find it.

The endless snowfall had turned my world into a wonderland. It kept snowing and snowing. I was amazed that the sky could offer so much of it. There was no sign of the road anymore. Our housekeeper, Anda, had made a path to the storage house at the back of the garden. Anda, who was making the preparations for Christmas Eve dinner, had help with all her chores that evening. Greta, an excellent cook, had been baking for days, and she'd also made bouillon and prepared the whole menu with great care, under Anda's supervision. Now and then Greta would run to the storage house for some additional ingredients to complete her recipes. By then the path was surrounded by a solid high wall of snow. Every time Greta came back into the house, she shook the snow off her cape, went back to the stove, and resumed her cooking, the procured ingredients at the ready.

Plates with gingerbread and all sorts of other cookies were placed on a special table near the Christmas tree. I admired how tall and fragrant the tree was with all the decorations and candles that covered the evergreen branches. The tree so enchanted me, I all but forgot about the cookies. How I wished that Lars could see the tree!

That Christmas, only Father, Atis (Anda's husband), and I had gone to the woods to bring home the tree. The roads were packed with snow, and so the tree had to be drawn home by horse, which was how Lolo, the horse from our farm, came into the picture. She looked so honoured performing the special duty. I never forgot to reward my beloved mare for all her hard work: I always gave her a few sugar cubes, followed by a big, tender hug. Lolo also got an extra cup of oats and was put into her shed to rest for the night.

The hours passed, but not fast enough for me. I waited with such longing to light the candles. That had always been the highlight of the evening for Lars and me. We would have a sort of "race" to see which one of us could light the most candles. The year before I could only reach the lowest branches; but this year, if I went up on my toes, I could easily light the candles on the two levels of branches above the lowest ones—if I used the long matches.

I swallowed back my tears, imagining what Lars would say if he were here: "Look at you, Lara! My little sister has gotten so big!" I lit one special candle for Lars. Its flame seemed much brighter and warmer than the others, and I basked in its glow, feeling how proud my brother would be of me.

Atis lifted me so I could put the angel on the treetop. She looked so lovely in her shimmering white dress, grasping the wand in her hand. With the angel atop the tree, all the preparation was done, and we each went to our rooms to dress for the evening. A very special dress had been made especially for me to wear that Christmas. It was white as a cloud and sprinkled with tiny stars. I put it on, adding the sparkling white socks and shiny new black shoes that completed my grand appearance, and then I looked at myself in the mirror. Again, I wished that Lars could see me.

Just then, in came Mikus, my big cat. I picked him up, holding him close to me, and twirled around and around. This made Mikus feel very special and mischievous, and he started to play with my hair. Anda knocked on the door, interrupting our little dance, and led us both downstairs. Mother came down, looking regal in her rose-coloured dress. Father looked so handsome in his dinner jacket. *If only Lars were here!*

I looked at the angel, and deep in my heart I felt that this was going to be a very special Christmas Eve. I'd always loved that magical moment when the spirit of Christmas filled our home, but now I waited for it with inexplicable reservation, even though I felt that this Christmas would be so special. I did not, and could not, know why or how this Christmas would be so special—or so different, yet I sensed that it would be exactly that.

The air felt heavy all of a sudden, as if dark clouds were closing in, choking off the air and changing the whole room into some sort of frightening hollow. I found it harder and harder to breathe, even though I could not understand why.

As I have described, this was the night when everything so abruptly changed for the worse. But I had no idea that would be the case; I only knew what I felt but could not understand. I was immersed in the unbearable uncertainty of that desperate time. Because I was so young, I did not know that what I was feeling was uncertainty. Needless to say, I could not possibly begin to know how to deal with it—I only felt that I couldn't breathe.

The times had changed somehow; I knew that much. Many memories flooded me that Christmas Eve in the suddenly changed and disturbing atmosphere. Countless occasions came to mind, all at once, like a never-ending film that I tried to stop but couldn't. Much tension had mounted inside me, which I had not released because I did not know how to do so. I didn't know how to ask for help. Everyone around me was very sad and preoccupied all the time. All those thoughts kept racing back and forth, and all the while I hoped that time would pass faster. I felt that an ill omen had invaded our home, and that it was taking away all our happiness.

Lars's long absence came to mind. Mother had cried a lot, and some people had followed Father, bursting into our home, searching all the rooms roughly, and going away very angry. That had happened not once but many times. On those days I just silently prayed that the bad people would not take my pianos or my books or my cat—my goodness, I could not even bear the thought of losing Mikus.

One day I saw Father give some money and his watch to a man. The day that Mother wore her pearls, one of the bad men ripped them off her neck. All the pearls fell on the ground and hid in the pile of the heavy rug. Mother stood motionless from fear. The intruders went toward the door, and as they were about to leave, they noticed me holding onto Mother's skirt. One of them hit my face with his heavy glove. I stood silent but kept looking straight in his eyes. My heart ached, burning with the righteous desire to demand of them, "Who gave you such cruel dispositions? Who gave you the power to think you have the right to scare my mother?" Yet, even at such a tender age, I had already learned that these were the times when one kept silent, holding all questions and opinions within. Finally the horrid men left, ugly grins contorting their faces as they slammed the door behind them.

I recalled many sad moments while trying to make the time pass faster so that the long-awaited magic of Christmas could begin. Those sad times had happened, but now it was Christmas Eve! The big snowstorm had turned the outdoors into a wonderland, and surely at least some magic would have to creep inside too. I further reasoned: *The mean, bad people will not be able to find us—not in all this snow!*

I held Mikus close to me and looked up at the angel on top of the tree. *Let this be a wonderful and peaceful night,* I wished silently. *Just one more Christmas, please, Angel. And let Lolo and Mikus always be with me and never go away!* That was all I wished for. I had known so many people who simply had disappeared. Vanished. I wondered why the happy days had gone away, all those lovely summers at the farm. As I began thinking about various occasions, my mind raced from one place to the other, but that was still far better than just waiting and waiting.

I looked at the angel; she must have been reading my thoughts, because she seemed to smile. It felt so good to see her smile, and for a moment I was not afraid anymore. The disturbing feeling faded, and it felt easy to breathe again.

I thought of a really funny story that I could never forget. It had happened during the summer when I'd visited my animal friends at the farm. Father had three mighty guard dogs whose job it was to make sure that his farm equipment was safe.

Nero was big and furry, with a short, stubby tail. He resembled an overgrown teddy bear, which made him easy to hug. Every morning I would brush his teeth with my own toothbrush. Mother did not agree that this was a good idea, but what was I to do? Nero had no toothbrush of his own! The two of us managed to sneak away to ensure Nero's proper dental care. Another one of the three dogs was Mister Speckle, the Dalmatian who had more spots than I could count and who willingly let me take my naps in his doghouse. Big Bruto, the third dog, was most likely the biggest—and nicest—German shepherd in the entire world. He always waited for me to wash his face.

All three dogs were my best friends, and they enjoyed my attention immensely, especially when I rewarded them with a sausage. They certainly showed their appreciation for the reward, standing on their hind legs and putting their paws on my shoulders. I was so small that my nose would touch their chests when they stood that way. I would rub my nose against their chests. Oh, how they loved that! I remembered the loud noise of all four of us flopping onto the grass—with me laughing happily and the three of them barking happily—followed by all three of them licking my face simultaneously. What fun that had been! The adults were petrified, assuming the dogs had attacked me. When two of the adults rushed to rescue me, they were almost eaten alive. The dogs definitely did not like that interference! I was the only friend they ever wanted. I treasured that happy, funny memory all the more now.

I tried to remember more precious moments like that one, feeling that the time had started to move faster. The dinner bell rang, breaking the spell. It was time to light the candles on the table. The crystals of the large chandelier cast beautiful rainbows, making the ceiling look like heaven.

All were seated, and Greta started to serve her wonderfully prepared dinner. Mikus found a comfortable spot at my feet; he knew that I would share delicious goodies with him, yet I was very careful not to attract anybody's attention. However, it was Christmas, and so no one would mind my giving Mikus treats.

It took forever to finish the dinner, it seemed to me. I became impatient. The tree was waiting for me! Finally the moment arrived, and everybody gathered around the tree, beneath which lay some beautifully wrapped gifts. Even Mikus noticed them and dove in to explore. I went to his rescue, but he had already managed to become tangled up in the ribbons.

The large grandfather clock that stood in the corner was in no hurry to move faster. Finally, and ever so proudly, it announced the magic hour: eight o'clock! All gathered around the Christmas tree, which looked delighted to be in the centre of the important night. The candles radiated lovely warmth, and it really started to feel like Christmas. All my concerns and disturbing feelings had disappeared completely; this was real happiness that we were feeling. *Please let it last forever, Angel!*

For me, the room was like a starlit heaven. In a moment the carols would fill the room, with me at the piano. As soon as I went toward the piano, Mikus raced to get there first and jumped up on the bench. I took my seat, and we both were ready to begin. As I played, everyone sang along, and soon carols echoed through the whole big house. They had been carefully chosen to set the sombre mood of the particular Christmas, when nobody knew for sure what would happen tomorrow—or if there would even *be* a tomorrow. Near the end of the last carol, I could hardly wait to play the final chord. The music filled me; I knew my eyes were shining as brightly as little stars—that's what the adults always said about me when I played. I just wanted to feel happy, even for only a moment.

I could not know how brief that moment would be—or how quickly my happiness would end.

After I'd played the last chord, all became so still that we could hear Mikus purring. There was an unexpected sound outside the window: very heavy footsteps—so heavy that the snow seemed to cry beneath them.

We heard a weak knock at the door. For a moment we thought it was the wind bouncing the shutters against the outside wall. But then somebody rang the chimes. The ring was ominous, not at all like it used to sound. Again came a knock, followed by the chimes, and then another knock.

I looked at the angel, begging silently but with all my heart, *Please don't let them take me away!* All I wished for was one more Christmas.

I rushed to Mikus, who had purred himself to sleep, grabbed him, and held him close, wanting to escape—but from what? I still was not sure where all the danger and uncertainty came from, or why we were in the midst of it.

Anda went to open the big oak door, and the cold air rushed into the room. For a moment there was absolute silence. In the doorway stood a tall person in a soldier's uniform. It was dark and not easy to distinguish his features; all I could make out was a very pale face filled with pain.

I stared for a moment longer, and then my heart jumped into my throat. It was Lars!

He was too weak to speak. At the time, I could not completely understand it all, but when I think back on that fateful night, I imagine that he had measured a long and fearsome road, sorrowfully parting from his fallen companions, covering them with a deep layer of snow, bidding them a final goodbye, and praying that they rest in peace for all eternity.

The claws of terror must have dug deep into Lars's heart. He had gathered his last bit of strength to get as far as the door of our home. The vision of coming home was all he had left. Leaning against the door, he had fallen back into the snow. He had struggled up again, trying to reach the bell, but his arm bled so profusely that he had fallen again. The large snowflakes had covered his burning face, soothing his pain. He'd heard the singing from inside the house, and, for a moment, he felt no pain. He'd tried to get up once more. *Just one more step, and I will be home!* Lars must have thought. Just then the door opened, and the Christmas lights warmed his heart. He was home. At last.

I wasn't old enough to fully comprehend all that my brother must have endured on his homeward trek. I looked from the door to the angel, certain that she was giving me a sign. "Go and greet the visitor, Lara," she seemed to say. The angel, too, could see that it was Lars! I ran toward my brother, put my arms around him, and whispered, "Thank you, Angel, for bringing my brother back."

I held onto Lars tightly, closing my eyes and wishing that the moment would never end. Then I felt something warm running down my dress. *My goodness! It's blood—my brother's blood!* In that instant, even as a small child I knew that neither storm nor danger could have kept Lars from coming home for Christmas.

Slowly Mother went toward him, tears running down her face. She seemed afraid to break the spell of the moment by speaking. She put her arms around Lars, leading him toward the ottoman, and they both sat down. Mother held Lars close enough to feel and hear his heartbeat. I watched them, somehow sensing that Mother would want to remember that feeling and that sound for the rest of her life: her son had come home to say good-bye forever.

Still it continued to snow. Lars had left a trail of blood leading to the house. Despite the pain, he had kept walking until he reached home. However, the sorrowful reunion did not last long. There was another knock at the door; this knock was not weak but infused with malice. The vicious men in their uniforms had come back, their faces still full of hate and ignorance—with the exception of one who was young and seemed scared; he had a big scar right across his face, and he kept looking at the Christmas tree.

I wondered who those men really were and why they would cause such harm—why they would even *want* to hurt people so badly. They took my almost-lifeless brother at gunpoint, not even allowing him to say goodbye, dragging him off and leaving the door open. I ran to the door, and Lars looked back to see me reach toward him as he disappeared into the dark, snow-swirled night. I could see the young soldier—the scared one who'd kept staring at our Christmas tree—run in the opposite direction, but it was too dark to see anything else. All I heard was a shot.

Not only did everything around me change forever that night, as

I've already explained, but everything within me also changed forever. A piece was ripped away from my heart, torn off completely, and my happiness was buried alive beneath inconsolable grief.

The grandfather clock struck ten. I took one last look at the angel on top of the Christmas tree. My heart was filled with gratitude for her having brought Lars back for Christmas Eve, and I silently pleaded with her to keep him safe. All the lights were turned off now. It was very dark inside the house, and the harsh wind kept banging the shutters. I covered my ears, thinking I could hear my brother's cries. For a moment I could not breathe, and I ran upstairs to my bedroom, collapsing on my bed and pulling the blanket over me so that I would not hear or see anything. I lay that way for a while; I cannot say how long.

The house was filled with darkness and silence. Everybody had already gone to their rooms. I got out of bed and stood for a while in the middle of the room, just staring out the window. The snowstorm had stopped at last, and the sky was clear. The stars were high in the sky, twinkling as they told their story to the moon. Did they share the story of my Christmas Eve? Had they witnessed my sorrow? I'd never noticed how bright the moon was before that night.

I felt so drained that I couldn't look any longer, and I went back to bed, falling asleep from sheer exhaustion. In my dreams I saw Lars, and I gave him the Christmas present I'd gotten for him: a little heart with an inscription that said, "Thank you for coming home for Christmas."

The events of that Christmas Eve did change everything, but time never stops. Spring still followed winter, but that spring would be without the fragrance or colour of the flowers, without the song of the birds; everything was so empty and so desolate because of the brutality of the war.

I never stopped believing in miracles. *One day Lars will come home, there will be happiness again, and nobody will take it away!* I let the words resound through my mind, believing in them fiercely. This strong feeling eluded any precise definition. I was far too young to define it, per se, or even to articulate how I felt. All I knew was that that feeling— the faith that happiness would return—was real and strong, and it dwelt deep within me. It was essential to keeping me alive. I knew it without knowing how I knew; I had begun to gain the uncanny wisdom that I've described as developing in children whom trauma forces to grow up too soon. The fact remains that the phenomenon of faith protected me; it kept me from becoming desolate and filled with despair, and it nurtured me, enabling me to be strong enough to live through the next day. Like little Helix aspersa, I, too, had developed a shell; however, mine was made of faith and music, and no one but I could see it or even know that it existed.

None of the wrapped presents beneath the Christmas tree were opened, but I treasured the little inscribed heart for Lars. It took time for me to fully comprehend the gravity of our situation, let alone the reason for all of it and all that would follow. I didn't comprehend it then, but I did feel that nothing would ever be the same again. I suspect the adults around me felt almost as lost as I did. And, intuitively, I knew that survival was in the hands of each person, no matter how young or how old. We each had to fight to survive. Alone.

★ ★ ★ ★ ★

The painful memories were etched deep within me; I watched their horrific images flash across the screen of my mind's eye countless times during the years that passed after the war. That night in my garden in Toronto, the sight of *Helix aspera's* shell did remind me of my own shell, did cause me to think about sharing my story with another who could empathise without being destroyed by the pain that I would unleash. But I could not say what it was, exactly, that had called forth the memories. My memories intruded, without warning or welcome, haunting my sleep and my waking hours. I could neither predict nor stop their arrival.

That night in the garden, after all the years that had passed, the visions of that long-ago horror sprang to life, as vivid and as harsh as when I'd lived through the actual moments as a child. The cruel lessons of learning how to stay alive flooded my mind. Most of the time, as young as I was, I'd been all alone, with nobody to tell me what to do or teach me the next step. I'd had to learn all about the bitter fight for life—the struggle for survival—all by myself.

More scenes from the past became vivid as I sat in the garden that night. As always, they were set off by some ordinary incident I experienced in daily life, working or watering the flowers in the garden; reminders were hidden everywhere. I will never know what, specifically, had triggered my memories that night. Nonetheless, the floodgates had opened, and I was helpless to stop the surge of images that surged through my mind.

I recalled that I had never been allowed to stay home and watch the war rage through the window. I had to attend school and seek provisions. The shortest walk could be full of danger, and the uncertainty and daily effort of staying alive became an enormous and constant challenge.

I learned soon enough that if I had to run, I should first look back and make sure that there was room to retreat. That was wisdom my father, who had been an officer in the army in his younger days, taught me. Often I was separated from my parents, and I had to make important decisions quickly—many times the choice before me meant life or death. Sometimes there was not even time to think, only to duck—more often than not, there was barely enough time for that.

Out of necessity, I learned to become quite comfortable hiding among the bodies of the *dead*. There simply was no time for me to pay attention to anything but finding a way to stay alive—for one more day, one more hour, one more moment. Inevitably, that became more risky as time went on, regardless of age. Experience and instinct were all I could rely on to help me make those critical life-or-death decisions.

At some point, even relying on instinct proved difficult, because no matter where I turned, a sea of flames gnawed at the landscape. I felt trapped because, as I tried to run away from the enemy, I ran into the arms of another evil. The roads were mined, and there were countless ditches filled with the dead and the dying. During one particular sojourn, I encountered the body of a woman with a crying infant still clinging to her clothing. I tore a piece off my dress and wiped the tears off the tiny face, stroking the infant's hand tenderly and whispering, "Don't cry, baby." The tiny hand gripped my fingers for the briefest of moments before the baby fell, lifeless, beside her dead mother.

My garden was filled with the dampness of night; it was summer and not really cold, but I shuddered at the memory. After that incident with the baby, the time soon came when my parents and I would have to leave our homeland—the only place that I had ever called home. It seemed to me, as the memories flooded my consciousness, that I had been a little girl one day and an experienced refugee the next.

The evening I came upon the infant, I could not see the sunset: the flames had claimed it.

The memories proved too much for me, and I fell asleep in the garden, exhausted by the demands of recollecting. I seemed never to have a single moment of peace, but only to relive everything over and over again. A loud noise awakened me, breaking the silence in the garden.

It was a thunderstorm. Lightning lit the night sky, slicing through the dark clouds. I was not afraid of storms; on the contrary, I let the summer rain run down my face and soak my clothes. Maybe it would wash away the memories of my past and of all the suffering. The whole garden was wrapped in a transparent veil; somehow the rain had taken away the dampness. I enjoyed watching the power of nature, and I felt a certain satisfaction in knowing that nothing could change its ritual in the continuity of life; in the face of nature, even the war had been powerless. The positive force always reigns supreme because it can survive the negative. I have believed that for all of my life, and I have come to live by it.

I noticed that my book was covered with raindrops, and little Helix aspersa had slid back into its shell. Had it told me its story? The tiny creature had followed the ritual set ages ago by its ancestors. I sat still, just enjoying the moment, feeling relieved that my waking and sleeping nightmares were no more than memories of the past.

I felt so humble being there, watching nature, grateful just to be alive. Many times what came to my mind was simple wonderment: What great force had allowed me to live through it all but denied life to so many others? I never found an answer. It was enough to be free, to be able to enrich the lives of my students. That was more than enough.

I felt happy. Gratified. I had been given another chance in my life, as long as I was not afraid to pay the price for being alone again.

Lars at the gate of the family farm

Me under the cherry tree with Mikus

3
Farewell

Throughout my life, I often wondered why I always ended up with unexpected responsibilities, but I took it all in stride, always happy to help out wherever I could.

Late at night, two kittens arrived at my door in Toronto: one was snow white and tiny, while the other was pitch black and quite a good size for a kitten. These two polar opposites were inseparable, and they quickly became part of my household. The two kittens somehow seemed to know that I would take care of them; they displayed the same innate trust that all my animal friends had always shown toward me. I was delighted, of course, and so began our joyous companionship.

I'd never even considered what it would mean to suddenly have the responsibility for pets at that stage of my life. The kittens might have arrived unexpectedly, but I would see to it that they had the best accommodations and care for as long as they stayed with me. That, quite simply, was all there was to that! I did have to decide what to call them. I chose the name Pinky for the little snowy puff and Mauser for her ebony best friend.

Pinky and Mauser both settled into my home immediately. Every morning, without fail, the kittens determined my wake-up time. With a mighty pounce worthy of a much-larger cat—in fact, I'd begun to wonder if the black kitten I'd taken in would become not a black cat, but a panther!—Mauser would dutifully jump up onto my bed, move in close, and look right into my eyes to see if I was awake. He never lost sight of the length of his whiskers, which he cleverly employed to assist him in "checking" on me. Little Pinky just sat on the floor, waiting for me to respond. If I did not move in response to pounce, stare, and tickle, Pinky would join Mauser on the bed, and they both would purr in my ear until I woke up. Neither stopped until they had successfully accomplished their mission.

Pinky and Mauser

To make the kittens' lives interesting, I had set up several birdfeeders, which I had to fill every morning. It was worth the additional effort, though, as birdsong filled my garden, and the kittens thrived.

One autumn day as I went out to fill the birdfeeders, the beauty of the garden's glorious fall colours struck me. Some bushes had turned a brilliant scarlet, others a bright orange, and still others a deep gold; the fall blooms that still lingered added more lovely hues to autumn's magnificent palette. The butterfly bush remained at its peak, and the monarch butterflies busily indulged in the nectar. *What a pleasant day!* I thought, feeling a broad smile form.

I finished filling the feeders, shivering a bit as the wind picked up. Perhaps the pleasantness of the early morning had deceived me. It seemed that the day might prove chillier than I'd expected. The wind blew some leaves off the big maple, strewing them across the patio. Turning toward the broom so that I could sweep the area before heading off to work—I taught piano to young children at a school in

Toronto—something caught my attention. It was a tiny bird sitting between the maple leaves, not moving.

Stepping closer, I saw that the poor creature had been hurt. I gently lifted it out of the leaves, cradling it in my hand. As the little bird quivered, I recognised that it was a goldfinch—a tiny one. Its eyes were open and it was quite alert, but it could not move other than to tremble, seemingly in pain. I had a few minutes before I needed to head off for the day, so I provided the bird with a small nest in the garage, and I left some seeds and water for it too. By the time I finished setting up its new accommodations, the goldfinch seemed to have come out of its daze. I was right: it *was* alive!

I just stood there, admiring the beautiful colours of its wings, and then I stroked its tiny head with my fingertip, pressing it to my face for warmth. I intended to settle it into its new nest for the day and then leave for work.

The goldfinch momentarily raised its head and moved on its side, but then it started to tremble and twitch. This activity eventually pulled all the remaining life out of the bird. Suddenly the trembling became weaker, the bird's eyes closed, and its movements were so slight that I had to strain to discern them. Although the little goldfinch fought valiantly, it inevitably lost the battle for its life. The poor little creature died in my hand.

I felt like someone had driven a knife right through my heart. The poor little bird had died; it would never sing or fly again, never return to its nest. Tears streamed down my face. *Have my emotions finally come back to life? Have I finally regained the ability to cry?* It had been so long since I had dared to let anyone see my feelings, so long since I had expressed emotion. Still cradling the bird, I walked back out to the garden, selected a nice, peaceful place, and laid the little goldfinch to rest.

My heart started pounding. I realised what was happening but could not stop it; I could never stop it—I was as powerless as ever when the memories of the gruesome past invaded my consciousness. From the spot where they lay buried deep in my heart, memories would surface at will and without mercy, tormenting me all over again. As if living through them had not been beyond unbearable, now my memories would force me to surrender this day, so many years later, to that long-ago horror and pain. It didn't matter whether a blizzard or a thunderstorm or a flower or a tree triggered my memories; something always did. That night of the summer thunderstorm, perhaps it had been the small snail;

but perhaps not. Today I knew what the trigger was: the helpless little bird dying in my equally helpless hand.

My memories were like a vortex that sucked me back into the past, back to those horrible times when the days and nights were unpredictable, except I could always rely on the fear that filled them. The continuous noise, day in and day out, numbed my mind. The air was always filled with noxious smells and horrifying screams, and soon I recognised that it was far better to be numb—that would spare me the horror of hearing what was around me. I could not articulate this as a child, of course; I simply did what I had to do to survive. It took me a while to find a way to hear my beloved music in my head, so I could shut out the awful sounds.

I became so used to it all, gruesome and terrifying as it was, that I learned how to fall asleep for just a moment to stave off total exhaustion and then to wake up just as suddenly and keep going—even though it felt like there was nowhere to go. The only hope left every day was that the house would still be there when I returned from wherever it was that I had gone. I started to accept the idea that this might never change, that somehow my home would remain intact.

I had no desire to think about the next day or even to consider what had happened the day before; I just moved along toward a nonexistent destination, always with the feeling of being trapped. I existed—it was not living, not really. I was simply in survival mode, my instincts having taken over—no more, no less.

★ ★ ★ ★ ★

One morning during those ghastly times I woke up early; perhaps I had never even slept—it was impossible for me to tell which. It was dark outside, and I quickly realised that it might very well still be night. Dark clouds covered the whole town in the dreariest bleakness imaginable. It felt as if darkness covered the whole world. Not until I was an adult many years later would I realise that, in many ways, darkness *had* covered the whole world.

The clouds, thick and ominous and saturated with a heavy, odious smell, stood motionless over the homes and the trees and the fields and everything else all around us—the darkness had captured us, and now it held us against our will. All at once, it resembled a place of concealment where one could hide, a prison where one could be detained, a monster just waiting to devour everything in its path.

I stared out into the darkness, wondering where it had come from and who had caused it. Darkness had not been so frightening earlier in my childhood, and I realised that the current fear resulted from the evil that had brought it about. In and of itself, darkness was not necessarily frightening: it was who you had to share it with that made darkness either frightening or safe.

Life as I'd known it had ceased to exist. We'd arrived at the point of misery, almost like captives encased within a narrow and deep tunnel, without the slightest chance of getting out. I'd often have nightmares—even in the midst of living a nightmare, day by day—where I'd been thrown into a dark hole so deep that it seemed bottomless. With each breath I took, I risked sliding lower and lower.

I forced myself not to think of the terrifying nightmares when I was awake; if I did, I might not make it through the day. But I couldn't help but wonder where the laughter had gone. Our lives had been filled with merriment—laughter, songs, music. It all had disappeared. Not just stopped but vanished, as if it had never existed at all. But I knew that it had, and somehow I knew that believing such times would return was the key to my survival. So I just kept believing, even if I didn't know why; I think I kept believing past the point where I even realised that I still believed.

I missed wearing my beautiful dresses and shoes; I missed having all my books around me; most of all, I missed playing the piano. I began to focus on hearing the music in my head and in my heart. Before long, I *could* hear it. When believing is all you have to hold onto, it becomes more real to you than anything else. Sometimes it's the only thing that keeps you alive.

Everything had changed. That included the fog, which looked thicker and denser than ever before. I only wished that it was thick enough to really hide me; on many occasions, I did not dare to move or even breathe out of fear that my heartbeat would give away my hiding place. That was when I most wished that the fog could be so thick that the bad people would not be able to even move through it, just as I'd imagined the snow would keep them away that fateful Christmas Eve.

Worst for me were the sounds. Perhaps it was the musician in me; perhaps it was just the composition of my soul. I had a very difficult time understanding how awful noises and horrid screams had suddenly become acceptable. I could remember when the only sounds that filled our countryside were those of nature, harmonised with silence in the night-time hours. The aggressors ravaged our land with brutality and malice, which saturated our beautiful land. Child though I was, I, too, felt saturated with it. People felt like hunted animals, unwitting prey that did not even know from which direction the aggressor was coming. In the rare quiet moments that did occur, it seemed as if the quiet were nothing but death stalking and homing in on its next victim. There was nobody to talk to; people kept to themselves, and the less one knew the better. Things were horrible, and horribly different from the fine way they once had been.

Many questionable activities took place all around me, and my days were filled with all sorts of things that I could not understand. I asked no questions; nobody would dare to answer such questions, if there were even any answers to give. I shut out the horrors in my waking moments—I could not get through the day otherwise—but sometimes they would come back to me in my sleep. One night I bolted awake, remembering the day when a man had held a hot light bulb against my head, making my hair fall out. I could still feel the searing pain, so sharp that it had ripped through my whole body.

I knew crying was forbidden. For those who showed any reaction at all, the punishment would just continue. When one of the newly appointed teachers dropped some heavy object on my toes one day at school, the long walk home was very painful. It was not wise to tell one's parents when such things happened. Even youngsters like me quickly learned not to discuss anything, because the complainant might be arrested or deported.

It was nearly impossible to constantly bear such distress all around me. I was a young child with no one to talk to and nowhere to go. My beloved brother, Lars, was gone—he'd always been the one I'd gone to with my troubles—and so all I could do was keep the pain within me, burying it as deeply as I could. That was the only way to ensure that my parents and I survived—the only way to escape the terrifying unknown evil that had descended.

There was nothing that had not changed. I tried not to think about it, but it was impossible not to notice. I could no longer have friends over to play because they had either been deported or were hiding. I felt quite alone without my friends and without Lars. I always held Mikus close to me; I wanted to run away, but to where?

The house had been raided many times, and it started to look empty. Only the very heavy pieces remained. The rugs had been stolen or destroyed, and hardly any of the chairs were still in one piece.

My room was the only one not yet vandalised. I had chosen to hide my books under my bed. I had to hide there on many occasions myself, always with Mikus at my side.

There were days when some people came and threw things around my room, but they never looked under the bed: Mikus and I were saved for another day. After they left, I would give Mikus an extra hug, stroking him tenderly and telling him what a brave and smart cat he was for not meowing or purring, which would have alerted the bad people to our hiding place. Mikus was all I had left, and he must have sensed how much I needed him; he followed me everywhere, willingly giving me his unqualified love and support.

The house was so empty that I began spending most of my days in the bunker with Mikus, who always found a nice spot for himself on a bench in back; this spot became my daily refuge of silence and solitude. The bunker had ample room for benches, shelves, and a small table. It was built of logs that Father and Atis had brought in from our woods.

On May 13 I set a table for three with my porcelain tea set, and I brought flowers in from the garden to decorate the bunker. It was Lars's birthday. I had saved a piece of the raisin bread from that morning for breakfast so that I would have something special to share with Lars and Mikus on the special day. All was finally ready. I looked at the lovely table and felt very happy. I had not felt happy once since Christmas Eve, which now felt like a lifetime ago

The sun had come out, and for a moment I didn't hear any shooting. In the distance the rumbling of heavy artillery continued day and night, but I did not pay any attention to it anymore. It was always in the background.

Suddenly I heard somebody approaching the bunker. My heart started to beat faster: maybe it was Lars! The steps stopped, and a mean-looking man filled the entryway, coming inside the bunker and roughly pushing me aside. He took some stuff from the shelves, and then he turned and smashed my tea set to bits. On the way out, he hit me so hard that I fell down. He left without remorse. I remained on the ground for a while, stunned. *Why did he do such a cruel thing?* I wondered. I wanted to run after him and ask him why; I felt compelled to know the reason for such brutality, such meanness. Of course I knew that I could not run and could not ask. I did not learn the reason that day or in the days that followed; I never learned it, and I never will. Quite simply, there was no reason.

That moment of cruelty was but one of many. It was better to be numb. Struggling to establish some kind of normalcy, it became my daily routine to count how many new holes appeared in the garden as a result of the attacks. Mikus and I were thus engaged one day, when all of a sudden it started to rain bullets again. We crawled to the bunker, hiding at the very far end.

It had been an exceptional summer for the garden. A huge pumpkin had grown, and it now covered the whole top of the bunker. I felt a violent vibration, and many things fell off the shelves. Dirt and dust blew in, and an odd, choking smell slowly started drifting inside. With Mikus clutched in my arms, I went back outside, only to see that the flowers and bushes had been blown apart by a direct hit. Where the pumpkin used to be was now a big hole. That pumpkin most assuredly had saved my and Mikus's lives.

That day passed. We had survived the attack, but no better days seemed to lie ahead; there was nothing good to anticipate. As with counting the holes, it had become a daily routine to investigate the damage all around. Mikus kept busy sniffing the ground.

I noticed that the little shed Father had built for my animals was gone! Because of Father's many responsibilities, the visits to our farm were less frequent than I would have wished. Knowing this, Father had a piglet, a rooster, a hen, a goose, and a turkey all brought from the farm to this house. He'd then built a shed for them—a sort of miniature barn—that stood at the far back of the garden. I walked around, hoping to find the animals hiding somewhere, but it was in vain: they all had been killed, destroyed. I found not even a trace of their remains.

Devastated, I just kept walking around the garden, Mikus trailing me. Nature, animals, and music all were part of the same delicate whole for me; together, they comprised what we call life. I didn't think of it in so many words as a child, of course, but I felt it, nevertheless, and quite keenly. Prior to the war, I had never imagined that life was anything but a beautiful melody that would play, undisturbed, forever. I still believed that life was a beautiful melody, and the sounds of nature gave life the same kind of tenderness found in homophonic music. It was war that disturbed the delicate balance of life and sound; it was war, with its harsh and ugly sounds, that intruded on melody and harmony. War destroyed the homophonic sounds, drastically changing them into the thunderous cacophony that resounded endlessly overhead.

In that moment, melody was lost, drowned out by the sounds of war as they sought to rise to a higher acoustic plateau, where they could dominate the world forever. But I believed that if I had faith, melody would return someday, and life would be beautiful again.

The very next moment would test my faith. In one of the holes I found a wounded bird that was barely alive. I picked it up and gently patted its wings. The bird started to quiver slightly. Blood dripped from its wing, and I pressed it close to me to keep it warm. I felt its pulse weaken and then slowly fade away. The blood had stained my dress, and a pool of blood lay in my palm. The bird had died.

I aimlessly walked toward the cherry tree, dug a hole, wrapped the bird in some leaves, and buried it. Gathering a few flowers that had not been destroyed, I covered the tiny grave with them. Most of the flowers in the garden were broken, like my own heart and spirit. For a moment I just stood there, with Mikus in my arms, and I looked up at the sky, which seemed so empty now that the bird would never again soar toward it, never again fill it with song. *Melody will return,* I told myself. *Life will be beautiful again.*

I continued to stand in the middle of the garden, with devastation all around me. It began to rain, and Mikus meowed a loud protest. I held him close to protect him from getting wet, though I did not mind the soaking. On the contrary, I wished the rain would wash away my sorrow, cleanse all the horror from our midst. The rain washed the bird's blood off my hands, but it could not wash away the odious smell that had descended all around us, and it could not wash away my heartache.

It was getting darker by the minute. I stood in the rain, dripping wet, with Mikus in my arms, shielded by my body. For a moment it was so quiet that I thought death might have paused, satiated from all the lives it had already consumed. The night and the storm had wrapped the town in darkness. The lights in the few remaining houses had either been turned off or disabled by the attacks.

Flames lit up the horizon, flashing like spears through the ruins and turning the whole panorama into a morbid and ghastly scene. The silence was short-lived; shooting and screams filled the air once again. I felt like I was watching the dance of death come closer and closer—soon it would take me away.

The already horrid conditions rapidly deteriorated to an unbearable degree. Soldiers were running, screaming, and shooting; they did not know whether they were standing in the line of fire, behind it, or facing it.

With Mikus still in my arms, I stooped to escape the threatening whistle of bullets overhead. It was too late and too risky to go inside the house, so I sat down on the ground, holding Mikus tight against me, using myself as a shield to protect my beloved cat from the flying particles.

We sat there for a very long time, just waiting. Finally the bullets stopped flying overhead, providing a chance to crawl back to the house. Eventually many bruises and cuts covered my legs, but I ignored the bleeding. The adults were so exhausted and terrified that most of the time they never noticed my absence. That night seemed no different.

In the middle of the night an overpowering blow shook the whole house. Mikus ran off into the garden. I ran after him, but I could not find him. Hours passed without a sign of him. The flames in the predawn darkness cast scary shadows. Standing in the middle of the inferno I still felt chilly. It was the same wickedness that repeatedly haunted us, making us shiver in fear. Nobody knew for sure who was who or why they felt obligated to do what they did and had done.

Back inside the house, the familiar odd smell was so overpowering that we went outside to investigate what had happened. To our horror, the part of the house where Atis, Anda, and their family lived was gone. Some of their belongings were visible, scattered amongst the ruins, but nothing else was left of them. I could not utter a word. Piece by piece, my life was being chopped apart. We did not even have any remains to bury—no way to say good-bye to the people who had been such an important part of our family life.

In the smouldering ruins, some wires sticking out were all that was left of the piano that Father had given to Atis and Anda's daughter Mara on her birthday. Father, Mother, and I just stood there in the ruins, stunned and speechless, as if under an evil spell. I surmised that my heart now refused to beat; how could it want to in this morbid silence that seemed to last forever, with the piano strings sticking up out of the destroyed instrument, the whole contorted mess dangling from the smouldering rafters? Looking at the scene, I thought, *After such a wicked deed, the mean, bad people cannot wish to do more! How could they?*

Yet, somehow, I knew that they could. Perhaps it was in that instant that I began to think of the attackers as assassins, as the living dead—I cannot say for sure. I did have a premonition that that would not be the last sorrow of the day.

I ran into the garden to look for Mikus again, but he was nowhere to be found. I'd prayed that he'd just been hiding, but now it seemed that he was truly gone. I felt deep physical pain overtake my body as a result of my grief: my beloved cat was gone forever. I was not quite sure whether to venture beyond the garden to search for Mikus or to run back inside the house in an attempt to stay safe. I listened carefully, hoping to hear Mikus meow, but all I could hear was the sound of the broken shutters bouncing against the outside wall.

Suddenly I noticed that the door looked strange: half of it had been blown off, and the hinges had been destroyed, so it could no longer be closed properly. The only place in the house that was somewhat clear of rubble was the largest room, where the two pianos stood, side by side, near the tall potted palms that partly blocked the view of the street.

Mikus was gone, but at least my pianos were still there. I wondered how much longer the house would offer any safety at all.

★ ★ ★ ★ ★

It was hard to tell what was left of the town, because it was still so dark. All sorts of strange noises filled the air, but I could not hear them anymore. All I wanted was for Mikus to return; I strained to hear his familiar meow, but to no avail. He did not come back. In the darkness I noticed a tall figure moving away from the house; I could just make out the sack on his back as he disappeared down the misty trail.

I began to wonder whether Mikus had gotten lost in the chaos or been stolen from my life, just like everything else had been. Frantic, I ran to the piano, desperate to play the piece I had learned a month ago. I so loved that piece, the most gripping composition by Frederic Chopin. The beautifully bound book was still in one piece, with no burn marks. It was a bit dusty, but the inscription in gold on the cover, bearing the title and my name, was still clearly visible. Father and Mother had always been most supportive of my studies, and every book I had finished was hardbound with the same material as the dress I'd worn that day. I sat motionless at the piano, tears running down my face, grief-stricken that another piece of my life had been destroyed by the ugly war, another piece of my heart ripped out.

The rest of that night, all three of us slept on the floor. I moved under the piano and fell asleep holding my music book. I was so used to the sounds of shooting that I easily dozed off, especially that night, when I was so physically exhausted. When the shooting stopped, I would suddenly awaken, listening to hear if anyone approached and pulling myself deeper into the nearest corner if I heard anything suspicious. It spooked me when the war sounds ceased, because it alerted me that danger was coming closer.

For a long time I had not had a restful sleep. My mind just raced fitfully through all the wishes that would never be fulfilled. During this most painful time of my life, even in sleep I had no peace: my dreams had become visions that scattered from incident to incident, often having no connection to one another at all.

Huddled beneath the piano in the wee hours of the morning, images flitted through my unconscious mind while my body sank into weariness, the kind that brings sleep without true rest. I saw Mikus sitting under the cherry tree. He and I started to run across the meadow, where he played with the butterflies. The brook was covered with beautiful water lilies whose buds had just sprung open. It seemed lovely and happy, and in my sleep, as often happens, I subconsciously thought, *What a pleasant dream!* Just then, Mikus jumped on a big leaf. I tried to run after him, but my legs felt so heavy that I could not move. I begged Mikus to come back and stay with me forever, but he only looked back at me for a brief moment before disappearing into the sunset.

★ ★ ★ ★ ★

Without Mikus, I arrived at the point of living from moment to moment. Continuous noise and fire were always around me. I grew accustomed to living on the edge of that inferno, but I could not abide feeling so lonely. Mikus and I used to sit at the window and watch the flames shoot up and eat the homes. Hardly any people were around anymore; either they'd been taken away or they were hiding. I felt as if the turmoil, by means of its evil, had spontaneously caused the unrelenting conflagration that kept swallowing the houses and all the people in them.

In daylight the streets were deserted. At dusk a few sad and melancholy people would try to move about, without any specific destination in mind. There simply was nowhere to go. Houses had been diminished to rubble and ashes, and empty ammunition cartridges and all sorts of other debris littered the whole area. The chance of stepping on a mine became ever more imminent.

For the past few hours the shrill sirens had not sounded any warning of air attacks, and so I just sat on the floor of my bedroom, staring up at the ceiling and wondering if the day would ever come when I would be free and feel safe again.

I did not have long to wait before the sirens started blaring again. After the latest of countless air attacks, I looked around the dust-filled room. All my books lay strewn on the floor. In the rubble I found the pencil I had saved for Lars. Originally, it was to be his birthday present, but May 13 had come and gone—I hastily pushed the memory of the bad man in the bunker from the foreground of my mind—and Lars had not returned. I'd decided to save the pencil anyway; I would give it to Lars whenever he did come home. I wiped the dust off a book and then started to write a note to Lars.

That was what I had begun to do in order to avoid becoming frightened. Sometimes it even helped me fall asleep. In my notes to Lars, I told him that if he ever felt lonely or scared, he should sing a song in his heart. I'd done that quite often by that time. Keeping the music inside protected me. I had built a kind of invisible shell around myself, even though I did not realise at the time that I had done so, and the music in my heart and head fortified that protective shell.

The daily routine never changed, but without Mikus I felt alone. Nobody talked to me; actually, there was nothing to say anymore, and it seemed the adults did not talk to one another, either. For a while it had been quiet, so I went outside to the bunker. From out of nowhere, bullets screeched overhead, forcing me to dive in. A cloud of dust and dirt arose, partly covering the entrance. The tremor was violent enough to cause many things to fall off the shelves, and some of them landed so close to me that they were almost on top of me. I picked my way around the fallen items and dug strenuously to clear the entrance, and then carefully I made my way back to the house. Nobody had any notion of what had gone on in the garden, and everyone was surprised to see me all covered with dirt.

As the bombardments intensified, our trips to the bunker became more and more frequent, and some nights we barely even reached it. One night I ran as fast as I could after my parents, but my legs were still only halfway in the doorway. A couple of bewildered soldiers running past pointed their weapons and were going to shoot, even though they were not clear about whom they would shoot. One of them noticed my legs sticking out and hurried the others away. Either he thought I was dead or did not want to waste a bullet on a child because ammunition was scarce.

We huddled together in the bunker until dusk, when we felt it might be safe to go to the house and salvage whatever was left. The siren went on again, and so we ran back toward the bunker to take cover. Right before our eyes, the bunker was blown apart. The wicked whistling of the bullets overhead forced us to crawl to a neighbour's shelter. I covered my head with my hands, petrified with fear: I was literally too afraid to even move. I felt something touch my leg. It was soft and gentle, and for the briefest moment I imagined it was Mikus, safely returned, but it was my mother checking to see if I had been shot. Mother was relieved to see that I was all right. Alive I was, but only physically.

The neighbours had built their shelter completely above ground, making the detonation of the constant shelling unbearable. As dawn approached, another enormous crash sounded quite close to me. Scrambling to look, I saw my whole world instantly disappear as the flames devoured what Father had worked so tirelessly for in order to ensure our family's well-being. Our house was on fire! Huge flames rose high into the sky, like enormous fiery fingers reaching to heaven in a prayer for help. The smoke seemed to cover all the clouds with soot. To the east, our wood was also on fire, and the distant roar and crackle sounded like the cries of a maddened crowd. Even the daybreak seemed to hesitate. I looked all around me: the bunker was destroyed, the house continued to burn, and everything was gone.

I started to run toward the house, but the intense heat kept me back. For a moment I thought that maybe I could save my pianos, but the flames came closer, almost setting my clothes on fire. Suddenly I wondered where everybody had gone. I stood stunned into numbness, all alone and helpless, not even knowing if my parents were dead or alive. The flames were swallowing everything. Separated from everyone else, I just stood in front of our burning home, wondering if the flames would claim my life as well.

I desperately started to look for something, anything, of mine in the still-hot soil. All I could find were my big porcelain doll, broken to pieces, and my scorched teddy bear. I dug and dug, but everything was gone. At last I found a small stone. Brushing off the dirt, I pressed the stone against my heart. This small stone was all that was left of my home. Amid the roar of the flames destroying the house, a soft and painful sound arose, growing increasingly louder. Was I crying aloud or was it the sound of my heart breaking? I could hear the sorrow that filled my heart: it seemed to say, "Farewell, Lara." My heart, my house, and my country all seemed to be crying together. That sorrow has never left me.

The fire lasted forever, destroying my heart piece by piece. It was as if I instantly grew old while estimating my great loss. Nothing could ever fill the hole inside me; nothing could ever replace what had been lost. Indescribable pain filled my body. It was too much to bear. I became like all the adults: numb to the chaos and evil around me, unable to find the words to express my grief and pain and horror. We had all grown too afraid to show the revulsion that had built up deep inside us.

It had been some time since anyone dared to speak. Anyone who broke down and showed frustration disappeared like dust in the wind. There was nothing anyone could do except keep running, moving forward and never looking back. All one could see were the twisted remains of those who had fallen amid carnage and rubble and ashes. Why would anyone even want to look back? All the dreams, all the hard work and achievements, were destroyed by the monstrous war.

I wondered what kind of power could be so ignominious as to remove people's dignity, discarding it in the dust to rot as if it were nothing more than garbage; in the nights that followed the fire, these thoughts would plague me. I developed insomnia. For so long I had kept everything inside me, never crying out loud, never voicing my fear or my pain to anyone, because I knew how easily we could all become the victims of fabricated accusations of activities that had never taken place. That was not a vague threat; it was all too real.

As those thoughts raced through my mind, I continued to stand alone. All I had left were the three dresses that Mother had made me wear in layers and the new ski boots that I wore to protect my feet. And the stone I'd found in the remains of our home.

The time had come to leave, but where would I go? The horizon was brightly lit by burning houses. There were fallen people everywhere. In order to move in any direction, I sometimes had to move the dead aside so that I could proceed. With every step I encountered destruction and death. I felt that if I took one step forward, I had to go two steps back, only to end up in the trenches filled with the bodies of soldiers and civilians. Sometimes I had to take cover behind or next to them, using them to shield myself from the bullets.

The insatiable power of the evil attackers—the living dead—had made me a victim. I began to distrust everything and everybody, and I wished that I could move along in the shadows where nobody would ever find me.

The long crawl through the ruins presented me with many challenges, one of which was trying to move past the corpses quickly, all the while keeping my head low both for my own safety and out of respect for the dead. I even played dead myself when an armed soldier passed by.

Finally I reached the far end of the property, where all was quiet for a moment. I was so exhausted, mentally and physically, that I fell unconscious on the forsaken ground. I had no idea how long I had been lying there when I awakened. It was raining, and my soaked clothing clung to my body. I started to shiver, but I did not have the strength to get up. I actually enjoyed the rain. It felt like salvation; maybe it would cause me to dissolve and become part of the soil. I wished that could be: then, finally, I would have no more pain or dismay.

Suddenly I sensed that something was strange. I felt no pain and heard no noise—had I become deaf, or had I died, or was I just dreaming? No screaming, no bullets—nobody was anywhere around. Finally I decided that I must have been freed from the catastrophic happenings: the war had claimed my life, and I was dead.

But perhaps it was none of that at all; maybe the war had died! Could war destroy itself, just like it destroyed innocent people? I cautiously moved my legs, struggling to get up. Maybe I could walk. I started to move slowly, and I realised that I must be alive. For a moment I just stood there, water dripping from my soaked clothes. The rainfall grew heavier. I looked up at the dark clouds, wishing that the rain would drown the war. Was this rain heaven crying for me?

I felt inexplicably safe, and I closed my eyes, wishing never to open them again until the war was over—but would it ever be over? I could no longer face the extent to which the brutal war had crushed my life. In spite of myself, my eyes fluttered open. I saw a white rose, the one thing still living in what had once been our lush garden. I could hear, as well as feel, the sorrow that filled my heart: it was the cry of the piano strings breaking in the intense heat of the inferno.

A lone bird flew west, toward the setting sun; the east was in flames, as were the north and south; the flames even obliterated the sunset in the west. The bird and I shared the inferno. I began to walk westward, clutching the little stone in my hand. I walked and crawled, falling as I stumbled over so many of those for whom it had become too late to walk. With the crackle of flames all around me, I took one last look at the ruins, whispering, "Farewell, my home."

Me with petunias

4
Trail of Fire

Life in Toronto was good. After one long but encouraging day at school, I came home enthused and delighted: enrolment in the piano classes had catapulted far beyond my wildest expectations. I loved teaching children, and my classes included a range of ages, from four- to ten-year-olds. The children inspired me, and teaching them helped me maintain the basics of musical composition and theory in my mind while I simultaneously developed a unique system for gradual, solid advancement. I came to think of this process as "the anatomy of music," because I always dissected the structure of every piece, bar by bar, trying to hear and understand the logic behind it, both compositionally and theoretically.

I thought of the children I taught as another garden. Young plants need care that is far different from that required by established vegetation: the gardener must carefully put new greenery in the proper soil, with all the necessary nutriments, hydration, and light. Too much of anything at once might kill the young plants; too little might yield weak stock. Such was the logic of nature as applied to agriculture, and I found that it worked with children as well. This was the main paradigm of my music-education programme, and my pupils seemed to respond to my ministrations as happily as my plants did. That day in particular, I'd observed that the children were noticing small details that had escaped them prior to joining my programme. They were making excellent progress, indeed, and I was elated.

As I've described, music and nature have always been intertwined for me, and I incorporated this concept in my programme. I taught my "garden" of youngsters to respect all life, often drawing examples from vegetation, in order to illustrate the circle of life in a way that the children could observe and easily understand. For example, I explained how the seed sprouted and then became a plant or a tall tree, which eventually would become a critical link to sustaining life on earth. I emphasised the necessity of oxygen to the existence of all forms of life, reminding the children that we humans are the only form of life capable of protecting and preserving our planet, which we share with all the other life forms. I taught them to respect one another and all living things, including the vegetation, animals of all forms and sizes, and even the insects and the "crawlers." Finally, I taught them that, in addition to our unique responsibility as protectors and preservers of our planet, we humans are also the most magnificent life form because we alone have the power to create—for good or ill. "Use your creative powers wisely, children," I exhorted. "Creating good is a miracle, but creating the opposite is something we all must avoid."

My explanations and examples activated their eagerness for learning. I could feel the nurturing transform them: their passion to achieve the best musical performance now included a respect for, and engagement in, the circle of life. In other words, they seemed to understand how it all comes together, how life goes on, and how nature and music are all part of the same organic whole that we call *life*. Most of all, it just gave me such pleasure to watch them smiling, full of joy, as all children should be. Giving to the children in my care somehow helped me give to the child within me who had lost so much that could never be replaced. The hole in my heart never closed, but teaching music to children was a salve that eased the ache and smoothed the seams where I'd patched my broken heart.

That happy day deepened to dusk, and for much of the evening that followed I collected material for the following day. It was such a pleasant evening, so warm and peaceful, that I did not turn on the lights. Instead, I sat in my study, enjoying the magical glow cast by the moon.

The piano was still open, and the moonlight was so bright that I could read the music quite clearly. The book of Claude Debussy's *Preludes* was open on the stand. On Tuesdays and Thursdays I held classes in my home studio for pianists preparing for their recitals. It was time for me to go through the different analyses of the compositions. Even though it was very late, I still had to prepare my editorial notes on the students' work, and those commentaries took quite some time to complete. I took my seat at the piano. As usual, Mauser pounced, panther-like, into my lap, while Pinky fell asleep on top of the stack of books on my desk. Mauser, too, was soon asleep. Their purring encouraged me to join them in dreamland.

More often than not, sleep was not a peaceful time for me, and my dreams were rarely pleasant. That night was to be no exception. Some memories seemed to recur in my dreams more than others, such as the moment of finding the small stone in the wake of the fire and the outpouring of emotion that finding it had engendered. As usual, I did not know what had triggered my recollections that night; it could have been any single specific thing or nothing in particular. Perhaps my work with the children, and my thoughts of them, led me to think of my own childhood, so cruelly destroyed by the inhuman attackers.

As I slept, the darkness and pain of the past loomed in my unconscious, returning to haunt me. The moment of finding the stone, once again, took centre stage in the theatre of my dreams. I understood the reason for this: the stone had been more than a memento. It was something real and solid that represented my home, something that I could hold tight and trust, which was so important to me as a child after all the deception and treachery that I'd found myself suddenly immersed in that I was helpless to change or to stop.

In my dreams I saw the little girl I had been, terrified and uncomprehending, standing all alone at the edge of the inferno. The ground was still sizzling hot; I could still feel the heat, even in my recollections, both waking and sleeping. I watched in my dream as my childhood self looked around, finding nothing but some shattered pieces of a porcelain doll and a scorched teddy bear. The rest was ashes. The house continued to burn, and the garden had been turned into a crater. The trees, engulfed in flames, seemed to cry. The roar of the fire shut out their natural music; I could no longer hear their melodious sounds. Frantically raking the ashes with my small fingers, I found one small stone, which I clutched in my hand.

Exhausted, I made my way to where the garden used to be, and I fell asleep on the hard ground. The rain woke me, and I could not tell how long I'd slept. I noticed a single white rose; it bid me good-bye from my childhood home, from the early years of happiness and innocence. Forever.

I saw a lone bird flying westward, and I followed it, picking my way amongst the ruins. I whispered a final farewell to my home, seeking to go on, though I knew not to where, or even why.

Me at the piano at home

★ ★ ★ ★ ★

I awakened in the midst of my nightmare, but my recollections did not fade; they just blended from sleep to wakefulness.

All had been quiet after the rain. In my heart I'd known the time had come to leave everything behind; I followed the lone bird winging ever higher, picking my way carefully through the remains of the dead and the wreckage of war. I had to leave the white rose, the last living thing in our once-lush garden; I had to leave the poor little bird that I'd buried; I had to leave so much that I loved. I had to leave the place that I called home, the place that I loved so deeply. I clutched the little stone, and turned back, headed for what was left of the house and garden. I felt drained and smothered by it all; the ashes and still-smoking remnants of our home choked me.

I didn't even know if my parents were alive or dead; I just stood, waiting; letting myself go numb so I wouldn't feel anything.

All my dreams had died in that fire; they were covered with ashes and debris, which, eventually, the breeze would blow away or the rain would wash away—and then nothing at all would be left of my childhood but my little stone, which I clutched even tighter.

I began to move around tentatively, searching different areas around the house than I'd been able to the night before. The rain had cooled things off a bit, but the smoke was still noxious. I kept walking and coughing, hoping—praying—that I would find something else to take with me. I would not let myself think about my parents or Lars or Mikus or anything at all. Now all I could do was survive. There was no time to think, or feel, or cry.

Something that seemed familiar caught my eye: a small loaf of bread. It was strange what the explosions did and did not destroy. I had grown accustomed to that, and I only felt relief that I'd have something to eat, at least for as long as the small loaf would last. I deposited the stone on one of my dress pockets, picked my way through the ruins, and pulled out the bread. Grasping it in one hand, I held it tight against my body.

My parents suddenly appeared before me. I blinked in disbelief at the miracle, and then I realised it was not my eyes playing tricks on me: they were alive. Mother and Father each held a small bundle, and they signalled me to follow them. Step by step, we moved farther away from the ruins; thus, we three, together, left the scorched remains of our home.

Clutching the bread against me with one hand, I reached into my pocket with the other hand and resumed clutching the stone. This was my desperate attempt to feel that I had something left of my brutally stolen childhood, even though I knew that I did not. I did not show the stone to Mother or Father, or even tell them about it.

Mother followed Father, and I followed her, and the three of us walked in silence. We had no choice but to walk in clear view of the snipers. Bullets rang out their song of death all around us, but, for some reason, none of us were shot or wounded.

We headed toward the city, trapped within both sides of combatants' lines of fire of . The all-to-familiar haze and odour engulfed the city: the miasma of war. The stench wafted through the air, filling our nostrils and nauseating us. The detonation of explosives infused the entire atmosphere, and the unnaturally thickened air clouded our minds and made it difficult to breathe. The road was deserted, and both sides of it were littered with the remains of the dead and the detritus of destruction: all the reminders of war and death.

There was nowhere to go: certain death faced us in every direction. We found ourselves perpetually in the crossfire, with the bullets whizzing overhead and all around us in an endless dance of death. This mayhem must be have been the game of the devil himself; it most assuredly put my parents and me through sheer hell.

In the midst of it all appeared hope, at last. *The bridge!* I thought, catching myself before I said it out loud. I thought I could see the bridge I used to cross so many times on the way to school. Before we could get any closer, however, four armed men appeared from out of nowhere, stopping us. I moved toward a tree to hide behind it. At gunpoint, the men ordered Father and Mother to hand over their bundles. One of the men pointed his gun at me, indicating the loaf. He pushed me down to the ground, wrenching the bread from my grasp. It didn't matter; the men were ready to shoot us anyway. I shut my eyes, accepting that this was the end of the road. I felt empty of all feelings. Even my fears had vanished, and what would have been the point of being afraid now? There was nothing left to fear.

After a few moments passed, we realised they weren't going to shoot us after all. They had other plans. The bridge was mined. The men just laughed, forcing the three of us, again at gunpoint, to step onto the bridge. We were walking toward a certain death, but we had no choice: if we didn't step onto the bridge, the men would shoot us.

I felt so cold. I'd placed my little stone in my pocket, and I crossed my arms, clutched the folds of the sleeves of my layered dresses, and began to walk across the deadly bridge. Bullets flew past, hitting the steel beams of the bridge many times. Father was slightly wounded by a ricochet, and blood began to seep through his shirt. The bridge was high and long, with some dead soldiers dangling over the railing halfway up. I could not understand war. Not just the soldiers' lives but also their dreams had ended with each of their assailants' bullets.

After witnessing horror for so long, I had lost all my precious childhood innocence. I no longer observed or thought like a child: I had become a veteran denizen of a war zone. What I had seen did not fit the concept of what I knew life was supposed to be. Because of all that I'd witnessed, I began to grasp the difference between good and evil in an all-too-real way—a way that no young child should ever have to see or understand.

After some time, which felt like an eternity, we crossed the bridge. We were still alive. I pressed my eyes shut, checked for the stone, and resumed clutching it in my hand. When I opened my eyes, I saw destruction in every direction. Corpses, the blood still oozing from their fatal wounds, lay scattered amongst the rubble and debris.

The walk through the city was slow and treacherous. Still-hot bricks from collapsed buildings lay strewn all over the streets, and the incessant bombardment continued. Dead people and their meagre belongings littered the gutters.

The next air attack made me lose my balance, and I fell over some wounded people. I lay near a sewer, watching in terrified revulsion as a stream of blood slowly ran down the filthy drain.

Clambering to my feet, I caught up with Mother and Father. In the chaos-induced stupor we all found ourselves in, they hadn't even realised that I'd stumbled. As the three of us continued our attempt to make it through the city, similar scenes recurred many times. Gradually, they all merged into a single gruesome tableau that I would never be able to forget; it would haunt my memories forever.

The walk through the city became a fight for our lives; we kept running, crawling, or hiding behind something or somebody; I could not even imagine where we were headed, as it appeared to be the end of the world, with no safe place to run to. I gripped my father's hand, looking up at him without saying a word.

What if all this is only a nightmare?! I wondered inwardly, keeping the thought to myself, knowing how much it would hurt Father if I said it aloud, because then he would have to tell me that it *was* reality—that we had no choice but to live through this hell, and there was nothing he could do about it.

Father appeared to be walking in a daze, not even turning his head, just holding my hand in his. He kept moving on, without paying attention to the burning factory that spit cinders all around us. I watched, helpless, as I realised that the ruined factory was Father's own. He didn't even cringe when another explosion sent debris high into the air. That was the end of it—all Father's dreams and achievements had turned into rubble and ashes. I noticed Mother turn her head away.

Stunned by the chaos and all that my family and I had lost, I forced myself to just keep walking. It was difficult to avoid stepping in the puddles of blood. Looking down at my bloodstained boots, I could have cried, but I had no time to cry, only to keep going. That was all I, or any of us in that nightmare, could do: move. But where were we to go?

The air attacks continued, unrelenting, and everything around us was on fire. Tired and emotionally numb, I just kept putting one foot in front of the other, stepping in the sticky, red puddles as I walked along with my parents. Fallen people, destroyed buildings, and flames stretched in all directions, as far as the eye could see. I was so tired that the hellish scene began to look like an evil dance of fiery vultures.

We finally reached the riverside, where the largest buildings had so many holes blown through them from the explosions that they appeared to be transparent. The street, littered with some partially burned papers and books, looked nothing like the busy hub I remembered from happier days. Soon we approached the second bridge: the only way to get out of the city. We knew it was mined and could blow up at any time, but, once again, we had no choice but to go across. Behind us was the burning city; ahead of us, the mined bridge. Mother and Father just kept walking along the river, and I trailed behind them. We reached the marina, where we could see Father's big sailboat anchored; its broken mast and torn flag symbolised the destruction we'd endured. All three of us looked at it, and then we looked away, as helpless as we had been at the sight of Father's burning factory. We had already lost so much that the sight of another loss merely added to the already unbearable grief.

We just kept walking, soon passing the music school that I had attended. The building emitted a sound similar to the one I had heard a few hours earlier, the same painful lament of our home crying a final farewell. I had no time to cry for my beloved home, or my beloved school, but tears streamed down my face in spite of that. I will never forget hearing the anguished cries of all the instruments within the Academy of Music as we passed the building. The sound of that pain has never left my heart; it will stay there forever. It was as if the instruments had created a melody to express the deep sorrow of such unimaginable tragedy, but it was a melody that should never have been written and never have been heard—least of all by any child. I longed to hear the natural melodies of the trees that would never again sing because the fires had destroyed them; I longed to play my beloved pianos, which the fires had destroyed. In vain I tried to shut my ears against the plaintive cries of the dying instruments, but I knew I would never stop hearing them for as long as I lived.

★ ★ ★ ★ ★

We were on the opposite side of the bridge, but I could not remember making the steps that had carried us across it. I was too numb to even feel grateful that we had made it across, that the bridge had not exploded beneath us. Looking back at the bridge, all I could see was the same thing I'd seen for I could not tell how long: people lying lifeless.

Horses lay lifeless also, their hooves turned skyward. The destruction had stopped the innocent creatures in the midst of their duties, and they would never again gallop in the fields, their magnificent bodies graceful against the wind, their manes flying free. The basic dignity that was so much a part of those beautiful beasts had been wrested from them, and the merciless wasteland where they had all taken their final breaths was a stark contrast to the serenity that they deserved.

My heart wrenched suddenly at the unbidden mental image of my beloved Lolo. Would I ever see my mare again? Had she succumbed to such a cruel and vicious end too? My heart ached for Lolo. She was even dearer to me now that Mikus had disappeared.

I forced myself to focus on what lay before us. All I could do was survive now; I had no time to dwell on my losses. The sun had begun to set, but without its usual brilliance. The western sky was a sombre, smoke-filled grey, and the sun looked like a ball filled with blood, trying to draw itself into the dark sea, pulling the entire world I knew—forests, valleys, and people—all down with it. I longed to follow the sun into the sea and never again emerge into the living nightmare of hell.

I kept walking, waiting for evening to descend. Knowing all too well the dangers of being seen, I became more comfortable in the darkness, which provided a protective wall that resisted the enemy's penetration. I could move around in stealth, cautiously gauging and planning my next step. I wondered whether I had been reduced to a crawler, a creature not even daring to walk upright. I was no longer aware of what I even felt inside. I needed to just stay numb so that I could go on, even though I did not know what that meant or where we would travel. Survival instincts had taken control of me; it was no more or less than that.

Reaching the land road, we kept heading north. Father led the way, Mother followed him, and I trailed behind the two of them. Whenever a military vehicle approached, all three of us swiftly dove into the ditches on either the side of the road. More often than not, the ditches were filled with the bodies of fallen soldiers and civilians, as well as all sorts of material that defied description. We disappeared amongst whatever already lay in the ditches, seeking only to remain hidden, undetected. It was impossible to avoid landing on whatever was already in the ditches. We did what we had to do in order to survive, moment by moment, not even thinking about whether the next day would dawn or how we would manage to live through it.

We must have walked for days and nights, but I lost track of how many. The sun rose and set, but we just kept walking toward the north, managing to catch some sleep at nightfall whenever we could. It was the peak of fall, and the fields were a beautiful carpet of changing colours: sometimes green, sometimes golden, sometimes the rich brown of fertile soil.

We'd been feeling hungry for some time, and the longer we walked, the greater a concern our hunger became. Father scanned the fields for what we might eat, but those who'd walked before us must have taken whatever was edible.

Dandelions filled the roadside, and I picked some blossoms, just to have something beautiful near me. Caressing my little stone, I deposited it in my pocket to keep it safe, holding my fresh bouquet in my hand.

Our walk seemed endless. Mother's foot began to hurt and swell. She'd injured it before we left home, and she had been wearing her slippers when the house burst into flame. After so many days of walking, her slippers were worn through, and the pain in her foot continued to worsen. Father gave her his shoes, and he walked barefoot.

★ ★ ★ ★ ★

After so many days and nights spent walking, I'd long since lost my sense of time. It no longer made any difference what day it was, anyway. One evening, when it seemed rather quiet, we dropped from sheer fatigue and lay along the roadside. The sounds in the field were so soothing—not the awful noises of war, but the beautiful night-time music of nature. The song lulled us all to sleep.

Morning arrived, complete with all the harsh sounds of the military display of power. The rumbling tanks awakened us. The tall grass hid us from view but did not prevent us from witnessing the brutality that unfolded before our eyes as the road turned into an instant massacre. I tried with all my might to shut my eyes and ears but in vain. The oncoming tanks rolled over the refugees who could not get out of the way fast enough. Their screams echoed long after their bodies had been destroyed. They could not possibly still be screaming—could not possibly still be alive—yet the sounds of their screams reverberated in my ears. The refugees, all in torn clothing, carried their children on their backs. They could not possibly outrun the murderous tanks; they'd had no chance of escaping—just as the three of us would have had no chance, had we not still been asleep in the grass that hid us. It was bright daylight by that point. Anybody who ran was shot dead or wounded, and those who stumbled were also run over by the tanks.

I was motionless and unable to speak. I started to scream, but no sound came out. Moving my hand in a feeble attempt to reach out to my parents, I watched it fall back, almost lifeless, as if it were the hand of some dying little girl, not my own hand at all. I looked up to see a small bird fly over the field, free and alive. It was the last thing I saw before losing consciousness.

I woke up to the sensation of streams of water running down my body. It had started to rain heavily. Eventually, the rain washed all the dirt and dried blood off my clothes and exposed skin. It felt so good to feel the rain stream down my face. I did not mind getting soaked, and I knew the sun would dry my clothes. Perhaps the rain would even remove the gruesome memory of the massacre that we'd witnessed beneath the clear sky. What if the rain could wash away everything— the war and all the nightmares it created? I wished it could. I tried to go back to sleep, but the visions of that morning's mass murder were so vivid that all I could do was spend the night lying in the tall grass, staring up at the sky, clutching my little stone tight in my hand.

The wet grass made the frogs become active, and I started to play with them. Some snakes slithered nearby. Despite my love of nature, I was afraid of snakes and mice. I would have screamed, but I was still in shock from the carnage I'd witnessed that morning. I didn't feel fear or anything else. The shock held me in a kind of bubble, removed from the reality before me. I was existing merely to survive.

★ ★ ★ ★ ★

It is impossible to gauge the depth of my wounds. Constantly witnessing such brutality had traumatised me beyond repair, permanently destroying my childhood innocence. I was in a state of unfathomable turmoil: the attackers had stolen my once-happy home and my once-happy life, but they had also robbed me of the ability to dream and to trust anyone. They had destroyed my idyllic life and butchered my childhood. By that time I knew they were worse than attackers: they were assassins; they were the living dead.

I had gone through so much in such a short time that it felt like many years of my life had simply disintegrated. Years that I could never recapture—never live—had turned into ashes and blood. I was a little girl who'd been thrown, unwitting and helpless, into the midst of all the other victims, equally unwitting and helpless, whether they were young or old.

The entirety of this tragedy, and all that I had experienced as a result of it, had utterly numbed me. I could no longer feel anything. It was an ordeal to live without the slightest hope of better days to come, and I could not cope with it for another second. My subconscious mind took over, forcing me to be silent until such time as I was in a safe place—if that time ever came. I had lost my ability to speak, but that did not cause me any fear. Intuitively, I knew that it was my only way to protect myself. My silence became part of my shell—invisible yet incredibly strong. Within its safety I could still hear the music I loved. Nothing could pierce my protection. I instinctively stroked the smooth edge of my little stone: it was not invisible like my shell was, but no one but I knew that either one existed.

My small self was covered with fresh wounds and deep scars, physically and psychologically, but I knew I had to keep going. My shell would protect me: all I had to do was continue to put one foot in front of the other. The days came and went. I just kept walking behind my parents. Mother or Father would sometimes look back to make sure that I was still there; they knew I had lost my ability to speak, but they could not do anything to help me. When I collapsed from sheer exhaustion, Father would continue to walk along, carrying me in his arms; sometimes he would carry me off the road, and then all three of us would rest for a bit.

All that I had to hold onto was my little stone and the profound beauty of nature in the glorious autumn. The meadows were fragrant, and the fields' golden hues grew ever deeper. Every so often a bird would fly overhead, and I would silently watch it arc through the heavens as the three of us kept walking. Deep woods lined the horizon, and as the day wore on, the sun would disappear, little by little, behind the tree line. Before long, night would fall, bringing us some respite. The darkness completely changed our surroundings, and the long shadows felt comforting. One by one, bright stars would light up the sky, signalling that it was time to rest.

One night I chose a spot near a dandelion patch, resting my head on the soft leaves and blossoms. I hoped to fall asleep quickly, but even more, I hoped that some night soon, all would be truly peaceful, and we would not wake up to another day of war.

I looked up, found the brightest star, and thought of my special angel—the same one who had been on top of our Christmas tree. Closing my eyes, I prayed inwardly, *Dear Angel, thank you for saving me one more day.*

The tiniest leaves gave me strength and nourishment, and I nibbled gratefully whatever I could find to eat. I was grateful, in spite of all the chaos and brutality, because it meant that I had lived another day. I had survived. Besides, the war was quiet now. I could see the stars, I had my little stone, I had my shell to protect me, and I felt lucky to be alive. *Maybe all will be better someday,* I thought. With that, I drifted off to sleep under the starlit sky as the crickets chirped their stories.

That night's sleep brought me the most wonderful dream: I was home again, with all my books, my pianos, my friends, and our huge Christmas tree. The candles were lit, and Mikus, as mischievous as ever, squirmed in my arms, his eager paws playing with the ribbons in my hair. Lars stood right next to me, happy, healthy, and strong, just as he'd been before the war. I felt so happy. We were all as we'd always been, and everybody was smiling. The angel descended from the top of the tree, trying to reach me, but as soon as she came close enough, the dream ended, interrupted by a loud blast very close by.

I woke up instantly. It was time to move on.

5
Field of Fear

After devoting considerable time, focused attention, and deep concentration, I had thoroughly researched and prepared a lecture devoted to explaining the enormous variety of scales in music. My intension was to prove the scientific basis for major and minor, as adopted by and used for various reasons within both Western and Eastern music. Such reasons include but are not limited to mathematical logic, early fundamentals (e.g., sixth century BC Greece), and even those reasons that remain untraceable by scholarship. The goal of the lecture was to prove that contemporary experimental music, comprised of multiple ingenious contrivances, was equally as important as the system of scales upon which all music, Eastern and Western, is derived, which provides the outcome that we have termed *melody*.

Rest assured that my story is not going to become a dissertation on music theory and composition. I include this information merely to show my passion for music, which has sustained me all my life and has kept me from sinking into despair over my intrusive memories of the painful past.

Because the lecture was designed as a presentation to other teachers, I had needed to carefully find and incorporate a large amount of factual resources into my theories before finalising my material. Needless to say, that had been a painstaking and time-consuming process. I had finally delivered the lecture, at last, and now was on my way home, pleased that the attendees, my fellow teachers, had responded favourably to my efforts.

As I travelled homeward along the familiar Toronto roads, I reflected that the positive outcome made all my time and hard work well worth the effort. It had been imperative to find the examples I needed in actual compositions, which had been a slow and tedious, albeit gratifying, research process, even prior to receiving the favourable response. Although the preparation had brought me deep satisfaction, I had undertaken the assignment gratis, and so the positive endorsement from my colleagues was especially important to me; collegial acceptance in Canada had taken time and been hard won, and receiving it now validated my efforts. The results of the grand undertaking far exceeded my expectations. I felt excited about future pedagogical opportunities.

Glancing up in the rear-view mirror, I smiled at myself. As I've described, my joy in music and composition—and in teaching children—continued to deepen and flourish, even though painful memories of the past never ceased. I had learned to be grateful just for life itself, for all the gifts that I *did* have, instead of focusing on what I could never replace.

As I drove, the weather changed abruptly. A storm came up from out of nowhere. Papers and leaves and other small objects, whipped by the wind, suddenly blew all about the streets. People tried to take cover but lost their balance as they fought the wind, helplessly falling into puddles. Larger objects like mailboxes became dislodged by the storm's fury, and those rolled around, hitting pedestrians, cars, store windows, and everything else in their path. I gripped the wheel, peering through the torrents of rain, and slowing my speed to a crawl. I was not afraid of storms, but I did seek to arrive home safely.

I drew in my breath, awed as ever by nature's raw power: the lightning bolts flashed rapid-fire, seeming to have cut a hole in the thick, dark clouds, through which an endless, massive rush of water poured nonstop. The thunder echoed throughout the city, and pedestrians continued to scramble for shelter, although many still stumbled and fell, rain-splashed, as they ran against the wind.

Nature's light show continued to hold me spellbound as I drove, but I managed to hold the car steady in the downpour and high winds. Perhaps this was because I had long since learned how to survive even in the midst of unrelenting terror. Besides, I loved and respected thunderstorms, which, for me, represented an atmospheric cleansing. They washed the area clean of repulsive behaviour, offering the opportunity for a fresh start. I did not spend a lot of time thinking about this or analysing it—I'd never had the time to analyse my emotions, and I'd never wanted to bother anybody with expending the effort necessary to listen to my pain or my pondering, so these thoughts remained in my mind, like all my other thoughts. For the most part, they were a major component of my subconscious; they dictated the way I related to the world, but in an automatic way that I did not think about on a conscious level. While driving, I simply felt reverence for the storm's power, just as I felt reverence for all of nature.

The roads soon flooded, resulting in many detours. Consequently, it took much longer to get home than it would have in ordinary driving conditions. I did reach my house eventually, safe and sound, and I parked the car and went inside. It was only three o'clock in the afternoon, but the inside of the house was dark because the storm clouds had eclipsed the sun. I flipped a light switch, but the storm must have knocked out the power.

Mauser sat before the window, admiring the illumination provided by the lightning. Pinky, however, was nowhere in sight, having hidden under the bed. I chuckled, knowing I would have to employ the usual coaxing to get my smaller cat to emerge.

As the hours passed, it grew darker, but the storm showed no signs of abating. With the electricity out, there was nothing for me to do. I thought about doing some work by candlelight, but all the work I'd done to prepare the lecture, combined with the weather, contributed to my feeling quite fatigued. I decided not to fight it; sometimes, when truly physically exhausted, I was able to sleep without the disturbance of intrusive images of the past—at least for a while. As the storm raged and Mauser remained transfixed by its electric splendour, I made myself comfortable on the sofa, with Pinky snuggled in my arms. Her purring lulled me into a relaxed state, and I felt myself drift off.

Fatigue was not to bring me peaceful sleep this time. Before long, my unconscious mind took me back into the midst of the war all over again.

★ ★ ★ ★ ★

It was early morning, before dawn, still as dark as night. Perhaps even darker. The grass was wet with dewdrops, and the occasional spider waited in patient silence on its gossamer, knowing its hapless prey would arrive before long to provide a meal.

As usual, there was nothing good to hope for in the coming day. I found awe in the scenes of nature all around me—grateful as ever for the gift of life—but, otherwise I kept walking dutifully behind my parents. Our single aim was just to stay alive each day. Father continued to head north, and Mother and I followed his lead.

We walked and walked, but nothing changed. The detestable firing from the snipers and planes overhead remained constantly, reminding me of the angry wasps that always seemed to appear without warning, arcing and diving through the summertime air. The revolting display persisted, the instruments of death and destruction following us as if they were our shadows. Our entire trek, sorrowful and tragic as it would have been under any circumstances, was a game of life and death. I imagined some vicious "player" up in the sky, taking sadistic pleasure and satisfaction in watching his helpless victims squirm. The bullets zoomed like tiny vampires thirsty for blood; we succeeded in dodging them solely by luck.

The road was mined, which left the harvest-time fields the only potentially navigable route. The golden wheat shimmered as the sun began to rise, catching the colours of the wildflowers scattered in the midst of the stalks of grain. Every now and then, the odd rabbit would jump up, startling me. The sharp stalks of wheat left deep cuts and scratches on my legs, making the walk painful.

The weather had been very favourable for the crops, and the grain grew tall and dense, higher than my head. I walked in circles more than once, eventually losing my parents. Mute from the trauma of the tanks' massacre that we'd witnessed, I could not call out to them. The sun beat down mercilessly by that point in the day, but I started to run as fast as I could to find my parents, regardless of the heat and glare. It was frightening to be alone in the middle of a place where I could see neither the beginning nor the end. The terror was worse than the discomfort, so I kept running until, at last, my feet gave out. There was nothing to do but crawl, and so I crawled, the sharp stalks cutting and scratching my arms as I pulled my body through the soil.

While I crawled, the weather changed quite suddenly. The sky darkened as a thunderstorm moved into the area. Pulling myself up to my knees, I watched as lightning struck a tree a short distance away. Everything began to swirl around me. My vision swam, and I grew increasingly dizzy, feeling my head overwhelmed by a buzzing sensation as blackness descended. The ordeal and hunger both had taken their toll, and I fainted.

★ ★ ★ ★ ★

The storm had simmered down, and I regained consciousness and felt raindrops falling intermittently on my face. I had no way of determining how long I'd lain on the ground, but I was soaked through to the bone. Instinctively, I felt for my pocket to reassure myself that

I still had my stone. Yes, it was there. I tried to resume searching for my parents, but my boots were covered with a thick layer of wet clay, making it increasingly difficult to walk. Somehow I just kept moving on, not knowing where I was or which direction to take. I was utterly lost but too numb to think about it. The warm rain continued to run down my face and body, comforting me: the rain was the first thing in a long, long time that touched me without the intension of causing pain or harm.

In the next instant, heavy steps approached me. Thinking and hoping that it might be my parents, I reached out, but I saw a strange and forbidding face instead of their familiar ones. It was too late to hide, so I closed my eyes and covered my ears, trying to avoid looking at the mean face.

He was very tall, and he used the butt of his rifle to push me down. I fell onto the muddy ground, and then he yelled at me to get up. No sooner did I manage to struggle up to my knees, than another blow followed, knocking me back into the mud. I lay perfectly still, pretending to be unconscious and not opening my eyes until I could hear him walking away.

An alarming sound arose in the distance, and I recognised my parents' cries. The tall, mean man had found my parents, who were no more able to escape his cruelty than I had been. Their cries will echo in my heart forever, hurting me more deeply than the physical pain of the wounds he'd inflicted on my body. I trained my ear toward the sound of the cries—my musical education enabled me to do this with precision beyond my years—and headed in that direction. I crawled through the tall wheat, finding Mother and Father seated on the ground, pale and speechless. Our reunion was sombre, with no words exchanged, but I could tell that they'd been looking for me for some time. Unfortunately, the attacker had found us first. This no longer mattered; all three of us were still alive, and now we were together again.

More time passed, and we all knew that we had to resume walking. I put my arms around Mother, attempting to comfort her because I could see how much pain she was in. All our clothes were soaked, but I tore off a piece from one of my dresses, using it as a bandage to wrap around Mother's bleeding head. Father had gathered some wet grass, which he put on his own wounds. The rifle butt had done far more damage to my parents than to me. Eventually, we gathered enough strength to start walking again.

We kept moving ahead, very slowly. All that mattered was having enough stamina to move on. I fought to keep my eyes open and not drop from sheer exhaustion and hunger. I was terrified of being left alone, and that fear was worse than feeling bone-weary or starved.

The field stretched to the horizon in every direction, so huge that it literally had no end in sight. We all felt too weak to keep moving, and frequently all three of us stopped in our tracks and sat down on the muddy soil.

All had been quiet for a while, and so we sat on the ground, nursing our wounds and relishing the precious peace. It began to get quite dark, and the air felt damp and chilly. We were all still soaked; the sun had never reappeared, and we felt cold. Huddling close together, we shivered in the night air. The shivering kept us awake, and we watched the blazing panorama beyond the endless sea of wheat: whatever was still left of our beloved city was being demolished.

Before daybreak, distant rumbling from the land road alerted us to trouble ahead. We had been walking through the fields for many days and nights, so we were no longer aware of all that went on along the road. The rain had stopped during the night, and the ground had begun to dry. It was time to move on. The sharp wheat stalks had irritated our wounds, which were now inflamed.

Suddenly the air was filled with planes that started shooting at us. The bulletscame close but never hit us directly. The deadly game had begun anew, trapping us in the field once again. We felt like pawns in the deadly game, or like prey hunted by a sadistic predator who had no intention to kill but merely delighted in seeing how much we could endure before we would snap and our morale would shatter. All we could do was duck, hoping to shield ourselves. The predator I'd imagined must have derived macabre pleasure from watching our desperate scramble for cover.

I was tired, and my limbs ached. I lost the strength to stand and walk, so I started crawling, which resulted in losing my parents again, as I could neither speak nor shout. In a panic I stood up, terror overtaking my pain, exhaustion, and hunger, and I started walking, regardless of whether I was in view of the snipers. I just didn't care anymore: I felt empty and numb; I had no feelings left inside me at all. The shell that surrounded and protected me must have been what kept me alive.

Exhausted, starving, and lost, I walked in a daze. I was utterly alone and devoid of emotion, but my survival instinct persisted. I kept moving, and some spark of the child I had been longed to disappear into the air itself, in the hope that my special angel would find me and take me to heaven, where the pain would stop and I would find peace.

I thought that I'd begun hearing things, and I wondered if I was delirious. No, I definitely heard someone call my name. *Mother? Father?* I started to run, but I stumbled and fell.

Next I heard steps. They kept moving closer. *What if it isn't Mother and Father?* My relief instantly turned to terror, and I hid between the sharp wheat stalks, which scratched my face. I was so afraid one of the attackers would hit me again, even though my body was covered with so many wounds, cuts, and scratches that there would be no place left to strike that hadn't already been hurt.

Bewildered, I stood up, wanting only to look directly into the assassin's eyes. After so much abuse, maybe this round would not hurt as much. Somebody touched my shoulder. I quivered involuntarily, pulling back. I would have screamed, but my ability to use my voice had not returned. All I could do was give myself over to fate, whatever it might be. Who would the attacker be this time? Wide-eyed, I turned around to look at the person who was about to mercilessly hurt me again.

The glare of the afternoon sun was right in my eyes, all but blinding me, and the tears it released blurred my vision. Blinking away the tears, I realised that the two people coming closer were my parents. They must have been looking for me all the while I'd been lost, just like the last time. *Mother! Father!* I tried to run toward them, but my legs gave out. I collapsed again, but Mother and Father had seen me, and they kept coming closer. I heard their voices, but I could not answer.

Some snakes slithered by, but I had long since stopped paying attention to them. They had become a common sight, and, besides, I had discovered that they were not the worst creatures one could encounter, which diminished my former fear. I was very hungry, and I grasped some wheat stalks. Tearing at them with my hands, which bled as the sharp stalks cut me, I tried to eat the kernels of wheat. Mother and Father found me then, and Father pulled me up from the ground.

At last we were together again. We kept moving forward, and I struggled to stay closer behind my parents, no matter how exhausted I felt: I could not bear the thought of getting lost again. The seemingly endless field of wheat ended suddenly, and we found ourselves in a crop of potatoes; a sea of emerald green strewn with tiny white flowers surrounded us. Thankfully, those plants were not nearly as sharp as the wheat.

The air attacks had stopped, but it did not take long for them to resume. Soon we had to scramble for cover, pawns in the devilish game yet again, but there was now nowhere to hide. The bullets tore the plants right up from their roots, and the soil sprayed through the air, blowing all over us. Mother, Father, and I looked at one another, and I was sure they must feel the same way I did: all three of us were hunted prey, just waiting for our moment to die.

In the midst of those frantic, desperate moments, I thought of Mikus, Lolo, Lars, and my pianos. I'd lost everything else, even the hope that I would come out of this waking nightmare alive. If I had to die in this potato field, at least it would be while I thought of my treasured memories.

Instinctively, my hand again sought my precious little stone. I was afraid that it might have fallen out of my pocket after all the crawling through the wheat field and the many times I'd fallen down, but, miraculously, it was still there. Inching my fingers toward it, I stroked the stone with a tenderness that bordered on reverence, and then I pushed it even deeper into my pocket. For the briefest of moments, this took my mind off the ever-present horror that surrounded me. I still had my cherished little stone, that small but solid symbol of my home and of all the happiness I'd once known. No one could ever take my stone, or my treasured memories, away from me.

As suddenly as they'd arrived, the planes changed course, enabling us to continue our unending walk. Beyond the potato field, some houses came into view. I dug up a potato with my hands, rubbed the dirt off on my thigh, and started to eat; I was so ravenous, I didn't even notice where my parents were. Half the potato remained when I heard a very familiar sound nearby. I swallowed bits of raw potato as the sound came closer and closer. I knew that sound, but I was incredulous that it might be what I thought it was.

In the next instant I understood that I'd heard exactly what I thought I'd heard: *Lolo!* Yes, there she was, my dear, big mare. *Lolo,* I thought inwardly, wishing I could call her name, remembering all the wonderful times that we'd ridden through the meadows during happier days.

After many days of walking, we had reached our farm. I'd never imagined it would still be there. I tried to run toward Lolo, but I fell.

Still holding the half-eaten potato, I crawled the rest of the way. Finally, I reached the gate, but I could not get up. I put my head against Lolo's leg and just kept patting it. She nickered in response. My mare loved me as much as I loved her, and she must have sensed what I had been through, because she knelt down as far as she could, softly snorting as she felt my familiar, loving strokes on her neck.

Crouching close to Lolo, I offered her the rest of my potato. I was still very hungry, but I would never neglect my beloved mare. I watched her eat the piece of potato that I had saved for her, knowing that she and I were equally grateful for each other. The sun started to set behind the barn; the long and painful day was finally over. Lolo and I were reunited, and I felt so safe and warm that I let myself forget all that had happened—even if the forgetting would not last long. Night fell, blanketing the farm in peacefulness. The song of crickets and the hooting of owls added to the tranquillity. Night sounded the same as it always had. I did not feel pain anymore; I felt like I was in heaven.

The stars started to twinkle, and I chose one for each family member and for each of my lost friends. Just as I had on Christmas Eve, I chose the smallest one for myself—I still wanted my own star to be so small that only happiness could fit on it, with no room for bad people. But I also wanted it to be so small that I could hide it in my heart and take it with me. Nobody would ever be able to find my star, just as nobody would ever be able to find my little stone.

I closed my eyes and let myself drift off. For just a moment before sleep descended, I imagined the peace of heaven penetrating my soul. My angel had found me! She was watching over Lolo and me. I slept under the starlit sky, imagining all the things I'd so loved during the precious moments of my idyllic, all-too-brief childhood: holding Mikus, riding Lolo, playing my pianos, watching the birds flying free, seeing and smelling the flowers in full bloom, and having Lars and all my animal friends around me. Mikus would want to know where I had been for so long. I could see him demanding this information, batting my hair with his paws as he listened to me recount all that had happened during our separation. He'd always been a good listener, and this time was no different. Sighing in my sleep, I did not even feel the cold air wrap around me. It felt so wonderful to be home again, the way it used to be, even if it was only in my dreams.

My treasured memories and the music I loved were woven into the energy that comprised my invisible shell of protection, fortifying it so that it would sustain me, and I felt safe within that protective bubble. I could feel the small stone, even in my sleep. I could feel my angel watching over me. Maybe I really was safe now.

6
Dark Night

A cool and gentle breeze passed through my garden in Toronto, blowing the leaves from the tall maple onto the patio. A few leaves found their way inside through the open patio door, landing on the music books that I had selected for my evening's work. It was just a bit before sunset, and I liked to gather my materials while sufficient natural light still came into the house from the outside.

As my gaze roved around the garden, I noticed that, although the maple had already seeded itself, it quite simply forgot to stop growing! The tree was always full of life, with birds frolicking, squirrels displaying their aerobatics, and raccoons scampering into their favourite hollow at nap time. This had never been more evident than it was on this particular late afternoon. I smiled to myself at the maple's vitality; it only slept during the winter, which would arrive before long. Tilting my head back, I scanned the sky. I loved to look at the cloud formations, which differed from season to season. Feeling as close to nature as ever, I reflected that nature and music were the things with which I had shared both the happy and sad times of my life.

Whenever I had the chance, I would walk to the park, where, for a few moments, I could feel free of all the demands placed upon me. While I was in the park I did not have to think about anything; I could just be, hoping that the tranquillity would not trigger painful visions of the past. I never knew for sure what might cause a trigger, but cleansing my mind in the midst of nature usually kept it at peace, at least for a while.

Spontaneously, I decided to go to the park. It was a short walk, and soon I was passing the brook where the duck family nested. That always inspired me. I loved watching the ducklings follow their more experienced elders as they all made ripples in the clear water. Further downstream a beaver had built a dam, and the freshly gnawed lumber spread a pleasant woody smell all around. A flock of Canada geese filled the air with their typical squabbling as they winged their way south to their seasonal retreat.

Nature's meticulous preparation of the seasons still fascinated me as much as it had during my childhood. It still seemed as if some "elder" went about to make sure that all creatures had settled down in their proper spots, whereupon he closed the gate for the winter. The sunset was brilliant, making the walk home delightful. Along the way, a couple of raccoons passed by, not minding my sharing the trail with them.

I looked toward the front yard as I returned home, noticing that many of the maple's leaves covered it. The tree was large, and its leafy canopy dominated the garden, extending over both the patio and the front yard. A couple of grey squirrels were busy running up and down the length of the maple's trunk, as if they had lost yesterday. It was leaf-gathering time, and the crisp leaves crackled beneath the soles of my boots. The pile of leaves had grown higher and higher, and I knew the time had come to bag them, but I kept putting it off. A sudden gust of wind blew across the yard, scattering the leaves all over the lawn.

That's what I get for procrastinating! I chided myself, but couldn't help chuckling. This was nature in all its glory, and I enjoyed its sense of humour. Nature always directed the scene, no matter what the scene was. It was human folly to think otherwise.

As the sky darkened, I went inside to prepare for the following day. The amount of work that I had usually took me beyond midnight, which was just what I wanted. The purpose of taking on extra duties, which involved long hours and a frequently overwhelming workload, was to be sure I did not have time to think about my personal burdens. I had come to understand and accept that my memories were outside my control, but my thoughts were not. By consuming my time with the responsibilities of my profession, as both teacher and musician, I was able to avoid my lifelong concerns and sadness—at least most of the time. As always, my passion for music and my deep love of nature sustained me. Together, they continued to help me maintain the invisible yet impenetrable shell of protection that surrounded me—but I felt better when I had as small an amount of time to think as possible. Having a few moments to enjoy nature's glory was beneficial; having hours to while away through the evening was not.

As I worked I felt tiredness creep up on me, but I resisted it, wishing to finish my tasks. Falling asleep was not always easy, so I usually did not fight feeling tired. I had learned through experience that being asleep proved to be worse, even when I fell asleep from sheer exhaustion. Before long, my painful past intruded upon my dream state, constantly bringing me back via memory to one or another ghastly moment from my war-ravaged childhood.

Palliative care was neither accessible nor affordable. The responsibility of providing the basic necessities—food, shelter, etc.—was my top priority, as I was a single person and my sole means of financial support. This left very little extra to provide for any of my needs beyond those basic ones. As a result, my colleagues tended to misunderstand the true reason for my professional undertakings, and they came to take me for granted. That eventually brought me great sorrow, because I realised that physical wounds heal with time and proper care, but emotional ones require much more than that. Some emotional wounds can and do heal, but others cannot and do not. My circumstances had forced me to learn how to go on, even though I could never move on.

The infliction of emotional wounds is almost always premeditated and almost always pursued at the exact moment when the victim is the most vulnerable. That was a truth that I had learned to accept at a very young age—too young—and it had become part of me. I had come to understand that there is a grave difference between feeling alone and being alone. I had lost my ability to trust people, with the exception of a precious few whose selfless kindness had saved me. Having learned as an adult that some people did not care about or appreciate my efforts, I nevertheless still felt mystified whenever I encountered people who seemed to think that I, or anyone else, did not deserve compassion and empathy. Yet, many of those I interacted with seemed to believe that because I worked tirelessly, I must have no feelings. This reality resulted in significant disappointment for me, which only served to reinforce my already weak sense of trust in others. I felt that those I had trusted in the past and those who I could trust in the present were few and far between; I cherished them, but I doubted that many more trustworthy people would enter my life. This also caused me to doubt my colleagues' praise and recognition of my efforts and successes, my well-received lecture notwithstanding.

Many times I felt like I was sitting all alone on an iceberg, expected to produce so that others could thrive, all the while keeping my own life on hold. It was as if the fight to survive from day to day during the extreme horror of my wartime childhood had extended into my adult life, and I would never have the opportunity to live life with any sense of ease or lasting contentment.

The efforts of the day and my mental meanderings had taken their toll, and I fell asleep at my desk before supper. Fatigue and hunger must have contributed to my sleeping even more fitfully than usual, and my subconscious brought me back to our last days at the farm during the war. I felt abandoned, all alone in the dark, as the veil of memory shrouded my mind and took hold of me.

★ ★ ★ ★ ★

In happier days, I had always enjoyed all the animals at the farm. There was big Rosie, the sweet cow. I had watched her deliver her calf, Moo-Moo. The piglets in the barn squabbled over the evening meal at the end of every day, and I loved watching them too. Father's shiny horses were magnificent when taken out for their daily exercise, and I always looked forward to that. I also enjoyed playing with the three big dogs—Nero, Mister Speckle, and Bruto. Most of all, there was Lolo, my beloved mare.

Even after our harrowing trek on foot from our destroyed house through the decimated city and onward to our farm, I still took pleasure in the animals. Headed out to visit my animal friends one day, I noticed that the barn door was open and some unusual activity had taken place. Big, odd-looking machines were lined up, and they started to move toward the woods behind the farm. I wondered what they were and where they were going in such a great hurry.

My parents had long since taken it for granted that I would look after myself. Everybody was so busy doing all the things they needed to do, running all around the farm, that they had no time to explain what was happening. Years later I realised that they could not possibly have explained it to me; they couldn't comprehend it themselves. As a child, I could not understand any of this. It felt like all the adults knew some secret, and I was just shut out. Abandoned. That was the part that hurt most of all. Because circumstances had forced me into such a cruel existence at such a young age, and because I could not understand the reason for what I considered a "secret," I started to develop an intense hatred of avoidance and a deep mistrust of those who did not honestly share the truth.

Several days passed, during which time trucks came and went, and I was left to just wonder why. I visited all the animals every day, whether they were in the stalls and sheds or out in the pasture. The lambs were in the pasture closest to the main house, so I took my scissors, intending to cut the grass so that I could feed them, as they were still a bit young to graze on their own. But as I approached the pasture, I saw that the lambs were gone. Looking around the barnyard, I realised that the geese and the hens were gone too, and I didn't see or hear the rooster, either. Something had changed drastically, but I didn't know what it was.

At least my three big dogs were still there. Nero, Mister Speckle, and Bruto all seemed to sense that I had changed. I had become quiet and sad, and the sudden, inexplicable change only made me more so. The dogs always wanted to be near me so that I could pet and hug them, and that day was no exception. As they surrounded me, eager for their daily dose of affection and unqualified love, I buried my face in their fur. To my sensitive, uncomprehending young heart, it seemed that my dogs and my mare were the only ones around me with any empathy, the only ones I could count on for unconditional love and constancy.

The big, strange machines were there, making the same disturbing noises that they always did before they disappeared into the woods. Everybody was running and shouting. As I watched, the commotion accelerated. I could see men in the woods, digging enormously deep and wide holes. They seemed to be in a great hurry; the tension mounted, and the farmhands kept running back and forth, carrying all sizes of planks. The longer I watched, the stranger the scene became, so I went to see Lolo.

I found my mare resting, and I leaned my head against her warm neck. Soon I dozed off. It was such a wonderful change to have a peaceful rest without any threat of intruders or attackers. Why could it not have lasted? Why could the assassins not leave us in peace?

I bolted upright at the sound of nickering. Horrified, I watched, helpless, as the men led all the horses into the woods and lowered the animals down into the freshly dug holes. The deep holes had been dug to protect them from being taken away by the enemy, but I did not understand what was happening; I only thought to protect Lolo, afraid that the men would take my beloved mare away from me and imprison her in a dark hole below ground. I held onto Lolo's leg with all my might, but one of the men pushed me aside, and then they led Lolo away, just like all the other horses. In despair, I ran after the men, trying to get Lolo back, but again, one of the men just pushed me aside.

I still was not able to talk, but I used body language in a vain attempt to plead for Lolo. I was so upset about what I considered to be my mare's abduction that I trembled. I had shed few tears for my other losses, but then the tears ran down my face. Nobody seemed to notice or care. I didn't bother to wipe away the tears. My grief had made me forget that I had no time to cry, but harsh reality would soon remind me.

Soon after that, the sun set. It quickly began to get very dark . I had to sleep in the barn that night because the main house where we usually slept had already been searched many times, and some of the young men had been taken away. The barn had a secret door in case of a raid or a fire, so it was safer than the main house.

We had gone to our respective makeshift quarters, and all was quiet. I could hear the wind whisper through the long alley of spruce trees that led to the main house; as always the sound reminded me of the flute's delicate chirp. These trees cast dark shadows that made it difficult to see if anything, or anyone, approached, and so one of the farmhands always perched in the tallest tree to signal any suspicious movements. Knowing this I felt safe, and I drifted off to sleep in my barn accommodations.

But my vivid, unpleasant dreams haunted my restless sleep. The images that flickered through my unconscious were not in any chronological order; instead, they seemed to appear in order of the severity of their traumatic effect. The repulsive deeds that I had witnessed, and to which I had been subjected, embedded themselves deep in my subconscious; images of them tormented me mercilessly, in both my waking and sleeping hours. They were worse while I slept. At my young age, all I could manage was to abide the situation that was far beyond my control. Perhaps the images tortured me because my subconscious rebelled against that which it found so intensely revolting. Even then, I knew intuitively—with that uncanniness of knowing without knowing how I knew—that my feelings of revulsion toward the malevolence, horror, and unjustifiable abuse were there to stay. I would never understand or accept such behaviour, no matter how long I lived; I would never want to—I would rather die than sanction the unacceptable.

I tossed fitfully as the recollections flashed through my mind in fleeting images. Initially, they were pleasant, such as the statues of the two lions at the farm gate, or the white columns in front of the main house that were so large that two people could not reach around them. Perhaps in disastrous moments I subconsciously sought refuge in memories of happier times, like the day when Father noticed Lars and me playing around the columns. Father had wanted to play a trick by hiding behind a column and touching our hands. I'd been amazed at how long Lars's arms had suddenly grown, not realising what Father was up to. Many precious moments came to mind, but most of the time an image from some painful event that I could not comprehend would intrude, overshadowing the pleasant memory.

My restless sleep continued, with the unpleasant overtaking the pleasant. The devastating memory of our last Christmas Eve with Lars supplanted the recollection of happier childhood play. Yet, even as my nightmares raged, even with all I'd already endured, I could never have anticipated the uproar that would occur at the farm during that dark night. It changed my life forever, ruthlessly throwing me into a life so unrelentingly harsh that, under the force of its cruelty, even the strongest would wither.

★ ★ ★ ★ ★

I was used to being awakened in the middle of the night and having to rush to a hiding place. Something had awakened me, but I couldn't say for certain what it was. I was already in the barn, and I knew where the secret door was in case the barn itself was no longer safe.

Peeking through a space between the boards in the barn wall, I saw some vehicles coming toward the main house. My heart leapt into my throat, my pulse raced, and my whole body trembled in fear. The soldiers were demanding horses and young men for mobilisation. I sneaked out of the barn and hid under a gooseberry bush; I'd noticed people take cover under bushes many times before. Only the elderly remained in the house to face interrogation.

The soldiers were very agitated as they stormed the house. I closed my eyes and covered my ears to avoid hearing the cries of old Otis, a man long loyal to our family, as he fell to the ground after one of the attackers assaulted him with a weapon. From my hiding place, I could hear it all through the open front door of the house, but I could not see it. It was very dark, and I needed to stay under cover. I heard the attackers leave. Otis must have heard, too, because he did not get up until after they had left. I recognised the sounds of his groans and his pained attempts to struggle to his feet.

The thorns on the gooseberry bush were sharp, drawing blood on the parts of my skin that were exposed, but I did not so much as wince. I'd long since grown accustomed to discomforts like that. The insects from the hay and bushes constantly got stuck in my hair, and sometimes they bit me most unpleasantly .A wasp stung me that night; I must have disturbed it, as they usually do not come out at night. The sting was painful, but it did not hurt anywhere near as much as the pain I'd already suffered. Besides, the wasp was a creature merely defending itself in the way nature intended; it was not a cruel, vicious assailant deliberately intending to inflict harm and terror. Wasps were not assassins.

In the next instant my heart almost stopped. I was absolutely petrified as I saw and heard the heavy boots of one of the attackers. *Did he hear me breathing?* I thought, panicked. He came so close that he almost stepped on my hands, which were on the ground to help me balance in my awkward position scrunched beneath the bush. I kept perfectly still, my breath bated, praying for him to move so that I could exhale. At last, he walked on, and I could breathe again. Relief flooded every inch of my body.

As I crept in stealth back to the barn, I struggled not to replay in my mind the scene of Otis's attack. But it was no use: what I'd witnessed that night etched itself deep in my soul. I'd already lost my childhood innocence, and I already knew nothing would ever be the same again. However, before that night, I had never imagined how worthless life was in the eyes of the attackers—the living dead could inflict harm so matter-of-factly because life itself meant nothing to them.

★ ★ ★ ★ ★

After what I came to think of as the "dark night," sleeping in the barn loft became easier to bear, especially as I became more accustomed to the insects and the mice. Some nights I would awaken to feel myself being pulled down from the loft and pushed through the secret door. One night the barn was set afire. I ran to the safety of the secret door so fast that I fell into the grain bin. Nobody noticed I was missing, so I had to crawl out by myself, along with dozens of equally frightened mice. As with the snakes during our trek through the fields, all that I witnessed helped me overcome my former fears.

Some days passed without any intrusion by the attackers. The farmhands were kept busy feeding the horses in the holes. I sat, horror-stricken, in one of them with my Lolo one day. I heard distant shouting and unusual sounds from the horses as they were led away. I tried to clutch Lolo's mouth to prevent her from responding to the cries of the other horses.

I visited Lolo many times every day, bringing my mare her favourite treat: carrots. Rations made sugar cubes impossible to procure, but Lolo did not seem to mind the switch. My three dogs followed me everywhere, always eager to be petted and hugged, and I was glad to comply. Interacting with my animal friends provided the precious affection and comfort that I sorely needed and which I was grateful to receive and return. Days such as those were at least somewhat endurable, but the nights were a different story.

Darkness descended quickly, smothering the farm in a heaviness that was as oppressive as it was inescapable. The darkness and the unrelenting threat of renewed intrusion and violence became the pattern of our daily lives. Even on days when the intruders did not appear, the threat that they might never disappeared. We were caught up in the midst of a raging war, helpless pawns with no way out.

In spite of the brutality all around us, life went on. One day at the far wing of the main house a newborn arrived. She was tiny and looked just like a little angel. Her little eyes opened, and she tried to cry but was not strong enough; all she could manage was something like the weak mew of the tiniest kitten.

The next day was Sunday, and a small group gathered beneath the big chestnut tree, the sun shining brightly. The air was still and silent, but we could never be sure how long that would last—the air attacks could begin again at any moment.

Chosen to be the baby's godmother, Mother held the frail infant in her arms. Little Dora opened her eyes, working her tiny mouth almost imperceptibly. A moment later her eyes closed, and they did not open again.

Dear Angel, please take little Dora to heaven, where she'll be safe and have no pain, I prayed inwardly.

* * * * *

Days came and went, but we never knew what the next day would bring, which made living increasing difficult, even for the strongest and most resilient people. I felt lost and alone, never quite sure of what to do with myself except survive for another day. Focusing on my animals, I just prayed that the nightmare would end soon, even though my fast-fading hope made that seem impossible.

One day as the sun set, some military vehicles rolled up the drive, stopping in front of the main house. It was too late to hide in the barn or under a bush in the garden. Someone pushed me into one of the deep holes where the horses had already spent many days and nights. Lolo was in the hole, and I put my arms around her neck, comforted by my mare's presence. My peaceful feeling was not to last long; a shot rang through the air, shattering any vestige of calm. It was my turn to comfort Lolo with my presence: I stroked her tenderly so she would not be spooked, and she remained quiet.

I heard a cry, which I recognised as belonging to Otis's wife, Anna. Their son, Peter, had been shot right in front of his mother and father. Peter had been trying to save the other horses hidden in the deep holes, but to no avail: the soldiers shot him dead and then took the horses. By some miracle, the soldiers had missed the hole where Lolo and I were hidden. I clung to Lolo, determined never to let go, and as dusk darkened the air above, I fell asleep.

I was used to the sounds of the woods, be it night or day, but the damp soil in the deep hole made me shiver. My own trembling awakened me. I huddled as close as possible to Lolo, afraid to fall asleep again. The night sky was very clear, and some bright stars peeked through the branches of the trees. Momentarily, I felt relief as I watched the stars twinkle and heard the soothing sounds of the nocturnal creatures in their habitats. As always, nature soothed me. I felt no pain and was almost content. I wondered if this had been one of those fortunate nights when I'd fallen asleep. At night it became difficult to determine whether I was dreaming or awake.

I watched the morning sunlight stream through the overhead foliage. A small loaf of bread descended, landing on Lolo's straw bed. I shared the bread with my mare, just as I'd shared the raw potato. I wondered how long I would have to stay in the pit.

Lolo and I spent many days and nights in the pit. The earthen walls were always damp, and they were high because of the depth of the pit. I played with the beetles and earthworms, rearranged Lolo's straw bed so that she would be comfortable, and used my finger to draw a keyboard on the damp, earthen wall. As my fingers moved across the keys from memory, I heard the music in my head, and the damp, dark hole filled with bright, beautiful sounds. My shell continued to protect me. I touched the small stone that I kept in my pocket, hugged Lolo's neck, and listened to the music that surrounded me. I was safe; no one could hurt me anymore.

I had no conception of how long I'd been in the pit, because it was dark most of the time. On sunny days, some light filtered through the overhead branches of the trees, but passing clouds and the sun's inevitable journey through the sky kept the light from lasting for too long. The moonlight was bright some nights, but I soon began to feel like a captive of the dark.

★ ★ ★ ★ ★

One night the moon was high and bright, and various strange sounds kept coming closer. A ladder was lowered into the hole, and somebody tried to lift me up and carry me out of the pit. *Will Lolo be coming up too?* I wondered, automatically concerned for my mare. I leaned over Lolo, patting her several times, but she did not move. Maybe she was sleeping. I could not speak, even to whisper in Lolo's ear, but I could see that her eyes were closed and she was not moving. I put my hand beneath her nostrils; Lolo did not seem to be breathing. A voice called down to me that I had to hurry. I tried to reach the ladder but slipped back. I preferred to stay with Lolo, anyway. I put some hay around her, hoping that she would wake up—she could eat some of the hay when she did.

Lolo and the three dogs were the last link to my once-happy life, and I could not accept that Lolo was gone. A pair of strong hands appeared at the top of the ladder, holding it steady, and I climbed to the top.

Once above ground, I could see that the large yard was empty. My legs felt funny after so many days and nights in the pit, where I couldn't really move around or stretch. I discovered that my parents and I were to leave the farm that night, before everything was burned down. The barn was already gone; only the foundation and some tools were left. It had been set ablaze while the farmhands were hiding in the loft. Some of them managed to escape the flames, but others disappeared without explanation.

I didn't let myself think about my three dogs. All I saw were their chains, so they must have been let loose to run off; otherwise, they would have perished by fire or bullets. This was too much to bear after losing Lolo, and so I just hoped they would find a safe place. That was all I could do for all my lost animals: pray that they were safe and at peace.

After surviving the war's destruction of our home by fire, I could not even think about watching our farm burn. This was more than just another night of unpredictable horror. This felt like the end, the absolute end. I felt like I had nothing left but my little stone. Feeling for it, I clutched it tight in my hand, pressing it as deeply into my pocket as I could.

Another long walk began for my parents and me. It was a damp and chilly night, and fog began to descend, wrapping the farm in its mystery. The glow of the moon was eerie behind the shroud of fog. As we came closer to the woods, we could see that fire had scorched some of the trees, and their barren trunks and branches cast ghostly silhouettes against the fog-shrouded moonlight. The darkness prevented us from seeing the ground, so as we traversed the trail through the woods, we constantly tripped over tree roots, as well as the bodies of those who had tried to escape but lost their lives before reaching freedom.

It was safer to take a few steps at a time, and then listen and wait, or hide behind a tree, until it was safe to move on. That night seemed to last forever. At some point the trail was so narrow that the tree branches scratched my face. I just kept walking behind my parents, one hand in my pocket so that I could hold my little stone.

This walk felt much longer than any other, and the darkness and the damp, chilly air made it seem to last for eternity. At first, I'd had no idea where we were headed—which made the night-time trek even more frightening—but then I caught some of Father's hushed explanations to Mother, and so I learned that we were to meet a train that would take us farther away from the front. Mother had brought some family photographs, but, otherwise we had left the farm empty-handed, as all the supplies had been stolen. Mother had our precious photos, and I had my stone—they were the only symbols of our once-happy life that we would keep. The three of us had the clothes on our backs and the shoes on our feet—and that was all.

I thought I saw an owl or another nocturnal creature with bright eyes. The gleam kept coming closer. Momentarily losing sight of my parents, I hid behind a bush. The gleam proved to be a flashlight: some soldiers were looking for something or someone. I did not dare to breathe; my heart started pounding, and I prayed the soldiers wouldn't hear it. The men passed without noticing me, so my heart must not have sounded as loud to them as it did in my own ears, where it echoed like the orchestra timpani. It was another lucky night. I remembered from our previous trek that walking in the dark made it easier to hide.

I still could not see my parents. Gripping the stone even more tightly, I breathed as shallowly as I could, in case any other soldiers lay in wait. *Keep me safe, Angel.*

After some time another dim light appeared in the midst of the fog, and it kept coming closer. *Should I hide again?* It came closer and closer, and grew larger and larger, and then I heard the locomotive engine. The train slowed down slightly, but it never stopped to allow anyone to get on. It just kept moving slowly ahead. I ran after it, but it kept moving away. I knew it was my only chance for escape, having no idea where my parents were at that point. Leaving the stone deep in the corner of my pocket, I ran as fast as I could. I tripped and fell, so my hands and knees were cut and bruised. With what little remaining strength I had, I got up, again running as fast as I could, but the train kept moving away. It must have been the will to live, pure survival instinct, that gave me the strength to get close enough to the train to hop onto the slippery step just before the speed increased again.

I clung to the handrail, and then somebody pulled me up and into the train. It was very dark; I peered all around me but could not see if my parents had made it onto the train. I searched in vain for them, praying that they had reached the train during the time that I'd been separated from them in the woods. Going through the cars, I saw many wounded people, some of whom had collapsed on the floor, making it impossible to tell if they were alive or dead. Through the windows all I could see were shadows rushing past.

I sank to the floor in despair and exhaustion; tears filled my eyes, and I felt totally lost. My parents were gone. All I had left was my little stone. I clutched and stroked it, but it did not soothe me. Nothing could soothe me now.

It was a very long and disturbing night. Some soldiers stopped the train, but they had no weapons; they did not shout or hurt anybody. I hid in a dark corner and pretended to be dead, just in case. The train resumed its course slowly; so slowly that it felt like it would take forever to get anywhere. I could not tell how many days had passed. Most of the time I either slept fitfully or just kept aimlessly staring out the window, wondering what would become of me.

I was so hungry that my whole body trembled in pain. The people next to me shared some food with one another but never offered me any. The only way to keep track of the time and days was to count the dark nights; eventually, I lost count.

The hunger and loneliness made me philosophical. I knew I had nothing left, as everything had been taken away, but I began to think about the elderly man sitting on the other side of me. *What had life been like for him when he was a child? Did he have a happy and carefree life?* I supposed that he must have; my childhood had been happy before the attackers stole it from me. Now I felt as if I were just like that old man. We both were refugees: the only difference was that I was near the beginning of my life, and he was near the end of his.

As the train moved along the rails, I kept thinking about what it would have been like if the attackers had not invaded, if they had not stolen everything from us and destroyed everything else. How wonderful it would have been to grow up at home, go to school, play my pianos, have all my animals around me, laugh with Lars, look forward to the next normal day—and never be hungry or feel afraid.

It was dark. In the dim cast of the overhead light I saw the old man crouched in the corner. I held my little stone in my hand and watched him closely. Before long I realised why the old man was so quiet and looked so peaceful: he had taken his last breath and left his days of sorrow behind. His journey had ended on the dirty boards of the train.

I turned away, too numb to even feel anything except my hunger. I closed my eyes and, mercifully, slept until morning.

7
Goodbye

Twilight had descended by the time I left the studio where I had recorded two piano works: the "Variations sur une theme Lette, opus 6" by J. Wihtol and the piano sonata by T. Kenins, both of which were soon to be released on LP. It had been a long and intense day, as the splicing had taken longer than anticipated. I decided to sit in the car for a moment to watch the raindrops fall on the windshield; the city lights of Toronto turned the drops into prisms that cast iridescent beams into the darkening sky.

The monotonous sound of the rain was soothing, and I felt completely isolated from any concerns. The sky turned darker by the minute, and the few scattered stars offered the bright city lights little competition. Although the day had been long and tiring, it had been inspiring too.

When I finally did arrive home, later than usual, I found the mailbox full to overflowing. This was no surprise. With the concert season coming closer, most of the mail was from my agent, who had just finalised my upcoming tour. This meant that my top priority would now be choosing the repertoire. I smiled in anticipation of my favourite time, to be spent looking through my scores, playing them, and trying to arrange the order of the programme and encores according to the cities where I would perform.

I had several bookings for practise sessions in New York. *That will be wonderful!* I thought to myself, recalling the last time I'd toured there. The many hours of intense work had brought me such delight at the time, and they still did; it was as if the beautiful sounds of my colleague's oboe, so brilliantly and deftly produced during our performance, still lingered in my heart. My mind sifted through heart-warming memories of other recitals in New York, when a different colleague's silver flute had filled every corner of the hall with its exquisite sounds—themes that only a master musician could produce. This same master had dedicated a piano suite to me. How I loved music! Music wafted through my mostly painful memories, and I felt grateful that I had pleasant recollections too.

I returned my focus to the tour. New York was, in a word, unforgettable. The boards of the stages in Town Hall and Carnegie Hall were electrifying; I could not wait to walk on them again. I could not wait to rekindle my love affair with the magnificent concert piano. Those hours spent performing onstage were worth all the sacrifices I'd had to make. My performances—both the pleasure of the music itself and the response of the audience—healed my wounds when nothing else could.

Me with soprano M. DeJardine in Town Hall, New York

Next order of business for the tour was my wardrobe selection, which had to be practical and the right colours. I never had time to think about my clothes once I was on the road, and I always packed an extra dress and my music in my carry-on bag, just in case the plane did not arrive on time. This had happened during several previous tours, most notoriously my last concert in Washington, DC.

My preparations went smoothly, and the time flew. Before I knew it, I was at the airport, waiting to board the Air Canada flight. The bold red *AC* on the plane's belly made me feel safe and free. The takeoff was smooth, and I settled comfortably into my seat. I looked out the window as the plane banked. This was my favourite time during a flight, when the fluffy clouds dusted the plane's wings and the land was still visible. How beautiful my adopted land looked—the woods, fields, rivers, and lakes; the roads like silver threads weaving through the valleys! It all looked magical, and the sight took my breath away. Canada was my home now, and I wished I could pick up the whole land and nestle it in my palms to protect it from all malice.

I felt my heart swell with pride and love for the country that was my new home and recalled how I had cried with joy on February 15, 1965, when the Maple Leaf flag proudly swayed in the wind. The church bells rang throughout the land, and all Canadians had joyously proclaimed the arrival of our very own symbol of freedom and faith. How gratifying that had been.

From my vantage point in the sky, I could see countless buildings with their flags hoisted. I swallowed back my tears, not wanting to alarm other passengers by crying. It overwhelmed me to have a country that I could call home, to have a flag that represented a positive perspective on life, to live in a land where I was safe and free. I continued to look out the window as the plane climbed ever higher; soon it was so high that the soft white clouds surrounded it.

I imagined that these were my own special clouds and that I could sink into them as if they were the softest bed—if I slept on these clouds, no gruesome memories of the past would haunt my dreams. The clouds would cradle me gently, and I would slumber in absolute peace.

★ ★ ★ ★ ★

The plane climbed higher and higher, eventually reaching an altitude above the clouds. Looking down, I imagined that the clear blue sky also belonged to me, that I could rest there safely just as I could in the fluffy white clouds. Far below my adopted land, a country of freedom and plenty, waited for me to return.

I continued to gaze out the window, transfixed. The plane seemed to float in the sea of eternity, where there was no beginning or end, only the vast and endless blue of the sky. Something about the endlessness of it triggered my memories; I felt the telltale shift in my consciousness. In my mind's eye I saw the wheat fields from our northward trek during the war—the endless stalks of grain whispering in the wind, shimmering in golden waves beneath the sun, as the air attacks, in violent contrast to nature's peace and beauty, hammered us relentlessly. The painful past had resumed control of my mind once again, and I sighed in acceptance, knowing it was pointless to resist.

What if the plane just keeps flying? I wondered as the past dominated my thoughts. *What if it continues eastward, giving me a chance to see Latvia again—my homeland and the country of my childhood?* Other memories streamed through my mind. Even in the midst of my contented existence in Toronto—and my love for my new country—I knew I would never be free of the past. Not really. Witnessing and living through horror and the pain and trauma that causes cannot ever be erased; they are etched into the mind, the body, the heart, and the soul, leaving indelible scars that never completely heal. I could never forget my past, and so I would never escape it. This, too, I had come to accept.

The captain dimmed the lights, and the flight attendants went to their stations. All became quiet and almost motionless. Only the humming of the engines filled the compartment, and the monotonous sound provided a kind of tranquillity that was too difficult to resist. As I felt sleep overtake me, I hoped that more memories of the gruesome past would not dominate my dream state, even though I knew such hope was futile.

The nightmares began all too quickly. My subconscious took me back to the times when monotony was not tranquil, when it was merely a momentary respite between the unceasing hours of deadly warfare, when every sound reverberated with terror. Sounds, not images, controlled my memory. Again and again, I heard the whistling bullets overhead, the endless artillery explosions, the blood-curdling screams that always accompanied the other sounds of war.

Far away from the freedom and safety of Canada, far away from the peace of the sky and the fluffy clouds, my war-ravaged childhood on the other side of the Atlantic ruled my mind and body. I had lost all conception of time during the war, so I did not always recognise exactly which event had assumed control. My memory retrieved a sharp sound, rough and metallic, and an engine's whirr, no means equivalent to the soothing hum of the plane's engine that my subconscious heard simply as "engine noise."

The metallic sound strengthened as it echoed through my mind, and my dream images flashed to the night of the harrowing journey by train, the night that my parents and I had fled our farm, going through the woods to catch the train that would take us farther away from the front. For me, it signified the night that the attackers had stolen our farm from us; the night that I'd been separated from my parents. I'd made my way onto the train but was forced to travel alone and afraid, lost and devastated.

Those dark, lonely nights on the train supplanted the reality of the plane to New York. The unimaginable hunger that had held me in its gruesome claws for so long ripped through my sleeping body. I tossed in my sleep, desperately trying to shake off the nightmare, but with no success. No matter how many more peaceful years I would live in Canada, the past would always haunt me.

The escape, first from our home near the city and then from our farm, dominated my psychological landscape—it was more vivid than the reality of the present. I had virtually forgotten that I was even on a plane.

It all came rushing back, flooding my mind with the usual sketchy details that defied any chronological order. The sounds and images were powerful—terrifying—and the feelings they brought up in me were far more real than those that I felt in the present. Anything at all could trigger my memory—a sight, a sound, an activity. Sometimes I could figure out the source of the trigger, sometimes not. This time it was two-fold: the sight of the endless sky had reminded me of the endless fields of wheat, and the sound of the plane's engine had reminded me of the sounds of the train. The specific trigger did not matter; something would always remind me of those awful, war-torn years—of the vicious assassins who had attacked my homeland and mercilessly stolen everything from my family and me.

My memory played havoc with me, instantaneously jolting me from the ghastly sounds and images of that train ride and taking me even farther back in time to happier days. I visualised our home near the city, seeing all the details of the big room, where my treasured pianos—a grand and an upright—had stood side by side beneath the tall potted palms. My beloved cat, Mikus, preferred the rubber tree. Its thick branches filled the far corner of the room, reaching the cabinet where I kept my music books. On many occasions Mikus would climb up the trunk, traverse the branches, and then jump, landing on my back so that he could play with my hair. Those were such wonderful days—so filled with joy and laughter and love.

I wish all my dreams could be like this one, I thought from within that semiconscious dream state, where I knew I was dreaming. I watched my mind's eye recall the beautiful upright piano, with its magnificent carvings of the muses on the front panel. Two brass candelabra in the shape of angels supported the stand. The piano was a portrait of sorts, symbolising the ascent of civilisation and the profusion of beauty that had resulted from it. *Why did beauty not prevent evil, not stop it in its tracks?*

That thought shifted my memories, and I recalled that the upright was the only piano I could play on the nights when all the lights had to be turned off early or disabled because of the war. The music cabinet had carvings of two mighty lions, which held the handle. I recalled the squeaky sound that the hinges made when I opened the cabinet door.

My memory drifted through the other rooms, and I recalled Mother's beautiful embroidery. In summertime, her fine stitches of apple blossoms graced the furniture; in winter, she changed it to the violets on purple silk. Our cushions always matched the season. I could feel the silken threads beneath my fingertips.

I continued to recall happy moments spent as a family in those rooms. Father and my brother, Lars, played the violin and mandolin. Those instruments were kept in the library, in a special cabinet engraved with the motif of a heroic saga of Latvia. Often they would play together while Mother sat reading or embroidering, smiling at the lovely sounds of their accompaniment. If I played the piano, Mikus would choose a spot where he could watch the sparks fly up the chimney.

The comforting flames in the fireplace instantly exploded into a full-blown conflagration, and the happy memories incinerated in the inferno. All I could see in my mind's eye now were the disastrous fires that had precipitated our flight. After our house near the city had burned, I had found my precious little stone in the ruins. Not knowing where my parents were or if they had even survived the air attack that had caused the fire, I had continued searching for them after finding the stone. They had appeared before me suddenly and miraculously, and all three of us had begun our trek through the demolished city, on through the endless fields, and finally to our farm. Before long, we'd had to flee the farm too. In the dark woods, we'd been separated again. Terrified but determined to survive, I'd managed to board the train. Alone.

My mind continued shifting, flashing rapid-fire images that swamped me, overwhelming me with their power. I felt the pain in the present, even after all those years.

I remember waking up inside the train that had pulled into the station after many tiring days of nonstop travel. I shivered in the cold compartment, too afraid to face the truth of having lost my parents. Clutching my little stone, I looked out the dirty window, but all I could see was devastation: some broken tracks and burning trains, plus boxes and all sorts of debris scattered across the platform. In every direction, flames filled the sky. A very small group of people stood on the platform, appearing to be dazed, fear etched into their faces.

We all were ordered off the train. Once on the platform, we had to move toward the station, which was nothing but steel beams sticking out of concrete rubble. The silence was ominous, and death lurked around every corner. An unspoken question hung in the air: Who would be the next to die, and when?

I slowly followed the group, not knowing which direction to take. My legs and arms were covered with dirt and dried blood, and my feet seemed to have forgotten how to move. Perhaps I simply could not walk anymore. I collapsed on the platform, and the others just passed on, not even checking to see if I were dead or alive. Such sights had become so frequent that people had grown numb to them; besides, who could help when everyone was on the verge of death?

I lay exactly where I had fallen, conscious but exhausted. Either the turmoil of the recent days or my extreme hunger was playing tricks on me, making me hear and see things which were not there. First, I imagined I heard someone call my name. The voice was familiar. It sounded like Mother. And then I imagined that I saw Father. I blinked in disbelief—once, twice, three times. Finally, I realised that my parents had managed to get on the train, just as I'd prayed they had. Now they were trying to make their way toward the station. They had noticed me lying on the broken cement platform, and they came toward me. Too weak to get up, I raised my hands in a feeble attempt to reach them. My voice had not returned, and so I couldn't call out to them. It must have been the power of faith that gave me the strength to get up and step closer, only to fall again. I was only a few steps away from them, and I crawled the rest of the way, falling into Father's arms as I slipped into unconsciousness. Father carried me, almost lifeless, through the rubble, toward the burning city.

★ ★ ★ ★ ★

My reunion with my parents always seemed like a miracle to me, and I valued it most of all. I never forgot how lucky I was, and I frequently reminded myself to be grateful. I had my mother and father; I had the will to survive. I had my precious little stone, my solid reminder of home, which gave me the strength and resilience to face just about anything; however, I never did know exactly what to expect. War made day-to-day events perpetually unpredictable.

My dreams replayed the moment of our miraculous reunion. When I opened my eyes, I saw Father holding me in his arms. Mother sat next to him, perched on a broken statue. We rested together for a short while, but we had to move on before nightfall. The city was in ruins, and some buildings still burned. The falling bricks and charred lumber made walking difficult, but we eventually reached a park. Nobody was there to remove the dead from where they had fallen in the park. The fires of war had scorched the trees, and still-glowing cinders covered the ground. We moved through the park as best we could.

The burned trees brought me deep sadness, but I still had no time to cry, and so I just walked in silence behind my parents, swallowing my bitter unshed tears. I could hear the trees' orchestral sounds echo in my head. Piano chords sounded particularly clear, and so I knew that one of those charred trunks once had been a magnificent chestnut. The chestnut trees always resonated the sound of the piano when their branches lifted in the breeze.

Opera House in Riga

The beautiful Riga Opera House came into view. Its silence pierced my heart. Sublime arias no longer filled the hall, resonating by means of the brilliant acoustics. The loss of those operatic sounds, so exquisite to the ear, saddened me even more than my own lost ability to speak. I could still hear beautiful music in my head; but without the opera, the building, once vibrant and teeming with people, was now empty and dead. I noticed that the white wall was marred with the stains of war—blood and dirt and smoke and char—and I forced myself to move faster so that I could pass it as quickly as possible and avoid seeing more.

We passed a stately monument: the Statue of Liberty, which had been erected in the heart of Riga in 1935 as Latvia's symbol of courage, faith, and freedom. It had rained, and it seemed to me that the statue was weeping for Latvia; the three gold stars that graced the statue definitely appeared less bright. Although I was too young to know much of my country's history, I had learned in school that November 18, 1918, was the date of Latvia's independence. Looking at the statue, I wondered why that independence could not last forever.

Statue of Liberty, Riga

We continued to walk, arriving at a lone building hours later. The roof was gone, and the top floor was barely there.

Father peered at the façade. "This is it: fifteen," he said to Mother, but the number was not clearly distinguishable.

Entering the building, we started to climb the littered stairwell. I thought the stairs would never end, and every step became more painful. Nobody was in sight, but some faint wailing and other all-too-familiar sounds of mourning broke the silence.

Finally, we reached the door with the number eleven on it. Father knocked, and from within we heard footsteps approach the door. At first, the door could not open because the hinges were broken. After much struggling from the inside, the door opened, but the broken hinges caused it to hang halfway into the hallway. Behind the door stood Nina, my parents' friend. Her smile was sad but welcoming. Father helped her with the door, and we greeted one another. Nina was alone now because her husband, a high-ranking officer in the Latvian army, had been shot a few days before.

The sunset cast ghostly shadows, and the flames of destruction shot high in the air; the revolting inferno swallowed everything in sight. Eerie shrieks pierced the otherwise silent darkness. Everything was gone: the war had destroyed it all, whether by explosion, fire, or some other deadly means. That night seemed to be darker than usual, even with the flames lighting up the vicinity; somehow the fires of war made the black of night blacker. I clutched my dear little stone with such fierceness that my hand grew sore.

There was nothing left in Nina's apartment—all had been stolen or damaged—so we all slept on the bare floor. It was cold, and there was nothing to keep us warm. I didn't mind: I could finally sleep in a real house again—or at least a real room. It did not matter to me that the roof was gone.

I must have fallen asleep for a while, because I bolted awake in the middle of the night when the sirens began blaring. Everybody scrambled to make their way down the steep stairs to the shelter. The lights had long since gone out. People were screaming, and articles fell to the ground and flew through the air. The scene quickly turned to full-blown chaos, with people falling on top of one another. The screams never stopped. It was only another air attack, but people had lost their nerve.

The hours we spent in the shelter passed slowly. Once it became quiet outside, those who were able to move started returning to their respective floors, assuming that those floors were still there.

With every new air attack, the building became shorter and smaller. Some of the walls were gone. Part of the stairwell was exposed and just hung by one side. Some people lost their footing during the ascent and fell off, landing on the rubble below. The only way to accomplish such a climb was to look straight ahead and try to ignore everything else. I imagined ballet class and how I'd learned to maintain balance by fixing my sight on a clear point straight ahead. And I did so as I began my climb. The only thing I thought about was that I had to survive.

As the days went on, the air attacks intensified. The shrieking of the bombs pierced the air, and Nina's floor was blown off. The path down to the shelter became shorter, but more dangerous, with each attack. There were huge gaps between each step, and any turbulence could cause them to break off. The blaring of the siren was overwhelming. It only added to the morbid recognition that we had nothing to go back to, so we remained down in the shelter.

It was difficult to find a spot to sit, because those who had lost their floors remained in the shelter, joined by the weak who could no longer walk. It was a cold night: some nursed their wounds; some stared into the darkness; some cried from emotional upheaval, even though we survivors all knew better than to show any emotion at all.

I noticed a pipe leading through a hole to the outside, along with some half-empty buckets used for drinking water. A very dim red light shone through a crack in the wall; it was the glow of a nearby building that was on fire.

The night seemed to last longer in the dark shelter. A thunderous impact again shook the whole place, covering everything and everyone with a cloud of dirt. Part of the ceiling fell in, and choking dust blew through the shelter. It had been a direct hit. In the next instant, what was left of the building collapsed completely, burying us all alive. Those fortunate enough to be sitting near the pipe took turns breathing through it, covering their heads with their clothing.

It was September 11—a day that would see horrific violence again, decades later. Although living through the war had destroyed my sense of time, I knew what day it was because it was my birthday. Mother had reminded me that morning that I was now seven years old. The shelter was very dark. All I could hear were a distant rumble and muffled voices coming from the other corner. All my hopes that life would be happy again had vanished, destroyed by this terrifying, bitter end. I felt around the rubble, found my father's arm, and held onto him with one hand, clutching my stone in the other.

★ ★ ★ ★ ★

The seconds felt like hours, so it is impossible to say how much time had passed. *What if it is still possible to get out of here?* I wondered, choking on dust. I was not afraid. Closing my eyes, I prayed, *Thank you, Angel, for saving me on my birthday.* At seven years old, I was too old to be afraid and too young to die.

With their bare hands, Father and Mother tried to dig our way out, which seemed to take forever. Stones and cement chunks kept falling back, blocking escape. After one last try, Father collapsed, exhausted from digging and lack of oxygen. Finally Mother uncovered a very narrow passage, large enough for me to get through. Father struggled up to help Mother push me through the passage. I started to dig as hard as I could to make it wider. Mother finally squeezed through. Both Mother and I were so tired that we could not move. Father was left on the other side of the passage to die.

I could not face abandoning Father, and I pleaded with Mother to try harder. It was so painful to hear Father's voice, to see part of him, and yet not be able to free him. With the last ounce of our strength, Mother and I resumed digging until the narrow passage was wide enough that Father finally managed to squeeze through it. Shaking off the dust from our torn clothing, we began walking away from the ruins. I felt sad that we had not been able to say goodbye to Nina, but she was never found.

After having been buried alive, I felt as if I'd been reborn.

We had escaped, but where would we go? The entire city was burning. Military vehicles rushed carelessly past, almost running us over. Another trek on foot had begun. By day we just kept walking; by night we slept beneath the sooty sky.

Gradually we came closer to the waterfront. The day was warm and sunny. It was October 3—I had managed to count the days after the building collapsed on my birthday. The few from Nina's building who had survived the air attack and dug themselves out had also come this far.

There was considerable unrest at the harbour. People who were still able to walk began forming a line near a makeshift desk. The wounded remained where they were to face their future. Loud explosions sounded in the distance, and terror closed in on the city.

A small ship was anchored at the harbour, its belly filled with prisoners. The deck was small and littered with ammunition. The three of us slowly moved toward the makeshift desk. An air of depression cloaked the harbour, as if we were waiting for a verdict of life or death. In a way we were, as little chance existed of our getting onboard.

Space on the ship was limited to only a few, so the three of us were flatly denied permission to board.

What will we do? I thought, in wordless panic. Even if I hadn't lost my power of speech, I would not have been able to say anything. The outskirts of the city were aflame. The enemy had cut off all exits from the city core. It became evident that there was no way to escape by heading farther inland, and on the other side was the open sea.

A twist of fate must have intervened. A soldier recognised our surname. Apparently, he and Lars had fought side by side somewhere in the trenches. As the family of a soldier, all three of us were then allowed to board the boat.

A very narrow plank led from the harbour to the deck. We took small steps and never looked down. The distance from the harbour to the deck seemed very long. Even with my plan to look straight ahead as I'd learned to do in ballet, I felt dizzy. My feet were swollen, which made every step excruciating. The slightest breeze could have blown me into the water. Clutching my precious stone, I just kept moving. I felt strongly that I had to protect my little stone more than myself. In my child's mind, the stone had become a living thing, and I identified with it because we had both been abandoned by fate, surviving horror by some sheer miracle; saving my stone had become tantamount to saving myself. I did not realise that at the time, of course. I simply wanted to save the last token of home.

Some of the elderly were so weak that they lost their balance; perhaps they just gave up. Only the ripples knew for sure what happened. Was the water cursed or did it just have a bloodlust for swallowing the ailing? Who would have had even the vaguest idea of the reason why? The water looked so cold and dark, and certainly it had no regrets. Nobody had the time or the means to save those who slipped and fell into the water. Thus, the water—ugly and smelly and dark—became the end of the journey for a few.

The sun began to descend. The crew raised anchor hurriedly, and the boat began moving away from the dock. The dreaded sounds of the air raid came closer, turning the city into a bonfire. The partly torn flag on top of the Old Castle swayed in a slight breeze. On deck a small group joined in solemn prayer and singing of the national anthem, "God Bless Latvia."

This emotional departure choked me, and in my heart I felt and heard my deep sorrow echo mournfully, just as had happened when our house burned. My heart cried out now, *Goodbye, my beloved homeland.*

Riga panorama

8
At Mercy

Although it was early October, the frost had already left its signature frozen lace throughout my garden in Toronto. The last fall blooms were encased in a rime of ice, and the grass resembled frosty spears. I imagined that the bird sitting on the edge of the now-frozen birdbath must be wondering what had become of the water.

I looked forward to my California tour, which began later than usual; I had a flight to San Francisco that very afternoon. Taking one last look around my garden, I stepped back inside to gather my things.

As always, the view from the plane was captivating. The sky was that particular azure of autumn, with only a few fluffy white clouds. Snow partially covered some of the trees, as the first snowfall in Canada can arrive far in advance of "official" winter—much like the Baltic winters of my childhood. As the plane flew over a stream or a small river—the altitude made everything below seem smaller, so it was hard to tell which—the thin layer of ice on the surface of the water shimmered in the sunset. With darkness about to descend, the street lights below came on, from my vantage point looking like little stars. Feeling as if I were suspended in the heavens, supported merely by a delicate layer of clouds, I sighed, spellbound as always by nature's splendour.

The flight was long enough to allow me time to review the repertoire for San Francisco. I far preferred to spend the time working rather than trying to sleep, which would inevitably propel me into a dream state featuring memories of the painful past. I had experienced that during the previous flight for my New York concert tour. I was immersed in my music, and the captain's announcement that we had begun our descent and would soon land seemed to come in no time at all.

My friends, Helen and Ward, were waiting at the airport when I deplaned. I had met Helen in Denmark, and we became good friends. After all these years of not having seen each other, we both cherished the reunion and exchanged warm greetings. Helen and Ward had planned a trip for the three of us along the California coast after my tour, and I looked forward to both my tour and our trip with happiness and excitement.

The drive to their home seemed to take longer than the flight, but the natural scenery was so magnificent that I was glad to have the time to enjoy it. Majestic redwoods surrounded the winding road, which seemed to cut right through the mountain. I opened the car window, eager to hear the sound of the redwoods and not a bit surprised that they resonated the deep, rich tones of the cello. Deer and smaller animals continually crossed the road, fully expecting to have the right of way, which Ward allowed them. It was so beautiful and peaceful. I wanted to throw my arms through the open car window, feel the full wind in my face, and hug every creature, every single gift of nature that I could enclose in my tender grasp.

At last, we arrived at my friends' home, just outside of Berkeley. The house, which sat almost on the top of the mountain, had no windows as such, only glass walls that provided a phenomenal view of the spectacular landscape. Thus, from anywhere inside the house one could see the tall trees swaying in the ever-present mountain breeze. To add to my delight, the grand piano delivered the day before stood waiting for me in the front hall. I could not have designed a more perfect atmosphere or situation; I could scarcely wait to feel my fingers dance across the keys while surrounded by such magnificent natural scenery.

Helen's Great Dane, Babe, slowly moved through the hall to cautiously approach me, looking like a mountain of sleek fur on legs. I could almost look at Babe face to face, which really amused me. *Babe just might be able to wear my slippers!* I laughed to myself, giving Babe a few friendly strokes in greeting, happy to see the huge dog warm to me. We would not be strangers for long! I so loved animals, but I was careful, lest my interactions with this new dog trigger long-held memories that were filled with pain. Everything here was so beautiful, I did not want the past to intrude and disturb my peace and joy. I could never tell what would trigger an intrusion; I could only wait and see—and pray that maybe, just maybe, my peace and joy would last for a while this time.

The few days I spent at home with Helen and Ward were special. As expected, being surrounded by such natural splendour while practising increased my joy in my music. The recital was held two days later, during which time I prepared for the whole tour. The tour went well, with performances every other night. Pleased with my success, I eagerly anticipated returning to my hosts' home so that we could embark on our trip along the California coast.

It was not until I returned to Helen and Ward's house after my tour that the past closed in on me. Looking out through the walls of glass, I watched the enormous shadows cast by the trees. The redwoods were so tall they dwarfed the house . As the sun set, its rays beamed through the foliage, drenching the ground in pure gold. It took my breath away.

It was the dusk hour that put an end to my contentment. The enveloping darkness triggered my memory, and I surrendered to the past, having no choice but to accept what I would never be able to change or erase.

California Pine

★ ★ ★ ★ ★

Our drive along the California coast commenced. Thick fog rolled in from the ocean, and it kept rolling—through the trees and all the brushwood and everything else. All the objects in our path, even the mammoth trees, completely disappeared from view. The fog seemed to swallow whatever came near it.

It reminded me of a long-ago foggy night, and I willed myself to keep at bay the terrifying images of the scorched woods surrounding our farm and my harrowing journey alone on the train.

Forcing myself to think of something pleasant, I recalled a recent event to distract my mind. During our coastal drive down the Seven Mile Road, we had watched a tree seemingly come to life when countless monarch butterflies took flight from within its branches. I smiled at the thought of the butterflies turning the surrounding sky an incandescent orange as they winged their way to a new destination.

Our coastal trip occupied my mind now, and I recalled the many wondrous sights. The amazing California pines that grew along the cliffs resisted storms by holding onto mere handfuls of sand between the rocky layers. The roots must be strong enough to drive themselves into the rock in order to stay alive. These trees held the same fascination for me that vegetation always has, but their tenacity particularly captivated me; I compared their will to survive with my own. Yet again, my bond with and affinity for nature both sustained and inspired me.

My thoughts drifted to the most marvellous rock formation I had seen on that trip: the majestic El Capitan in Yosemite National Park. Reminding me of a monument or a huge guard, thatnot only reached toward the sky, it seemed to almost touch it. This loyal sentinel had kept watch over the surrounding land for countless centuries. It looked to be as old as time itself. I knew that if I could get close enough to hear it whisper, it would have amazing stories to tell me—its *basso profundo* sounds floated toward me on the breeze, wrapping me in a veil of velvety warmth.

Every inch of the park was God's creation and a testament to nature's perfection. The reflection in the lake mirrored the scenery as a mirage. Small chalets along the winding road hung onto the cliffs like birds' nests. I stood on the balcony of one of the chalets, enjoying the breathtaking view. The clouds seemed to divide the earth from the sky, and I felt like I was in heaven. All too soon, we had to leave the park and return to Helen and Ward's home.

Yosemite National Park, California

The drive back to Berkeley became quite an adventure, and I felt fortunate to be alive and able to reflect on the journey! The mountain roads were narrow and winding, as if they had drilled themselves through the rock. On one side were very old trees; on the other, a frighteningly steep drop. In one of the clearings below, I noticed a car that had gone off course and landed down in the valley. On the way down from the mountain the brakes of our car failed, and we rolled down to a clearing where there was one gas station and a very long saloon carved right into the rock.

Needless to say, it was a relief to get back to Berkeley alive and in one piece! I was also glad to be able to enjoy the beautiful redwoods again. My room in Helen and Ward's house was on the ground floor, and it had a glass door leading to the garden. Small crawlers always skidded along the slippery rocks. Larger animals occasionally crossed the mossy walk, trying to enter the house. They were quite confused upon discovering that the transparent glass was not the same as the outdoor world of their own existence, and I enjoyed watching their puzzled realisation.

The dusk began to cast shadows, and a ghastly fog descended, enveloping the whole area in its thick grey cloak. *More fog!* My heart hammered, and my pulse raced. The ocean was very close, and the constant sound of the tranquil waves felt soothing. After our long car trip, we all were weary and chose to retire early. I hoped that my exhaustion would keep me in a deep sleep—so deep that my memories would not dominate my dreams. I always hoped, but usually my hopes were for naught. Tonight would prove to be no exception.

Water, darkness, and fog: the combination of those things made my sleep restless, despite my physical weariness, as my subconscious mind shifted to our voyage from Latvia. All those nights on the open sea while crossing the Baltic from Riga still haunted me. That small vessel had been filled with tears, suffering, and death; the boat itself had grown weak, almost as if it could barely continue its voyage. Even as a child, I'd wondered what had really weakened the boat. Was it the damage it sustained from the air attacks or from the continual storms? Or had the burden of the refugees and prisoners it carried caused the boat to grow ever weaker?

★ ★ ★ ★ ★

I heard cries coming from below the deck—feeble, thready sounds filled with pain. The largest part of the deck was covered with barbed wire through which the prisoners below reached up, begging for water. My mother, devastated by their desperation, risked her own life to help them.

The only container she could find was a rusted can, which she kept filling with the water that washed up on deck. Throughout her attempts, the guards struck her frequently, and she almost lost her balance more than once; yet, nothing could prevent her from handing those meagre drops of water to the prisoners down in the belly of the boat.

Mother looked down into the dark, overcrowded bowels of the boat, peering amongst the prisoners. "Lars!" she called, hoping that, against all odds, her son would answer to the sound of his name. I, too, hoped that maybe Lars was there, but Father just stared out at the sea, showing no emotion, unable to bear the burden of hope that would undoubtedly prove futile. Alas, Mother and my hopes were all in vain. There was no sign of Lars. Mother kept kneeling as low as she could to reach the prisoners' hands. "At least I'm helping another mother's sons," she whispered to me.

The darkness and the cold wind made the sailing as treacherous as it was morbid. Some refugees became so ill that they collapsed on deck, only to be washed overboard into the black sea. No one could save them. For me, the dark, watery depths of the sea became a monster. The waves were its jaws, and it patiently waited for the victims that would satisfy its ravenous appetite. The monstrous waves swallowed the ill and infirm in gulps so mighty that it seemed those people had never even existed. All through that voyage, I felt as if we all were at the mercy of the monster.

Flares with a glare far brighter than daylight were thrown from the planes overhead, turning the night garish. The waves were tremendously high, and they kept rolling closer and closer, seemingly ready to swallow the whole boat in yet another monstrous single gulp.

Amidst the crashing waves, suddenly all was silent. The sounds of death broke the silence. Nobody moved. Expressionless faces stared into the darkness. We all wondered what the next moment would bring. For some, the tension was the worst of all, and so they jumped off the boat. The ones who remained simply lived from attack to attack.

As the bombing intensified, the boat appeared to sail on a sea of fire, not water. Many vessels were hit, briefly lighting up the horizon before disappearing from view as they sank beneath the surface of the sea. It looked like daybreak, but the bursts of light came from the war's inferno surrounding us, not from the natural glow of the rising sun as it wakened the world. The bombing came closer and closer, until the whole sea seemed to be continuously on fire.

The cries from below became weaker by the hour, as many prisoners died. Reaching the grille of barbed wire had become very difficult, because they stacked the deceased against the mesh; some had been shot, while others had been beaten to death with the guards' rifle butts. A storm came up suddenly, becoming quite violent, and eventually affecting even the guards.

The next night the sea was unusually calm—so calm, in fact, that it spooked me. There was no sound and no fire. The whole boat was engulfed in treacherous fog. Child that I was, I was also a veteran of war zones, and the silence and fog terrified me far more than the screams and the chaos and the destruction. I clutched my little stone, and prayed, *Angel, please save us to live through this night, to survive another day.*

★ ★ ★ ★ ★

A dreadful sound shook the boat, and the engine stopped. The waves crashed against the sides of the stalled boat, tossing us about aimlessly. It was so dark that the only thing we could distinguish was the boat's broken mast. I knelt down and gripped the barbed-wire grille, but my hands were so numb with cold that I could hardly hold on. The awful sound we'd heard had been either a mine or a bomb that had almost sunk the boat.

Over the next few days a larger and more violent storm took the sea in its powerful grip. I imagined that the storm was an even greater monster than the sea, and the two of them were engaged in a battle.

I felt weak all the time. We had nothing to eat or drink, and so I drank the water that the storm had washed on deck. Days came and went without any change or movement of the boat; there was only the storm-whipped sea all around us and the sky above, so it was difficult to know how many days had passed. I had ceased to be afraid of the monsters of sea and storm; war was the most evil monster of all, so what was there for me to fear from the sea and the storms?

Miraculously, the engine was repaired, and the boat started to resist the pull of the waves. It was peaceful for a while once the boat began moving again, and I fell asleep, soon dreaming that I'd fallen into the sea and was drowning. I could not breathe because the waves kept pulling me lower and lower, all the way to the bottom of the sea. I saw Lars trying to reach me. I reached out, but my arms were too short. In the next instant he disappeared. I abruptly awakened when I felt something grasp me. Somebody from below had reached a hand through the barbed-wire grille and held onto me so that I would not roll off the deck into the water. I saw a very gaunt face through the mesh; he could hardly move his lips as a result of the cold and anguish he had to endure. Not a single word passed between us. Neither the prisoner nor I was able to speak, but my look into his eyes expressed my deepest gratitude to him for having saved me from the waves. His brave kindness proved to me that the voracious monster's jaws I feared, indeed, did belong to the war, not the sea.

It was draining, both physically and psychologically, to spend so much time at sea. I began to believe that this was the way life was going to be forever. With all the horrors I had witnessed and all the pain I had endured, I was thoroughly traumatised. I just hoped it all would end soon, and it no longer mattered to me how it ended. I just wanted peace.

Holding onto the barbed-wire grille with one hand and clutching my little stone in the other, I drifted off to sleep again. This time I had a lovely dream of birds flying free in the blue sky. My special angel touched me ever so gently, whispering, "Lara …"

I woke up again and blinked my eyes in disbelief. There before me stood a woman with the most beautiful golden hair. She smiled at me and gave me a tiny piece of bacon. *Real food!* I could hardly believe it. I so wanted to save it for Lars, knowing how hungry my brother would be when we finally were reunited, but the golden-haired woman sat next to me and waited for me to finish her generous, life-saving gift. Extreme hunger blurred my vision, so I cannot say what this woman actually looked like—to me, she had the same golden hair as my angel because the small bit of food she gave me provided some desperately needed nourishment. I was saved to live another day, and that is what mattered. Life itself is the greatest miracle of all.

★ ★ ★ ★ ★

All the days and nights were identical. The boat began to float aimlessly. The storm had wreaked havoc, damaging the engine and washing more refugees off the deck. The air attacks increased in both frequency and severity. We all sat on deck, helpless. There was nothing to do but surrender to fate.

I lay down at the grille, resuming my usual position: holding onto the barbed wire with one hand and clutching my little stone in the other. And then I just waited for a final blast to blow the boat apart.

The sky was never blue anymore; it was a perpetual, dingy grey, smudged black from the smoke from explosions or seared orange and red from the infernal glow of their flames.

★ ★ ★ ★ ★

The surface of the sea resembled the water in a boiling pot. I felt such a void deep inside me that there was no room for fear any longer. Everything seemed senseless; it was as if only the sea knew for sure whom to claim next.

After countless nights and days, the boat pulled into a North Pomeranian harbour. The sea had claimed many. Full of sorrow, I found it difficult to forget the ordeal on the Baltic Sea. The harbour was littered with all sorts of debris. There wasn't even a single house left. The city near the harbour was totally destroyed, with the lone steeple of a church overlooking the ruins. The view was ghastly. It was as if we'd entered a ghost town, or the world had ended—or worse, someone had ended the world and taken away everybody who was still alive.

Looking at the awful scene, my innate appreciation for life once again surged within me. I felt that I had been given the greatest gift of all: life. My life. I was still alive; I had survived another day.

The sky was dark, with motionless clouds suspended in it. A strange odour and miasma hung in the air, choking us. It seemed to seep through every crevice, pervading all that existed. It was as if only the earth's parasites remained, and their task was to infiltrate every single part of every single thing that human dedication and hard work had achieved for the advancement of culture and civilisation. Once those creatures had accomplished their task of infiltration, it was time for their next task: destruction. An endless line of maggots gnawed away at all the treasures of art strewn about the harbour, until nothing remained.

This site of destruction was the once-glorious city of Danzig. It was a hellish reminder of war's handiwork, a nightmarish vision that I would remember forever. A combination of pain and disgust filled my soul, along with deep compassion for the loss. At some level, even then, I realised that tyranny, because it acquires everything by means of force and brutality and cruelty, can never retain its might for long. Only nature, whose force is good and wholesome and God-given, can retain its power eternally.

Instinctively, my hand gripped the little stone even more tightly. I kept it safe in my pocket to spare it from witnessing the atrocious sight. My precious little stone had become my silent companion, my symbol of home, and my amulet of protection—all rolled into one. My clothes were still soaked from the days at the sea and I was starving, but my little stone gave me the stamina to keep going.

The stone remained my secret. Nobody knew I had it, and I made sure that nobody would ever take it away from me. When somebody approached me, afraid that my pocket might be checked, I stealthily put the stone in my mouth. I recalled the day when a man had asked me something, but I could not talk. He'd hit me, his smack falling hard on my face. I'd let the tears run, gritting my teeth to keep my mouth shut tight. The little stone did not fall out; I saved it, just as it saved me.

Somehow, I knew that my precious stone sustained me, although I could not have explained how I knew at the time. It was my duty to protect my stone, because it had become a living thing to me. Deep within me, I believed that if I kept my stone safe, I would stay safe too.

★ ★ ★ ★ ★

The harbour at Danzig was a mountain of ashes and fire. At least I had lived another day. Even if it was filled with uncertainty, it was one more day that I had survived.

My parents and I were put on a train that smelled like a farm. As the train started to move out of the ruined station, I caught one last glimpse of the boat that we'd sailed on from Riga. It was slowly sinking into the dirty water of the harbour. All I heard were faint, futile cries coming from the belly of the sinking ship. Those sounds remain etched deeply in my mind, an inconceivable reminder of the cruelty and arrogance of tyranny.

The walls of the train cars scarcely held together, and I could see flames around us in all directions. Shortly after the train left the station, an air attack levelled everything in sight.

The trip was very long, and the train never stopped moving, day and night. Sometimes a shaft of light would peek between the boards, and I would guess that it must be daylight, but most of the time it was so dark that I felt like I'd been buried. It was cold, and in the constant darkness, my sea-soaked clothes never dried. I kept shivering, and I stayed close to my parents. Everybody was quiet. What was there to say, anyway?

Nevertheless, I had been chosen to live. I never forgot to be grateful. I caressed my little stone in silence, praying inwardly, *Thank you, Angel.*

★ ★ ★ ★ ★

In the morning Helen knocked on the door to my room. I opened my eyes to see the early light glint against the glass wall. For a moment it felt surreal—almost like my life was suddenly realigning itself. All the dark memories disappeared, vanishing in the clear light of day, in the healing warmth of the sun.

I got up and walked to the glass wall. The fog had lifted, leaving crystal-clear droplets suspended at the end of the tree branches. The rays of the sun grew brighter, first peeking through the trees and then streaming in full beams of light that made the droplets fall gently onto the fertile forest floor. Here was nature in charge again, coaxing the sun and the rain and the vegetation to work together, just as had been true since time began.

9
Beyond the Chill

It had snowed all night, and the temperature had dropped well below normal, even for winter in Toronto. I went to the window to look outside, but every pane of glass was completely covered with ice particles. The icy rime was so thick, in fact, that the window appeared to be an opaque surface that obscured the view to the outside. The wintry squall had deposited enough snow to block the door. I tried to force it open, but strong gusts of wind buffeted the door. I couldn't fight the snow and the wind. Nature was in charge, as always. The patio door was not blocked, so I went outside to estimate the chances of being able to safely drive to school. The blizzard's handiwork up to that point, compounded by the still-falling snow and still-gusting wind, told me that I would need to change my plans for the day.

I loved my work teaching children to learn and appreciate music—and nature and life, for all are one—but I also cherished spending time at home during the winter. That was very special to me, and I always managed to arrange it. Everyday activities seemed to vary in the wintertime, as the cold and snow and ice of that season created far more challenges to daily living than warmth and sunshine, or even summer thunderstorms. Winter weather could make it difficult to get to school, but I was always there on time to receive my students. Appreciating my diligence, they always managed to arrive on time, too, although their windblown faces would be red with cold, their coats covered with snow. My pupils were always happy to begin their lessons, no matter the weather. Because sound and weather are all part of the same whole that is nature, music triumphs through sunshine, gentle rain, bitter cold, swirling snow, or thunder and lightning.

This was my day to enjoy the winter at home, and I acceded to the weather. I planned to work on some projects, practise some pieces, and watch the snow. After a while the blizzard ceased, and I was amazed at how deep some of the drifts were. Some spots in the garden had drifts that easily reached more than four feet. And it was a heavy snow, I realised, observing the signs left by wildlife. The paw prints of rabbits and raccoons had left distinct indentations in the masses of white. A small squirrel darted across a drift but, apparently, hit an air pocket and plummeted through a cascade of snow. Shaking the frozen white crystals from his thick grey fur, he looked about, quite confused. In a moment he scampered off again, bits of snow flying from the fluffy question-mark curl of his tail.

I moved across the patio. The sky was clear and blue; the cold air crisp and refreshing. This was my favourite part of winter. My face melted into a smile as I made my way to the garden, my boots sinking deep into the dense snow. I joyfully made a snow angel, watching the sunlight turn the pure white surface all around me opalescent. I deeply enjoyed the feeling of being free and happy; overhead, clouds sailed by, puffs of white as pristine as the snow.

While thoroughly enjoying the snow, I reflected how long time it had taken me to reach this state of winter delight. In my early childhood before the war, I had adored the winter; but the war changed that, just as it changed everything else.

My first winter in Toronto had been far from enjoyable. After my years in Denmark, where the climate is much kinder than it is in Latvia, the Canadian winter catapulted me back to the war-ravaged wintertime, especially the one in northern Germany. I had stood at the window in my new home, gazing at the snow-covered ground. All was quiet and calm, without even the slightest breeze to disturb the tranquillity, yet I started to tremble and feel faint. *Why?* I had wondered to myself. *This is Toronto, not Riga—not the Baltic crossing, not northern Germany.*

Although my body was physically in Toronto, my memory had taken control of my mind, transporting me back to my flight as a refugee. Winter's cold had triggered my memories of those bitter, frigid days during my parents' and my flight from our homeland. More real than the scene in front of me on my patio were those days when I had struggled just to survive; I was so much more fortunate than those whose attempts to get through the day had proved futile. So many had been unfortunate. I counted my blessings as a child, and I count them still.

Canadian winter was reminiscent of those bone-chilling days in northern Germany that had followed the terrifying voyage across the Baltic Sea.

★ ★ ★ ★ ★

We Latvians were accustomed to the harsh Baltic winter, but our clothes were still wet from the storms at sea, and the frigid air made us feel excruciatingly cold. Nevertheless, all of us refugees were loaded on the train. Some could not even stand because the heavy toll of daily horror and pain had depleted them of all strength. They remained behind, crouching pitifully on the destroyed platform as they watched the rest of us board the train.

The small group of refugees still able to walk began to move toward the train, our own feet hardly able to carry us any longer. Some wore boots, some had only socks, and some were barefoot. We moved like phantoms, our pained steps taking us closer to the train, which was filthy and full of bullet holes. Some of the cars no longer had roofs; others had part of their walls blown off.

I was petrified of the train, which looked to me like yet another heinous monster waiting for its meal of helpless humans. Standing aghast at the sight, I hesitated for a moment. A guard shoved me inside. I did not feel any pain as a result of his roughness, or for any other reason. Already emotionally and psychologically numb, the cold had numbed me physically as well. My legs were so cold I felt like I was walking on frozen stilts. Once inside the train, I kept close to my parents. I clutched my little stone; it was safe, so I was too.

Reminding myself that the only monster worth fearing was the war itself, I struggled to overcome my fear of the train. The locomotive had trouble starting. For a brief moment I thought that I might still be able to jump out, to run somewhere far away. Far from the war. But I knew I could not outrun the war; I could not jump off the train. I could not escape what I feared.

Commotion ensued, with screams and shots coming from all directions. In the midst of all this, I did not notice that the train had begun to move away from the station. Some boards from our car were shot off, and I could see soldiers blowing up the train station. The air filled with shattered objects and remains. I forced myself not to think about the refugees left behind crouching on the platform. Despite my numbed state, I trembled in terror.

★ ★ ★ ★ ★

Time passed slowly on the train. It seemed like we were on an endless journey to nowhere. Half the occupants of our train compartment looked barely alive. Nobody moved or talked. What was there to say, anyway? We all held the same unvoiced question in our minds, and we all knew that question had no answer: Why? We all just continued to live in a capsule of misery. Many times the engine gave up and stopped, leaving us to silently wonder if the train had been deserted—if we had been left to die. In the cold, dank train compartment, our sea-drenched clothes remained damp. Some of us began to cough; others cried mournfully. It was utterly demoralising. I moved away from my parents, shrinking into the darkest corner of the compartment. I shut my eyes tight and forced my ears to stop hearing the dreadful sounds all around me. Secluded in the corner, I instinctively checked for my little stone. Yes, it was still in my pocket—still safe. Relieved, I breathed a bit more easily.

The train's engine problems made the sudden starting and stopping even worse. As soon as distant shots were heard, it would try to stop, resulting in a journey filled with lurches and jolts. This continued for many days and nights. I kept the stone as deep in my pocket as I could, lest it fall out while I dozed off. Every time I checked, it was there, and that comforted me.

Sometimes a dim light would appear through the cracks in the compartment walls and between the train cars; most likely, the illumination came from the fires of a recent bombing or explosion. I preferred the darkness to the glare of the fires of war, and I had not seen real daylight for many days. A few times the train slowed down, and the heavy door pulled open for a bundle to be rolled out into the deep snow. Frigid air mixed with snow would gush into the compartment, making it even colder than it already was, but at least it was fresh air. Our bodies were frozen with cold, but we gulped the clean air gratefully. Many such bundles had to be discarded; sometimes the train did not even slow down for this task. I knew what such activity meant, but I could not accept the bitter truth of it, and so I forced my ears not to hear the heavy door as it rolled open again and again—not to hear the telltale sound of the bundle falling into the snow.

The only way to survive was to stay numb to everything around me. The war had already made me mute; now I pretended to be deaf to what I could not bear to hear. I pretended to be indifferent to what I could not bear to feel or accept, even though apathy was something

I could never truly attain—I valued life far too much. No matter how hard I tried to stay numb, every time the door opened, something died deep inside me. My soul longed to cry out in desperate pain, but it could not.

Whenever scant light did come into the compartment, all it illuminated was devastation. It would have been better if the light never came in at all, better if I did not have to see the misery and destruction all around me. There was no end to the war and our suffering in sight. I started to wonder how long such misery and horror could last.

Where did the blue sky go? Where is the sun? Where are all the beautiful trees and flowers? Is this another world, or is it the absolute end of the world we have known? Has war ended life? My unanswerable questions shifted to a prayer as my fingers, once again, instinctively found my little stone. *Help me, Angel.*

★ ★ ★ ★ ★

As the endless train ride continued, I began to turn more and more to music as a way to pass the time and fill the deepening emptiness inside me. Within the confines of the train, I sorely missed my connection to nature, and I needed my music more than ever. Gripping my stone tightly, I focused as hard as I could on the music I remembered, singing in my heart all the songs and pieces I knew. My invisible shell of protection still surrounded me, and I let the beautiful sounds I loved fill that space. Running my thumb tenderly over the smooth surface of my precious little stone, I let the music fill my heart and mind, and my soul felt content and at peace. I still could not speak, but it didn't matter; music, whether played or only heard, expressed my feelings far better than words ever could. My connection to music became the voice of my soul, a counterpoint to my loss of speech.

I could endure what I had to. It was bitterly cold in the dark corner of the train compartment, and my damp clothes made it more so. My boots were wearing out, and I noticed my sock peeking through a small hole in the sole. I tore off a small piece of my dress and stuffed it into the hole. Who could say when I would be able to get a new pair of boots, and the makeshift insulation would at least offer my foot some protection from the elements.

Finally the train stopped. The big, heavy door swung open, and everybody had to get out. The Baltic winter had not abated, and a severe blizzard raged. Powerful gusts of wind whipped the snow into our faces. There was no trail to follow. We could not even see the ground—or anything else, for that matter; the blizzard obliterated everything. It seemed that we were walking into absolute whiteness that was opaque, yet not solid, as if the air itself had taken on a different quality. Walking into the blackness of night was far less frightening than entering this whiteness. *This must be the way "nowhere" looks,* I thought to myself, as the swirling snow consumed me in a more intense degree of cold than I had ever experienced or thought possible.

None of us had the clothing to withstand the severe winter conditions, least of all me. I was so cold that I did not even feel my damp clothes turn to ice in the frigid air. We walked and walked on through the blizzard. Our eyes had adjusted somewhat, and we could tell that the soldiers were directing us toward some buildings in the distance. It was hard to tell what they were because the snow around them was so deep that all we could see were the rooftops and chimneys.

We all started to slow our pace, from the cold-induced pain that filled our bodies as well as from fear. Arriving at these buildings meant the end of one situation and the beginning of another. Would the next one be better or worse? Veteran refugees that we were, we knew that worse was far more likely.

A woman fell, her eyes half closed, her face swollen. She briefly raised her hands, but they fell back to her sides. A soldier pulled her away so that the others could pass. A small girl who had lost her mother began to cry. I remembered how it felt to be lost and totally alone. This little one had even less than I. Keeping my parents in my sights, I clutched the little stone in my pocket. With my free hand, I reached out to the little girl, taking her hand in mine, and we continued walking.

Eventually, we reached the buildings, which turned out to be barracks. Deep snow blocked the door. We all used our bare hands to clear away the snow, desperate to get inside and out of the cold and wind and frigid wet snow. At last the door was open, and the soldiers rushed everyone inside. The small girl broke away from me and ran to an elderly woman. I heard her cry, "Grandma!" as she embraced the woman. The grandmother held her granddaughter, letting the girl weep quietly.

My parents and I stepped inside. It did not matter to me that we were in military barracks. It felt like a real house, with no holes in the walls! Beautiful ice crystals that looked like little stars laced the windowpanes. I could have stayed there forever—it was so nice to be in a place that was clean and warm and dry. This was particularly precious to me after our harrowing flight from our farm, during which I had felt forsaken, all my prayers and gratitude for surviving notwithstanding.

The snowstorm simmered down as the hours passed, and the night was quiet. The moon rose, its glow through the ice crystals pure silver-white. The small room was divided amongst the refugees; we were not a large number, as so many had not survived the journey. I stayed in a small corner, continually watching my surroundings. This spot would become my "place" for an unpredictable length of time.

I was so tired that I did not even feel how hard the floorboards of the barracks were. It was just nice to feel warm and dry, to be in a place where there was no immediate threat of bullets whizzing overhead or bombs exploding all around. I sank into the quiet and fell easily asleep with no screaming to shatter my ears and nobody around me crying out in pain —and I began to dream the first pleasant dream I'd had in a long time. It was the most wonderful dream, really. The ice crystals on the windowpanes turned into tiny dancers in white dresses, identical to the one I'd worn when Lars came home for Christmas Eve. *Lars!* Perhaps my brother would be in my dream too. As I watched the dancers twirl in my dream, I remembered feeling very happy to see Lars, but his departure had been so cruel, so tormenting, that I knew those painful memories would last a lifetime.

Is happiness always so short-lived? As my dream-state thoughts shifted, the dresses of the dancers turned red, as if soaked in blood; the tempo of the music slowed, and the sounds became warped and ugly. Suddenly the sound stopped entirely, and I heard loud noise. The dancers fell to the floor, disintegrating as if the ground had eaten them alive. All turned dark, and I heard the dancers cry as they sank into the voracious red mud. A deafening noise pulled me up to consciousness and into shock. People were screaming, desperately trying to get outside, but the doors were frozen solid. The air attack was somewhere nearby; we could see the flames shooting high into the air. The ice crystals, glowing red in the reflection of the fire, had melted in the heat and streaked in small rivulets down the windows. Even the ice appeared to cry in the blaze.

After a while things calmed down, and we all sat speechless, trapped in the cold barracks and wondering if we would ever get out. Had our attempted flight to safety merely taken us deeper into the line of fire?

Winter held the countryside in its icy grip for a long time. There was nothing to do but stay inside the barracks, watching the bare walls and waiting—but for what?

Every night I retired early. I was still wearing my layers of three dresses, torn and dirty, but they kept me from freezing. My hand always found my precious little stone, safe in my pocket. Caressing it lovingly, I would pray inwardly, *Thank you, Angel, for saving us another day.* Pulling the skirt of one of the dresses over my face, I would curl up tight and manage to fall asleep for a while—that is, until hunger woke me up.

Eventually, the door was forced open, but there was nowhere to go. I felt like a captive in a field of ice.

★ ★ ★ ★ ★

There was not much to wake up for every morning; my will to survive was what motivated me to keep going. I still valued my life and felt grateful for every day that I was still alive. However, that did not change the fact that it was not easy to live in the military barracks, which were crowded and uncomfortable, even though we were a relatively small group.

The other refugees did not know that I had lost the ability to speak as a result of the horrors I'd witnessed and the trauma I'd internalised. Consequently, they ignored me, assuming that I was mentally deficient My father was sent to work at the army compound, doing eighteen hours of hard labour every day. At the time I did not understand most of what went on—I felt shut out of the world of adult secrets, abandoned and alone, much as I had at the farm. All I knew was that I did not see Father much, and Mother was ill, becoming weaker by the minute. Watching her lie on the floor with a high fever, I felt helpless, but I was unable to communicate, and the other refugees were wrapped up in their own problems, anyway. Thus, the days were long and lonely, and I withdrew ever deeper into my shell of protection—holding my stone and listening to the music that I could hear resonating magically through my heart and my head.

On the rare nights when I was lucky enough to fall asleep for a while, my dreams would often begin peacefully. Sitting under the cherry tree with Mikus next to me, I would see images of home. Lars would start to come toward me, but as soon as he got close, a sudden storm would whip up and take him away. That would jolt me awake, and then I would sleep fitfully, plagued by awful dreams—if I were able to fall back to sleep at all.

One morning I woke up to the smell of bacon. *Am I still dreaming, or is this real?* I wondered. Getting to my feet, I emerged from my corner. The remaining family of the little girl whose hand I'd held during the blizzard sat around the small coal stove in the centre of the barracks. The grandmother was frying bacon.

I was so overcome by hunger that it was too difficult to remain in the same room where I could smell food cooking, and so I ran outside as fast as I could. The cold crisp air cleansed the aroma of the food from my nostrils, and I swallowed hard a few times to get the smell off the back of my tongue and out of my throat. I had grown accustomed to the pain of hunger, and I was able to live with that emptiness deep in my belly—it was not easy, but I had learned to manage what I was not able to change or control. Nevertheless, I was still but a child, and the frustration of seeing and smelling food that I could not eat in the midst of such unrelenting hunger was unbearable. It was the cruellest form of denial that I have ever had to face.

For many days following the morning of the other family's bacon breakfast, I did not see my father at all. He did not return from working at the compound, and I did not know what had happened to him. I couldn't ask Mother because she was so ill; I didn't want to upset her, and she wouldn't have had an answer anyway. I felt trapped: I was not able to speak, Mother was gravely ill, and Father seemed to have disappeared. I did not know what to do, and I began to panic.

I became so terrified that I could no longer breathe inside the barracks, and so I stumbled outside. A soldier stood guard, rifle at the ready. Suddenly I knew that I had to take action to help Mother—especially if Father might not ever return. This single-minded purpose was stronger than anything else, even my terror.

Approaching the soldier, I used sufficient gestures to convince him something was very wrong, and then I quickly pulled him inside the barracks. Pulling him closer to where Mother lay on the floor, I pointed toward her. I watched his face carefully, certain that he could see how desperately ill she was. He raised his hand, and I cringed, afraid that he might hit me, but he did not. Instead, he took my hand, trying to comfort me. He opened the door to call another soldier, and a few minutes later, they brought in a stretcher, moved Mother onto it, and took her away.

I watched, horrified, as they all disappeared behind the barracks. *What have I done? Now Father and Mother are both gone! I've lost them both … just like in the woods.* I'd had no choice, of course. Mother could not survive in the barracks; she was ill and continuing to worsen, and Father was not there to see how ill she'd become. I did what circumstances forced me to do. I was simply too young to have known for sure that I'd done the right thing—the only thing I could have done.

I was all alone again. All I had left was my precious little stone, which I clutched with all my might, never letting it out of my grasp, day or night.

A large truck began stopping by every so often, doling out a small loaf of bread to everyone, which was meant to last a few days. I saved mine for Father, praying he would return soon. Sometimes the truck would have a large soup pot attached it. The soup was really just boiling water with a few meagre shreds of kohlrabi floating in it. I was so very hungry, and I could not save the soup for Father; it would only get cold and do him no good. I took one of the small bowls that came on the truck and brought it to the soup pot to have it filled. I drank it in a dreadful hurry. The consequences of my desperate, ravenous haste would last the rest of my life. I had severely burned my mouth.

★ ★ ★ ★ ★

Eventually, Father returned, much to my relief. One day he came back earlier than usual, bringing a few potatoes with him. "Lara, go outside and get some snow," Father told me. He cut the potatoes in small pieces, put them in a metal pan that he found near the coal stove, mixed in the melted snow that I brought him, and placed the pan on the top of the stove. It took a very long time for the mixture to cook, but Father had made something like bread.

Father broke off a piece of the bread and handed it to me. Having learned my lesson with the soup, I let it cool a bit before taking a bite, even though I was very hungry, as usual—it seemed I had not eaten my full since the Christmas Eve that Lars came home. The bread felt warm in the palm of my hand, and I cradled it tenderly. The warmth of the piece of fresh-baked bread curled in a tiny plume of steam, and I breathed in the aroma appreciatively. I put a small piece in my mouth, feeling my taste buds come alive to the flavour of food. This was the best bread I had ever tasted—the best bread anyone could possibly imagine!

Everything was wonderful now that Father was here. I wasn't all alone anymore, and Father and I had the best bread in the world to eat, but there were only the two of us to share the whole loaf. *I wish Mother were here to share it with us. I wish Lars were here too, safe and sound. I wish ...* I stopped myself. I couldn't think about all that I'd lost. I had to be grateful for what we did have: for this bread Father and I had to share; for our very lives. *Thank you, Angel, for this bread and for saving us another day.*

I broke a small piece off from the bread Father had given me, and I walked over to the little girl who shared the barracks room. Extending my hand to her , I offered her the piece of bread from my portion. She made a strange face at me, turning it down.

I was puzzled. Wasn't she hungry too? It did not matter to me that they had not shared their bacon; I knew what it felt like to be hungry, and I always shared the little food that I did have—just as I'd shared my potato in the field with Lolo. Even in the depths of starvation, we can still be kind and generous. Intuitively, I somehow knew that by doing so I was honouring life and denying triumph to the assassins. I never did understand why she did not take the bread I offered, but I could not wonder for long. Surviving takes a lot of focus and energy. Eating the piece of bread myself, I walked back to Father, staying close to him until he had to return to the compound.

I was relieved that Father was there, but it was hard to not have Mother with me. I constantly wondered where she was and whether she would come back. I spent most days all alone in my corner, holding my little stone and waiting for Father to come back to the barracks. Sometimes one of the others would check to make sure I was still alive, but for the most part they left me alone. There was nothing to do. The little girl I'd tried to be kind to never wanted to play with me, so I remained with my stone, recited my music in my head, sang songs in my heart, and thought of home. Those days in the barracks still seemed much better to me than many of the other days of the recent past.

Father did not say much to me when he came home from the compound. He was exhausted from the hard labour, and he knew I could not speak. What could we have talked about, anyway? He would ask me to bring him some snow if he'd found more potatoes, and then we would just sit together waiting to share the bread that Father had made for us to eat.

I realised that Father and I did not need words to tell each other how we felt. Our eyes told each other everything. He could see how thankful I was for his efforts to make the bread, and I could see how thankful he was for my smile. We were equally grateful just to be with each other. I no longer feared that Father would not return, and so I always greeted him with a big smile, hoping this would make things easier for him. We would eat together if Father could manage some food for us, and then he would drop down in our corner and fall asleep on the floor. All that mattered to me was that Father was there.

I missed Mother a lot, especially during the day when Father was away at the compound. Sometimes I would leave our corner to go outside. As far as the eye could see in all directions there was only snow—mountain after mountain of snow. I was accustomed to the rigours of the Baltic winter, but the weather seemed even harsher here than in Latvia.

One day, despite the falling snow, I decided to go outside to look for Mother, reasoning that she must be somewhere behind the barracks, as that was where I'd seen the soldiers take the stretcher. Running as fast as possible past the coal stove where one of the families that shared the barracks room sat feasting on their prepared meal, I went out into the storm. The blizzard had created huge snowdrifts, the air was bitter cold, and the snow still swirled. I felt like I was running into that absolute whiteness again, just as I had when we'd walked from the train to the barracks. I made my way behind the barracks, only to find nothing but more snow. I kept going; I had to find Mother. Finally, I reached a road. The snow was not falling quite so hard anymore, and I was able to see. In the distance, I saw tall buildings surrounded by a huge gate. *Mother!* Maybe that was where the soldiers had taken Mother.

I kept running and running, not even feeling the bitter cold anymore. I had no coat, but at least my feet were not cold. My socks had worn out, but Father had given me newspaper to wrap around my feet. With my boots over my paper-wrapped feet, I felt generally warmer and better than I had in a long time. *Father must be the smartest man in the whole world!*

As I got closer to the gate, I realised it was an army hospital guarded by an armed soldier. I tried to open the gate, but he pushed me away. My heart almost stopped from fear. I only wanted to find Mother, but

I could not tell him that because I could not talk. I pointed at the gate, pleading, tears welling up in my eyes. Standing still in the bitter cold, I began to shiver. I reached into my pocket and gave the soldier a small piece of bread that Father had made a couple of nights before, which was the last time I'd eaten. I had saved some of it, not knowing when we would have food to eat again. The soldier saw how upset I was. He smiled at me, declining my offer.

I sensed some glimmer of kindness in him. Maybe he would help me find Mother. Hesitantly, I began to move my lips. It felt so strange after not being able to speak for so long. I managed a faint hint of a sound, barely a whisper: "Mother …" I tried again, pointing to the gate. I tried so hard to say more, but the words froze in my throat; I could feel them strangling me from within.

Watching my face carefully, the soldier now understood what I was saying and realised why I had tried to enter the compound—why I was so desperate. Leaning his rifle against the gate, he picked me up and held me close to keep me warm. I had not felt such kindness for a long time. Clinging to him, I wept—partly because of the relief I felt in that moment, briefly safe and warm, and partly because it just felt good to know that someone cared. Again, I offered the soldier my small piece of bread.

With a smile, he put it back in my pocket. Wiping my tears compassionately, he set me down on the ground, and then he opened the gate. The yard was so big that I was sure the whole world could fit into it. I started to run as fast as I could; some other soldiers caught me. They were about to push me outside the compound, but I fought to remain inside, determined to find Mother. During the struggle, a very tall officer arrived. He took me by the hand, ordering the soldiers away. Utterly numb with fear, I looked up at him, incredulous. Because of the soldier at the gate, a small amount of trust had begun to grow in my heart. I took the piece of bread out of my pocket and gave it to the officer. He smiled, and we started to walk toward the hospital.

Some guards opened the doors for us, and the officer led me inside. The hospital seemed to be a large house, and it was nice and warm. I looked all around as we walked through many long corridors. My feet gave out, and I sank to the floor. The officer picked me up, carrying me past many rooms filled with wounded soldiers.

At the very far end was a small and dim room. The officer stopped and set me on my feet, motioning me inside the room. The light was so poor that I could scarcely see anything, but at the far wall I noticed a person who looked quite pale. I could not tell who it was, but, somehow, I felt warmth radiating.

Mother? Yes, it was! *Mother!* I saw Mother trying to reach me, she was speaking softly and lifting her arms, but they fell back on the bed because she was so weak. I ran to her bedside. Some food was brought in for her. She offered it to me, but I declined. Mother needed it more than I did. She needed to regain her strength so that she could come home and live with Father and me in the barracks.

This reunion was a very precious moment for me. I felt very happy and relieved. Mother was all right. Maybe the war was over! Or, if not, maybe it would be soon.

After a while, the officer took me by the hand and nodded toward the door. It was time to leave. I had to say goodbye—not another goodbye! I clung to Mother's hand, refusing to move. I felt my heart would break again—that is, if there was anything left to break. Mother stroked my hand gently. I remembered the kindness of the officer and the soldier at the gate. I would be able to visit Mother again; she would come back to the barracks soon. Father would come back to the barracks tonight. Everything would be all right.

I followed the officer out of the room.

★ ★ ★ ★ ★

The officer gently took me by the hand, and we walked through more long corridors and up many steep stairs. Finally, we reached the attic. Within it was an enormous loft, a huge open space but poorly lit. I was suddenly afraid that he would leave me there forever. But he smiled, pointing to the far end of the room. Near the small window stood a piano.

A piano! The chords began to sound in jubilation in my head. I started to run toward the piano, but I tripped and fell. My legs were just too weak to carry me farther. I had not eaten in a while, and having to leave Mother had upset me terribly, especially after our long separation.

The officer picked me up and carried me to the piano, telling me to play.

My fingers were so cold and numb; initially, they hurt moving across the keys, and I had to play very slowly. My joy in the music warmed every part of me, even my frozen fingers. I began to play all the pieces that I could remember, hoping Mother would hear. *Chopin will make you well again, Mother!* I thought to myself, as I played the waltz that was Mother's favourite piece.

I closed my eyes, imagining the whole family at home—Mother embroidering, Father and Lars playing their violin and mandolin, me playing the piano. I imagined Mikus curled up beside me on the piano bench, and I could see the angel at the top of the Christmas tree, smiling down at me. The lights on the tree were shining like a thousand stars, and we all were smiling and happy as I played. I played and played and played. I could hear Lars singing in his velvety baritone to my accompaniment; I could hear the rich strains of Father's violin. As I played the piano in that attic loft, something deep with me shifted: I was home again, safe and free.

Many hours had passed when I awakened, still sitting at the piano, exhaustion and hunger having taken their toll. Suddenly the door swung open, and the officer rushed toward me, picking me up, clearly relieved that I was still alive. I was alive, but the dream was over. I had come back to the harsh reality of war.

That day was very special for me, not just because I'd found Mother, but also because my faith and trust in people had returned. I had never stopped valuing life, and, deep down, I'd always maintained a positive feeling, believing that everything would be good again. But it was so difficult—if not impossible—for me to understand all the malice, as there was no reason for it, and it brought only suffering and sorrow.

Meeting the officer was a turning point in my life, and I would come to understand this even more so as time went on. From a small window in the attic loft I was able to see the landscape. I would look outside before I played the piano, gradually realising that the surrounding topography provided a natural shield for the barracks where we now lived. Neither Father nor Mother could possibly have guessed how prudently this officer had planned our escape from the advancing front. He tucked our group of refugees away in the valley, with a wall of snow all around to provide an extra barrier. This shielded us, but it also prevented us from being aware of what went on farther away from the barracks. Nobody had a premonition of the impending danger.

Weather conditions, too, limited our awareness. The winter had been so long and so cold, with no end in sight. Snowstorms raged almost every other day, it seemed. All the roads and paths had been destroyed by mines or bombs; the ones that remained were usually impassable because of snow and drifts. I had to make a new path to the hospital every day. Some days the wind whipped the snow mercilessly, and I would find myself walking in circles, having lost my bearings in the swirling snow. The freezing crystallised snow cut my face, as if each flake were a tiny blade of ice.

Many times I arrived at the hospital but was not allowed to see my mother. No one every explained the reasons for this, and I could not speak to ask Father—and would not have burdened him with greater worry if I had been able to speak, anyway. On those nights I did not sleep; I would just lay awake, wondering if Mother had grown worse. Was she still alive?

★ ★ ★ ★ ★

Time passed, and I felt that I truly had every reason to be happy again. I knew where Mother was, hoped she was getting better and growing stronger every day, and was able to see her most days that I went to the hospital. Father was with me every night; he usually arrived late, but he always made it back to the barracks to be with me. I had my little stone and the music in my heart. When I went to see Mother, I also had the chance to play the piano; the attic loft had become a magical place for me. Sometimes I had to pinch myself to believe that I was really playing, not just dreaming of playing.

One day I awakened to more light than usual peeking through the boards in the barracks. Venturing outside, I saw that it was a wonderful sunny morning. Even the weather was changing for the better; soon it would be spring. A small town was a short distance from the barracks, and I longed to walk there. As with my walks to visit Mother, the soldiers did not pay much attention to the refugee children; it was the hard labour of the able-bodied adults that interested them.

The town seemed to be a peaceful place, hidden away from the world as it was by the valley and the tremendous snow banks. From the barracks, only the smoking chimneys were visible, but as I neared the town I could see more. Some children played in the snow, reminding me of happier days. I stopped to watch them, stuffing my hands in my pockets to keep them warm. My hand instinctively found my little stone, and I held it tight, swallowing unshed tears at the memories of playing in the snow with Lars.

The smallest girl in the group of children approached me, wanting to play. Putting my stone deep in my I pocket, I pulled out my hands. The nice little girl saw that my hands were nearly frozen; my fingers had begun to turn blue. She offered me her mittens, but I was suddenly afraid. My sense of trust was tenuous at best, and I was unable to accept this gesture of kindness from another child. Turning away, I quickly ran inside one of the stores on the main street of the town.

What a beautiful store it was! There was food on the shelves, real bread, fish, and many other things. I must have stood there for quite some time, just looking at the bread. Many people came in and formed a line; they handed over their coupons to receive their weekly rations. It must have been the only place in the area where people could go for their rations. I had no coupons and no money, so I just stood in the corner, watching people come and go. It had been so long since I'd participated in a quiet daily activity like going to the store—even with a ration coupon—and I just stood in silence, transfixed by the normalcy I'd forgotten existed.

Lost in my daydreams, I suddenly noticed that I was alone in the store, except for the man behind the counter. He was elderly, with a kind face, and he watched me looking intently at the small heel of bread left on the counter. I could practically taste the bread—the crunch of the crust between my teeth and the taste of yeast and grain and salt on my tongue. It was pointless to look at the bread or dream of its flavour: I had neither the ration coupons nor the money to buy even that small end of bread.

With a sigh and a deepening pang of hunger, I turned to look out the window, surprised to see that a new snowstorm had whipped up while I'd been lost in thought. The morning had been so bright and sunny, I'd never expected such a drastic change in the weather. It was time to go back to the barracks, and I needed to hurry, or I'd risk getting lost in a blizzard. Putting my hands in my pockets in preparation of facing the harsh weather, I started to walk toward the door.

The nice old man behind the counter smiled at me, motioning for me to wait. Turning toward me, he gave me the small heel of leftover bread. I wanted to thank him, but I could not yet speak. I smiled, and he seemed to understand the look in my eyes. He could feel my gratitude, I imagined, as he also gave me a handful of the tiniest fish I'd ever seen—they were so small, I had to put the whole fish in my mouth and eat it, guts and all. The man demonstrated this, and I mimicked him, delighted by how delicious it tasted. It was a real treat, one that I wished to share with Father, so I saved the rest of the fish and only ate a small edge of the crust of the bread. Giving the man another wordless thank-you with my eyes and smile, I left the store.

The air was frigid, and the wind was fierce. Snow swirled all around me. It was hard to follow the road because the snow was already deep, and it continued to fall. I walked as carefully as I could, but I still fell into a deep ditch concealed by the snow. Keeping my hands deep in my pockets, I held my stone tight in one, and the bread and fish in the other. I wanted to save the food for Father. They fed Mother in the hospital, thankfully. I would not be able to visit her today, as my walk to town had taken so long because of my daydreaming and the snow.

I should not have stayed so long in the store, but it was worth it to have the treats that the kind old man had given me. Father would be so pleased and so surprised! I brightened at the thought and kept trudging carefully. Walking became more and more difficult, and I had to proceed slowly to avoid falling. Seeing another store peek through the curtain of snowfall, I realised that I hadn't even gotten out of the town. The store was open, and I decided it would be better to go inside and wait until the storm passed.

This was a different kind of store from the first; the shelves were lined with all kinds of small bottles. It smelled of medicine, and I wrinkled my nose. I passed a young woman as I entered the store. She stood in front and handed everybody who entered a small tube of something. As I took the tube she gave me, I saw what looked like small pieces of candy inside it. A smile formed deep inside me, warming every part of me before it even came to my lips. *Candy!* The thought of the sugar filling my mouth was even more tantalising than the bread had been.

After a while the storm passed, and I hurried out of the second store to make my way back to the barracks. I tucked the small tube into the pocket that held the bread and the fish—my stone was special, and so I kept it safe its very own pocket. The walk through the deep snow was dreary, and I kept thinking about the candy in my pocket. The temptation was too great, and I surrendered, easing the tube out of my pocket gingerly so as not to disturb the feast I was saving for Father. I turned the tube between my fingers, reading the label: B

VITAMINS. Unsure what that really meant, I decided that anything that so resembled candy had to be good. I decided to try one, and I placed it on my tongue, finding it delicious. Before I knew it, I'd eaten all but two. *I must save these for Mother and Father; it will be a special treat, just like Christmas Eve!* I told myself, firmly replacing the tube in my pocket.

I kept walking toward the barracks, despite the difficulty of trudging through the deep snow. I was very tired, and in many places the snow was waist deep. Suddenly everything began to spin around, and the dizziness forced me to sit down in the snow. *I must have had too much vitamin B—whatever that is,* I conjectured, feeling guilty that I'd so indulged. Now I felt ill, and there was hardly any left for Mother and Father.

When the spinning stopped, I resumed walking, arriving at the barracks just before darkness fell. Father arrived just after I did. We shared the fish and bread, and then the two of us dropped on the bare boards of the barracks, utterly exhausted.

★ ★ ★ ★ ★

Days came and went without much change, in the weather or otherwise; that one morning's sunshine proved not to be the harbinger of spring that I'd hoped for. Because of the kindness of the officer, I was free to visit Mother most days. Mother appeared calm, always asking me to play the piano. She said she could hear it, so I would climb the stairs to the attic loft and play for hours—while I played, I would dream of better days to come. The kindness of the officer had restored my spirit, and I believed the war would soon end and life would be happy and good again.

The attic loft grew dark, meaning it was time to leave. I walked through the vast, dim space, but I was not frightened. Reaching the door, I saw a lone soldier slouched in a chair. I had not known anyone else was there listening to me play. He hadn't made a sound, so I suspected he must have been so tired that he hadn't even moved in his sleep. Opening the door as quietly as I could, I began to tiptoe out to the attic stairs. Just then, he fell off the chair and onto the floor; he still did not move. I had seen enough death to know that the poor soldier had died. It was different than the other deaths I had witnessed, though, because I had been playing the piano all that time. The soldier had departed this earth, and I believed that he had taken my music with him to eternity.

Clutching my little stone, I exited the loft and descended the attic stairs. Somehow I knew that the soldier's death was not the only farewell of that day: I sensed that it was the last time I would play the piano in the attic loft.

★ ★ ★ ★ ★

A continuous rumble always hung in the air, but after encountering the dead soldier in the attic loft that day I heard a particular rumbling that kept coming closer and closer. I felt unsettled by what I'd seen, and a sense of foreboding overwhelmed me, although I couldn't have expressed it as such at the time.

Trying to shake the feeling of distress, I decided to take a walk to the town. All the stores were empty and closed, and only a few people moved about in the streets. Rather than easing my distress, the walk to town had intensified it. I turned to walk back to the barracks, but the road was gone! The town had been snowed in, and I could not find any trail or tracks anywhere.

To stave off full-blown panic, I just kept walking, telling myself I would find the barracks. I wasn't that far away. *Please, Angel, just get me back to the barracks. Please! Don't let me get lost again ... don't let me lose Mother and Father!* I prayed with all my might, clutching my little stone for dear life. It had become my lifeline.

I walked and walked, but the barracks never came into view. Somehow I must have wandered off in the wrong direction. It began snowing again, and in no time at all a wall of snow surrounded me. *How will I ever get through?!* I was lost, but giving into fear would not help me. I had to wait out the storm before I could figure out what to do. Eventually, the storm simmered down. I was able to see a thicket of trees ahead: spruce covered with a deep layer of snow, brilliant white against the dark blue-green of the spruce.

Finding the smallest tree in the thicket, I sat beneath it, comforted by the silvery-flute sounds of its whistling in the quieting wind. The clear moon made the snow sparkle on the ground. Looking all around me at the glistening sea of white, I felt happy. I was lost and utterly alone, but I was alive! Surviving had forged an indomitable spirit deep within my child's body, and I knew that I would make it through. I reached inside my pocket and found the tube with the B vitamins. I'd forgotten to hide them in the barracks so I could save them for Mother and Father. I was so hungry—always so hungry—and my need to eat overtook my wish to have a gift for my parents. I ate the remaining two vitamins—which still tasted like candy to me, even after the dizziness that followed eating them the first time.

This can be my very own special Christmas Eve! I thought to myself, with the kind of quiet, private joy that young children seem always able to muster, even the midst of circumstances as appalling as mine. Caressing my dear little stone, I heard the carols of my childhood resounding in my heart; I felt my angel gazing down me. Despite the bitter cold night, I felt warm and filled with peace. I fell asleep, dreaming of happier times, when my parents sat with Lars and me, telling us all about the first Christmas tree, which had been decorated in Riga in 1519. So long ago! I slept beneath the shelter of a tree just like that one, though it was far away from my homeland and stars, not candles, illuminated it in the darkness of the wintry night.

I slept peacefully, not waking until it was light. When I opened my eyes, I saw that the early morning sunshine had turned the vast field into a shimmering, crystalline carpet. Distant voices were coming closer, and I crawled closer to the base of the tree to better hide myself within its lowest branches. Peeking through the branches, I saw three men, who were awfully close to the thicket. A few more steps, and I would be able to see their faces. The bark of the trunk was rough, but I was grateful to the tree for protecting me. The men turned, and I was able to distinguish their faces, one of them especially.

Father!! I crawled out from my hiding place as fast as I could, but I was numb with cold, and so it was difficult to move.

Seeing me, Father rushed to the tree, the other men following him. It was such a happy reunion! They had realised that I must have gotten lost in the snowstorm the night before; at daybreak, they'd set off to find me.

My feet were so cold and numb that I could not walk. Father placed me on his back, carrying me all the way back to the barracks. I pressed my cheeks against the warm spot between his shoulder blades, wrapping my arms around his neck. I was safe, and I would live another day.

★ ★ ★ ★ ★

With each passing day, the rumbling noises grew louder. The war was coming closer. One dark night some army trucks arrived, and the soldiers ordered everybody in the barracks to get into the trucks. They pushed us to move quickly. Instinctively, I checked for my little stone: it was gone! Panicked, I hurried back into the barracks. I could not leave without my stone. I found it on a small ledge near the corner where I slept; it must have fallen out. I picked it up and stuffed it back into its spot deep in my pocket. *You stay there, where you belong!* I admonished it, filled with an odd mix of relief and anger at having lost and found what I so dearly loved. That was what I would have said to Mikus if I'd found him in the garden the night of the fire. The stone was like a living creature to me, and I gave it all the love I could no longer give to the ones I'd lost.

With the stone safely deposited, I quickly ran outside to get back in the truck, but it had left without me. I looked around, but there was no one in sight. Father was gone, and so was Mother, recently returned from the hospital. The three of us were finally together again—or, at least, we had been—and now I was alone. Abandoned. Lost, all over again.

I stroked my stone, not knowing what else to do. I had no voice with which to shout or cry out, and even if I could have spoken, no one was there.

A new blizzard whipped the air; sharp ice pellets cut my face. Yet another wall of icy snow was closing in on me. Soon I would be buried in snow. A strange, airy feeling came over me. It was similar to when I had fainted in the wheat field, but now the rumbling noise drowned out the buzzing in my head. I saw a hand reaching toward me; I tried to run away before it could grab me, but my legs would not move. Just then, the face that went with the hand became visible: it was the same officer who helped me find Mother and let me play the piano in the attic loft. Catching me as my body began to sink, he carried me to a nearby ambulance.

Once again, the officer restored my faith with his kindness: he had rescued me in more ways than one. It felt like a dream from which I never wanted to awaken. Mother and Father were in the ambulance, sitting at the far end. Father tried to keep Mother warm, as she was still quite ill and was running a fever. The officer brought me to them, and then he got into one of the trucks.

I was determined *never* to lose them again, and I held onto both of them with all my might. I did not dare take my eyes off my parents now that I'd found them. My little stone was safe in my pocket, and my other pocket held a small piece of bread. I had my parents. I felt enormously grateful and fortunate as the whole convoy set off, heading westward.

The larger trucks were able to plough through the deep snow without much difficulty, but the ambulance laboured to follow. Suddenly the road disappeared, and we were snowed in. The driver tried to turn around, but it was no use.

Gunfire suddenly erupted from the nearby woods, . Luckily, it was very dark, so the snipers did not have a clear view of us. I jumped out, picked up some snow, melted it in my palm, and cupped my hand so Mother could have some water. We moved on, but the road became increasingly treacherous. All attempts to move resulted in the vehicle rolling from one ditch to the other. Finally the driver managed to make it back onto the road, where the tanks had made deep tracks that he could follow.

It was a sad and scary drive. For long stretches, the snow was not white anymore; it was filled with dirt and blood. Ammunition and fallen soldiers were scattered along the roadside. The sight of it all made me feel ill, as memories swamped me—the Christmas Eve when Lars had come home wounded, the massacre on the road, the building collapse, and so many horrible images. I couldn't stop them from flashing through my mind. The agony of my grief was overpowering.

The vehicle suddenly lurched to a stop, and we heard a kind of choking sound. The petrol tank was empty; at some point during our escape the tank had developed a hole, and all the petrol leaked out. The driver quickly vanished, leaving my parents and me in the middle of nowhere. A mass of snow surrounded us, extending all the way to the horizon. The three of us were left there to perish.

The next day was clear and sunny. I got out of the ambulance to get more snow for Mother. Something seemed to moving toward us. Was this real help or just an illusion? It was real, I saw as it came closer: a convoy of trucks.

★ ★ ★ ★ ★

The convoy was the same one that had left the barracks without me, and it moved along the only remaining road, stopping at the stranded ambulance. Mother and Father were put in the back of the truck. The other passengers scrambled to keep their seats on the truck, roughly pushing me aside. Separated from my parents, I was left standing in the road. The truck began to move away, and, in utter despair, I ran after it. With the last ounce of my strength, I jumped onto the back of the truck, barely making it.

And then I looked toward the side of the road in helpless panic, watching my precious little stone fly from my pocket and land in the deep snow as I jumped onto the truck. *My stone! My dear little stone! It's gone forever.* My heart almost burst from the force of my pain and grief. The only thing I had from home was gone. I felt like I was losing each of my animal friends all over again; that little stone had become my life line and my closest companion, my fast friend through thick and thin, beside me in the deepest moments of peril. I had given it such tender care, even dashing back into the barracks to rescue it, and now it was gone. Forever. I felt as if my hope and strength had deserted me, and I had nothing left to help me get through the hardships that awaited. I was all alone again. The stone had become not only a symbol of home but something to believe in: if I kept the stone safe, I would be safe too. And I had been; I'd found kindness even in the depths of the nightmare. Every act of kindness was a propitious omen, a sign to keep believing in survival—to keep believing in life. I had learned not to let the scourge and din of war distort my motivation to live or my appreciation of the gift of life; I had kept the ugliness around me from penetrating my soul. My music filled my heart and my mind. I still had my shell of protection—I still had my music. I would survive, even if my poor little stone was gone. *Keep it safe in the snow, Angel. Help it go on without me, just as I must go on.*

I had come to achieve great wisdom at far too young an age, but I recognised that I must never let the negative overshadow the positive. And I never did.

The ride on the convoy was long and difficult. There was not enough room for both my legs, and so I had to just hang on for dear life. It was so cold that icicles formed in my hair. Corpses filled the sides of the road. The journey was to become even more harrowing.

From the back of the truck came a heartrending cry. A newborn had died. The young mother's pain echoed through the truck. A small bundle wrapped in rags was passed toward the front, eventually reaching me. Barely hanging on myself, I held the body of the baby in my free arm. The baby's eyes were closed, and the face was pale and lifeless.

Even if I hadn't heard the mother's cries, I would have known that the baby was dead. Still, I longed to save the tiny thing—I could not bear another loss.

Somebody yelled and hit my arm so hard that the baby fell out, landing in the deep snow. *Just like my dear little stone!* Overcome with sorrow, I closed my eyes, surprised to feel no welling tears. They must have dried up for good. *Angel, please take care of the poor little baby. Take her somewhere safe and beautiful, where there is no war or pain.* A combination of grief and pain pierced my body like the sharpest knife, penetrating every cell. I only wished I could follow the baby to heaven.

As always, I had no time to cry.

The day went on, and the convoy continued moving. Those who died along the way were pushed off the truck into the snow; I shuddered each time. Eventually, the convoy arrived at a small town. Even from the outside, the houses looked beautiful. Everyone remaining in the trucks was asked to go inside one of the houses. The inside was even more beautiful: fine rugs covered the floors; numerous paintings hung on the walls; lovely objects and furniture adorned the rooms, and one windowsill held a plant, still green, with buds about to bloom. More army vehicles arrived, and tired soldiers filled the rooms. The house looked meticulously managed. Flames crackled in the fireplace, radiating warmth into the large front parlor, at the centre of which stood a black grand piano—one of the largest I'd ever seen.

I approached the magnificent instrument, letting my fingers hover over the keys before I began to play. Once I started, I kept playing—all the songs and pieces that I was able to remember, I played. I released my need to express my grief through my music. Nothing else could ever ease my pain, anyway; music was my true and only curative.

The soldiers began to cluster around the piano, some with tears in their eyes, some far away in their thoughts, some completely motionless. One soldier gave me a small piece of chocolate. I wanted to save it, but it started to melt. I gave it to Mother, who needed to eat more than I did.

That night passed without any sirens. I was very tired but would not sleep; I stayed up far into the night playing the piano. The fatigue and drama of the day eventually took over, and I fell asleep under the piano. It was a restless sleep, filled with torturous images of war and pain and death.

Before daybreak, the soldiers gathered all the refugees together and loaded us onto the truck, which took off in a hurry. There was now more space in the truck, and I had room for both of my legs, so I didn't have to hang on. I could even see my parents sitting at the far end. For many more long and hard days we just kept moving along the seemingly endless bloodstained road.

All the roads were littered with weapons, ammunition, and death. It was a treacherous ride. Sometimes the truck would slide from ditch to ditch, and the bodies of the dead were cast off more frequently.

I had no idea where the journey would end—maybe the land of nowhere. How long would a journey to the land of nowhere take, and who would be left to reach the end? There were only a few people left in the truck, and I could then move closer to my parents. I sat right beside Mother, putting my arms around her and hugging her close. I kept watching her face, silently pleading with her not to close her eyes. She understood even my silence, kept her eyes locked on mine, and managed to give me a faint smile.

10
Serpent

It was recital time again, which I always enjoyed. Usually it began in September, just when the beauty of Canadian autumn was at its best, and continued until the end of June. I spent the summer looking forward to touring, and the better part of fall, winter, and spring delighting in performing.

The only part of touring that ever presented a challenge was the travel. Most of the time I travelled alone, but occasionally I went with an ensemble. The upcoming tour would be an ensemble of six, and we would appear throughout northern Ontario. The means of travel always depended on both distance and weather conditions. So far the winter had been harsh, and this caused great concern, as travel by air and most roads was subject to frequent cancellations. Under no circumstances could the contract for the tour be broken, which left only one reliable travel option: the train.

Snow had fallen for many consecutive days, but we had to embark for the tour of northern Ontario. On the day we were set to depart, the railway tracks to Sudbury had been cleared. The train left on time in the early evening, and all seemed well. Without any premonition that we had set off on what would become a long and extended haul, my ensemble group and I settled into the comfortable train seats. We were a pleasant group of colleagues: three vocalists—a soprano, a baritone, and a bass—two string players—a violinist and a cellist—and me, the pianist. We had a special car on the train, both for our travelling comfort and also so that we could practise more easily.

It was such a pleasure to sit in comfort, to feel safe and warm, while the wind howled outside, whipping the snow and frigid air. This was quite different from the terrifying train journeys of my wartime childhood. I held myself steady, listening to the banter of my colleagues, focusing on the music—I knew the train travel would trigger my memories, propelling me back to the painful past. I could never stop that from happening; the best I could do was pray that I would endure it. Determined not to let it ruin my present joy in the tour, I willed my mind back to the conversation, turning away from the blizzard outside that so reminded me of northern Germany.

Our pleasant conversation, combined with the vocalists' practising, drowned out the irritating noise of the engines. After a while, the engines sounded to me like they were on the verge of breakdown, but nobody else seemed to pay any attention. At first I thought that might be because they were engaged in happy conversation or singing, but then I questioned whether, perhaps, my memory was triggering remembered sounds of those awful blizzard-borne train rides. Believing it was more likely the latter, I settled back again, enjoying the warmth, safety, and comfort.

Some more time passed, and the monotonous whistle of the locomotive began to reassure me that all was well. This was modern train travel in Canada, not a long-ago flight of beleaguered refugees. The train dutifully ploughed through the storm. All one could see in any direction was white; a wall of snow surrounded either side of the train. I felt like I was racing through dense clouds, almost like air travel, except that the clouds in the sky were lighter and fluffier. I relaxed even more, amazed by the number of songs, jokes, and anecdotes my companions could call to my mind as a way to pass the time.

I was not sure how much time had gone by when I noticed that a thick layer of ice covered much of the windows. The ice was less thick in some spots, where beautiful flowers of frost illuminated by the dim light inside the train sparkled magically against the dark sky. I smiled, awed as ever by nature's exquisite presence.

The train had all the modern conveniences, including a private bathroom. I decided to get ready for the night. The bathroom door was wide open, and there at the sink stood the majestic bass vocalist, washing a sock. "I'll just be a moment, Lara," he told me cheerfully, using his index finger to steer his sock around the filled sink.

"No hurry," I said, puzzled as I got a closer look at the sink. "May I ask why only one sock?"

"But of course! I washed the other one yesterday." He grinned at me. We musicians possess a logic all our own!

The evening was most enjoyable, and soon we all were ready to retire, wishing to have sufficient rest before our upcoming performances.

All was quiet and peaceful, except for the thunderous snoring that came from the far end of our private car. The vocalist whose golden bass had brought many opera-house audiences such joy now entertained his colleagues and fellow travellers with his powerful snoring. However, I must note that he never failed to stay on pitch mid-snore! The tiny diva kept running back and forth, practising her recitative in her crystal-clear coloratura soprano, all the while complaining of not being able to sleep. Her high notes were so brilliant that I feared they would shatter the glass in the windows, letting the frigid air and snow into the compartment; her voice was so beautiful, I wondered that it didn't melt the ice right off the windows. Both snowing and snoring continued through the night. From the very far corner soothing passages of Brahms filled the air as the gifted violinist practised the sonata, rocking us all to sleep, except for the cellist, who sat up puffing on his cigars.

None of us could have guessed what the next few hours held in store.

In the early hours of the morning day, the conductor announced that we had become snowed in. Nobody had anticipated that a supposedly ordinary and uneventful trip would come to a sudden halt in the middle of a mountain of snow in Ontario. The train did not have a dining car or any provisions, as this was to be an overnight journey by train. We'd already planned where we would have our breakfast when we got off the train, a little place two blocks from the station that a friend had recommended to the cellist.

Alas, our plans were not to be. Inured to the vicissitudes of life more than I imagined my colleagues might be, I remained quiet. We all made the best of it, singing and telling jokes to pass the time and stave off boredom. Eventually, fatigue set in, and I nodded off.

★ ★ ★ ★ ★

My sleep was restless, as usual. The previous night on the train I'd been lulled by Brahms, but today the past haunted my subconscious. My dreams took me back to the night-time truck convoy. We had almost reached the border of Denmark, and all the refugees who had survived the harrowing journey to that point had to board a train. The whole station was in turmoil, and the train seemed on the verge of falling apart.

All through the night we journeyed by train, an endless and terrifying ride. I felt trapped, a prisoner of the dark, as if it were a dungeon and not a train at all. *Where have the days disappeared to?* I wondered. *Will the sun ever shine again?* I had thought of all this many times before that, but I never could get over how dark it always seemed or how cold and hungry I always felt. I willed myself to believe that things would get better—that the war would end, and we would be safe and happy again—but I began to feel that safety and happiness were things that I longed for, more imagined than real, as my actual memories of living in safety and happiness retreated ever farther into the past.

The spaces between the boards were too narrow for light to pass through but wide enough to let in the freezing air. Bone-chilling cold filled every inch of the train car. I caught myself instinctively reaching for my little stone, cruelly lost in the snow banks when I'd had to jump onto the truck. My fingers stopped at the edge of my pocket, gripping a fold of fabric. How I missed my only remembrance of home—my only companion.

Mother and Father are here, though, I consoled myself. *Let us live another day, Angel.*

No longer did it matter where the soldiers took us; Mother and Father and I all were together. I would never let anybody take them away from me again. *Ever.* Finding my parents' hands in the dim light, I held on tight. *I will never let go!* I prayed inwardly, still unable to speak except for infrequent and barely intelligible whispers.

Mother was still gravely ill and running a high fever. I desperately tried to keep her warm, fearfully watching her face and silently pleading with her not to close her eyes. Mother pressed my hand in tacit understanding, keeping her eyes open for my sake, despite her own exhaustion.

All the crying and mourning that filled the train car overwhelmed me, quickly becoming intolerable. I shut my eyes and inwardly hummed all the melodies I knew until music filled my head and my heart. This drowned out the unbearable wailing, and then I invented stories to cheer myself—these were variations on happy recollections of life before the war. I felt so grateful that I still had my music and my happy memories when so many of my friends had just vanished from the face of the earth. I treasured the gift of my very life, humbled. I continued to reassure myself that happiness would return. So many people, young and old, became sad and very ill in strange ways when they did not hold fast to this belief. I came to see that when one loses perspective and the wish to live, the spirit suffers. This diminishment is how the living dead gain power through tyranny; people who value life will never succumb to evil or brutality. Even as a child, I intuitively knew that and cleaved to it. That is how I survived. I also came to understand that no one can receive happiness: it must come from within. *Why are adults not able to see the beauty of a single flower among the ruins? Why do people always need more than what they have? Why did the little girl in the barracks not take the bread I gave her?*

I had grown quite philosophical, remembering the beauty of the single white rose amidst the devastation of our once-lush garden. It was more beautiful juxtaposed against the charred waste than it ever would have been at the height of a peaceful summer. *Count every lovely green leaf, not the ruins,* I told myself. Peace surrounded me for a moment, and I drifted off to sleep.

My all-too-brief serenity was shattered by my dream-state image of the trains lined up like venomous serpents waiting to attack their prey. A few emaciated figures, some walking and some carried by others, moved toward the partially dismantled and demolished train. Chaos and commotion erupted, frightening a few, who ran back to the station. Their terror cost them their lives, for, in the next instant, an explosion shook the station, incinerating it all into ash and dust. Some of the trains were set on fire. Screams, fire, explosions, and fallen soldiers were all that I could see and hear. I thought the whole earth would disappear into the craters created by the bombings, yet the thought that I might fall into one of those pits never entered my mind.

I was so determined to live that my will burned away my fear. It never occurred to me that my life, too, could end right there in that station, on that train. My life was too precious to me; I would never submit or surrender. I would live, no matter what. As one disaster followed another, I had no time to stop, no time to think, no time to cry. All I could do was keep going, knowing that life itself is all we ever have that is truly our own.

★ ★ ★ ★ ★

My new philosophy and my music sustained me then. I felt so strongly that it was my obligation to live and to move on intrepidly that I shut out everything else except Mother and Father. I just focused on every step, putting one foot in front of the other, for that was the only way to survive. There was hardly anything left of the little girl I had been before we had to flee; I'd been forced to take charge of my own life and fend for myself at such a young age that I'd ceased to be a child. I did not even think like a child anymore but like an experienced refugee.

It had been difficult to board the dilapidated train that looked so dark and reeked of such an awful odour. I only got on the train because somebody struck me on the back so hard that I'd practically flown inside. It was too dark to see who shared the car with us, but I could see that some of the occupants were curled up in a corner and covered with spotted sheets. The noxious smell intensified once the doors closed, and I felt nauseated. But I had to get one of those sheets for Mother; I had to keep her warm because she was so sick. Braving the smell and the darkness, I went to the far corner to find a sheet. One person was covered from top to toe, not moving, and his hand lay lifeless at his side. Realising the reason for the sheets, I moved back to Mother and Father.

The train started to move out of the destroyed station, which was still burning. Explosions sent debris sky high and partly covered the tracks with red slime. The heavy door slid open to one side, and a limp body rolled out onto the tracks. An old man crawled to the corner, took the available sheet, and wrapped himself to keep warm.

Mother doesn't need the sheet that badly, I told myself with a shudder. *I will keep her warm.*

Trains no longer seemed like monsters to me, but they did remind me of metallic snakes. This one continued to slither slowly toward an unknown destination, all the while feasting on its prey. It sucked the life out of weakened humans and then let their carcasses fall out through the open jaws of its heavy doors.

The trip seemed to last forever, with no end to the tracks in sight. Every so often the mighty door swung open so that the serpent-train could expel another corpse. I shuddered every time a body rolled out onto the ground beside the tracks.

Whenever the door opened, snow and cold air rushed inside the car, numbing us. I held my breath in the hope of keeping warm. The most important thing of all was to keep Mother warm, and so I would hold her hands in mine or wrap them in the folds of my layered dresses. Even though she tried hard to stay awake for my sake, sometimes Mother drifted off, and I would gently stroke her face just to make sure she was still there. She always found a shred of strength to smile, even if she was too weak to open her eyes.

Days and nights passed without any change, and the pain from hunger and sleeping on the bare boards became unbearable. A crude kick would often awaken me, as the guards constantly checked to see who was alive and who had died.

Despite all this, I knew that I had to block out all the pain and horror and gruesome sights. If I let all that swamp me, the negative would overtake the positive, and I would never be able to survive. So I forced myself to stay positive, to think about the things that made me happy—the things I loved. I kept reciting to myself all the music I knew, singing in my heart and playing in my head; I kept thinking of home and of our farm; I kept rereading all my books, page by page. I would do all this over and over again until I fell asleep or something happened that required action.

★ ★ ★ ★ ★

One day, as the endless journey to nowhere continued, my ritual of music and recollection was abruptly ended by a deafening explosion. Some windows in the train car shattered. Many more blasts followed the initial one, and the chaos of the station began all over again for those remaining refugees on the train.

This was the moment of truth, so to speak: the train either had been hit by a bomb or had gone over a mine. There was no way to find out which, and it didn't really matter, anyway. What did matter was that the train had been blown off the tracks; it rested on one side in the snow. The impact had thrown some out of the train, and they lay on the platform, injured and shaken up, at best. Others were barely alive; some were dead. My parents and I had been sitting at the far back of the train, so we were thrown about and dazed, but we were alive.

The sparks and billowing clouds of smoke were so dense that it was hard to see how many had been killed. Contorted pieces of metal, bodies, and body parts lay strewn all about. I covered my face, unable to look, believing that it must be the very end of the world. Again, it did not occur to me that it could have been the end of me. I clung to my belief that I had to survive—that it was my duty to survive. It seemed as if others fell victim to destruction, but I remained unharmed. I believed my angel watched over me, which made me more keenly feel my duty to survive and honour life.

Not many survived the attack. All the buildings and storage places were left in smouldering ruins. On the far side of the platform the train cars were completely torn apart. As it grew dark, the cars began to look airy, as if they were not made of metal at all. Even my will to survive could not help me muster the strength to face it all over again. I knew that I would be forced to board anothertrain, the fires would start, and the entire dreadful experience would recur—war was just one fire after another. What we had been forced to endure would haunt us forever; there was no escape.

I was in such physical pain from the guards' kicks, from being thrown about by the explosion, from my endless hunger; I just wanted to run away. But there was nowhere to run, nowhere to go. This was the point of no return. All seemed to be spinning around me as I reluctantly walked over the bricks and twisted steel toward the train. I looked back, thinking that the whole world had disappeared right in front of my eyes. In a way, I suppose it had.

★ ★ ★ ★ ★

Some people had collapsed and some were blown apart. I witnessed but still could not comprehend how little life meant to the aggressors— the assassins, the living dead who took perverse pleasure in soaking the earth with the blood of innocent people.

Suddenly I wondered again about the little girl from the barracks. *Did she make it onto the train? Did she survive the explosion?* I could not see her anywhere, and I had to hurry to get on the train before it left without me.

The damaged train began to move out of the station, continuing the endless trip to nowhere. *Where are we going? When will this all end?*

Forcing my mind away from the unanswerable questions, I willed myself to think of what made me happy. I could not ever let my hope wither; I could not ever stop believing that life was a gift to treasure; I could not ever, and would not ever, submit to the deceitful and destructive forces of evil and brutality.

★ ★ ★ ★ ★

I kept my dream alive: at the end of all this madness, there would again be happy days, everything would flourish, and I would be free of all misery. My positive attitude was all I had; I had to remain strong in order to live through the madness—in order to survive.

A side had been blown off the train where I now sat, and I could see the vast snow-covered fields. I smiled at the trees that rose tall and proud above the land, the silhouettes of bare branches or evergreen boughs like mighty, tireless sentinels. Sometimes a hamlet was tucked within the shelter of a thicket, and I would wonder what the town and its people were like. The train kept moving, day and night. I just kept dreaming that at the end of the war and all the suffering it caused there would be peace. The rest of the trek I cannot recall. After so many days of hunger, I slipped into a deep sleep again. All that kept us alive was the snow we scooped into our hands and melted in order to have water to drink.

All of a sudden a shrieking voice pierced my subconscious, alerting everyone to get off the train, which had no time to come to a full stop. I was barely aware of all this, having not actually fallen asleep but fainted from hunger. For the same reason, I could hear but not quite comprehend all shouting. I just wanted to stay on the bare, cold boards where I'd collapsed. Those who could not walk had been carried out or left behind, I slowly realised. Father carried Mother out first, and then he returned for me. I struggled to stand and walk, but with a "Hush, Lara," he scooped me up in his arms and pulled me to safety.

I returned to unconsciousness, but on the periphery of my awareness I heard snatches of conversation. The partisans had planned to blow up the whole train because its markings indicated it was a military convoy .. Hearing that, I woke up with a jolt, and then I heard Mother cry for help. She was burning up with fever, even higher than before, and she spoke muddled words that the strangers did not understand. I did not see where Father was, and I could not speak to tell them what was wrong, even if they could understand our language.

As I looked around, it became clear that there were civilians amongst the military. A few men dressed in black suits came closer, and I noticed their jackets bore a small flag: a red field with a white cross. *Where are we?* I struggled to move my limp body closer to the window. I could neither walk nor talk—even if I hadn't lost the ability to speak, I had no energy. There was so little left of me. I couldn't think or move or even feel. I was almost afraid to believe the truth of what I saw outside as I leaned my face against the window. But it *was* true! I managed a strangled whisper: "Denmark."

Mother's condition had worsened. Burning with fever, she started to gasp for air. I felt so helpless, and panic began to overwhelm me. *I might lose Mother! No! Not now.*

We had survived the unbelievable. How could Mother die now? Why? It would be so awfully unfair. I withdrew even deeper within my shell, staying in self-imposed concealment until the dangerous stage of Mother's illness had passed. I felt so helpless and afraid; all I could do was keep looking at Mother, terrified because she could scarcely keep her eyes open. I moved closer, put my arms around her, kissed her hands, and tried to keep her warm. That was all I could do. The music I heard in my head was sad and sombre, as my heart prayed only for Mother to get well.

★ ★ ★ ★ ★

I glimpsed outside the window. It must be another world, because there were no ruins or fire, nobody lying dead. *Maybe I died and am now in heaven.* A man came toward me, handing me a bottle of milk and a piece of real bread. For a moment I just held it in my hands. I checked to make sure my parents had some food. They did, and I thought of saving mine for Lars. Much to my dismay, I knew that he was far away. I drank the milk, held the bread close to me, and again slipped into unconsciousness.

★ ★ ★ ★ ★

When my eyes briefly fluttered open, I lay wrapped in a piece of canvas near some sort of shack. I blacked out again. Hours must have passed, and when I woke up again, I saw that Mother, Father, and I had been loaded onto another train, which began to move.

It was not a dark and scary train but clean and light, with nobody sitting on the floor or shouting. It was so nice to be there, though I wondered if maybe I was just dreaming. The people on the train spoke in a language I did not understand, but they spoke softly and smiled at me, so I was not afraid.

At daybreak the train pulled into a very large railway station. *Will this change into an inferno?* I thought suddenly, all but overcome by panic. I knew that I did not have to be afraid, but I was overwhelmed, traumatised, and too exhausted to fully comprehend reality.

Mother and I could not walk on our own, and so the people on the train carried us to the truck that was waiting. It drove through the centre of a large city, stopping at a gate guarded by soldiers. The gate opened, and in the yard there were many barracks, one for the refugees and the others for the army. Mother was put into a makeshift hospital. I looked around, realising that this would be our home for a while.

Days passed. Mother was much better, and she grew stronger every day. Another truckload of refugee families arrived. All was peaceful, and I began to feel safe. Gradually, my voice started to come back. I did not say much, but it was comforting to be able to murmur some words to Mother and Father. There was no one else to talk to; all the other refugees had to mend their own fractured feelings and heal their own wounds.

Among the new arrivals was a boy named Ray, who was about my age, and we soon became good friends. We played with the stones and pine cones in the yard. Having heard my story, Ray found a little stone like the one I'd lost in the snow so far away. I will never forget his sweet, unaffected kindness.

The compound was a huge place, filled with tall trees and singing birds. There were countless chestnuts, and so I heard the piano soaring on the breeze. It was so good to be there!

The staff in the compound kitchen prepared meals for us. I was never hungry anymore. It is impossible to describe how it felt to actually have food to eat every day after spending such a long time in the cruel grip of unrelenting, desperate hunger.

Some days after Ray and his family arrived, more refugees came to the compound. They seemed to receive less attention, perhaps because the compound was understaffed. Mother worried about the children in much the same way as she had pitied the prisoners on the boat when we'd crossed the Baltic Sea. "We cannot let these children go hungry, Lara," she said. Taking some of our portion in stealth, she went over to the recently arrived refugees and fed the children. Mother's compassion inspired me. Throughout my life, I have always done what I could to help those with less than I had; I never forgot what it felt like to be starving and cold and lost and alone—to have nothing but the will to survive.

More days passed. The rest and food nourished us, and we began to feel alive again. The compound even had a bathroom with a bathtub. It felt like a dream to sink into the warm, crystal-clear water and then to sleep in a real bed with clean sheets, a pillow, and a soft blanket. I put my new little stone that Ray had found for me beneath the pillow every night. Sometimes I did not even want to fall asleep—I was afraid all this was just a dream that would vanish when woke up, which would be unbearable. Once that fear subsided, it just felt so good to be safe and warm that I wanted to relish the feeling and make it last as long as possible. As the pillow touched the side of my face, tears would flow, unbidden. My gratitude for surviving and being in that place was boundless, and it filled me with a deep and peaceful contentment that only the survivors of trauma can understand.

As more time passed, I was even able to sleep through the night without nightmares haunting me.

One night three young Latvian soldiers dressed in uniforms crawled through the barbed wire into the compound. The adults amongst the refugees burned the uniforms and dressed the soldiers in a tattered hodgepodge of spare civilian clothing, scraps of blankets, and other fabric. If the soldiers had been caught, they would likely have been shot. The three brave men tried to crawl through the barbed wire again and back into the city. It was the same night that the guards fell asleep; the disguised soldiers managed to pass a message to the Danish Red Cross that one of the military barracks was occupied by civilians—we refugees.

Additional ammunition and soldiers began to arrive in the compound. Some of the soldiers were marines, very disruptive and brusque. They moved about the compound without any respect for anything or anyone. These changes were unsettling, but I tried to ignore them, continuing to play in the yard with Ray every day.

The days began to come and go aimlessly. One day I could not find Ray anywhere. Puzzled as to what had happened to my friend, I asked another refugee who knew Ray's family what had happened. Much to my dismay, I discovered that Ray had almost been shot the night before. Another refugee had asked Ray to sneak through the compound yard and steal something from the army storage. Not fully comprehending the danger and trusting the adult, Ray had agreed. Luckily, the guard on duty had realised that Ray was a refugee and a child, and so he had not shot him. Once the guard identified him, Ray had been sent for questioning; after he revealed the perpetrator who'd planned the theft, he was released.

I felt so sad that my friend had been used as an accomplice to a crime by an adult whom he trusted. That was what the assassins had done to good people. Children could no longer trust the adults in their midst, and my innocent friend might have lost his life. Nothing was the same for Ray and me after that.

★ ★ ★ ★ ★

Winter finally melted into spring, and that brought a very special day for all of us—May 4, a day I would never forget. Everything changed. The capitulation had come, heralded by alarming shots that rang through the compound. Many more marines had arrived, creating a noisy and dangerous brawl. They broke into the civilian barracks, smashing the windows with their empty liquor bottles. Totally intoxicated, they were out of control, and nobody could stop their rampage. Mother ran into the hall, screaming for help, but the marines pushed her up against the wall. They pushed Ray's father against the wall, next to Mother, and then they shot him in cold blood. It was awful.

At last the war was over, but it ended quite bitterly for us. The price we had to pay was inestimable, and it still was not truly over, for my family or for me. Many hurdles still awaited us before we would live in freedom again.

Summer followed the end of the war, but the transition time that separated war and peace seemed odd to me, almost unchanged. All around me were the reminders of war: barren soil and bitter people who sought revenge—understandably so, but revenge and bitterness cannot breed peace. Only forgiveness and compassion can.

Refugees now had permission to walk around the city, but where were we to go? Denmark, so recently liberated, still needed to settle itself, to heal the wounds created by the brutal atrocities of the invading attackers. The Danish people needed all their strength to rebuild their own country and their own lives; they had no surplus energy for the refugees, and that was understandable. Consequently, the Danes did not trust any foreigners, including the refugees, who merely sought safe haven after the destruction of their own homelands. For me, a safe place was enough. More than enough. I prayed that the other refugees would be compassionate toward our hosts, knowing that mutual understanding and kindness are the first steps to building trust.

The five-year-long invasion of Denmark had ended, but that occupation had been gruelling and filled with horror. The Danish people struggled to heal from the staining of their soil. I had faith in their goodness, and I knew that they would come to accept and trust us when they were ready. I just kept praying, and my faith in goodness and in the value of life sustained me, as always.

The answer to my prayers came even sooner than expected.

The Danish people were so strong, in both body and in spirit, that their sterling faculties and high standards soon carried them above their pain and grief. They began to see that we refugees, though dressed in rags and physically impoverished, were spiritually as rich and strong as they. After all, we all were Baltic peoples, and they realised that we would do anything to help them heal their wounds and restore their country. The Danes slowly warmed to us, giving all the refugees an opportunity to start anew in Denmark. I for one have never forgotten this Danish benevolence, and I hope and trust that my fellow refugees have not, either.

The Danes realised that we refugees were the victims of the same ruthless aggressors who had invaded their land; we were every bit as deeply scarred and tormented as they, perhaps even more so, for so many of us had no homeland to which we could return. We all were the helpless captives of the same tyranny, the same libidinous power that had brought the Western world to its knees, brutally attacking everything in the path of its juggernaut. And now we all were equally depleted, equally demoralised.

Ironically, the heinous tyrant's monstrous attempt to reign over the entire world destroyed the history and values not only of the conquered but also of his own people; he absurdly destroyed the intellectuals of his own country as well as those of the occupied nations. The mad power and avarice of that tyranny systematically destroyed its own country and so many other countries, leaving all of Europe in ashes.

★ ★ ★ ★ ★

Denmark had long been a cultural centre of Scandinavia, and enduring the plunder of its treasures and the murder of its scholars resulted in pain and grief that only refugees could understand. Thus, before long, the Danes opened not only their homes but also their hearts to the people in rags, realising that, beneath our meagre habiliments, we were trustworthy, honest, and capable and would lend our expertise and effort to our welcomers. Together, we would re-establish productivity, helping Denmark to thrive and prosper once again.

That wonderful country became my new home, and the people treated me with the utmost tenderness. My dreams had come true: I was alive, free, and contented. I had the chance to have a happy future.

Life in Denmark left an indelible impression on the latter part of my childhood, but this mark was positive, unlike the scars of war that would never fade and could never be erased. I fell in love with the country and its people, enchanted by their tenderness, their earnestness, and their love.

I could not know that I would never experience such true tenderness again. I suppose it is similar to first love in its absolute magic—and the utter belief that the magic will last forever. No one can ever love in quite the same way again after having sustained pain and disappointment; we learn to guard ourselves afterward, not before. Perhaps it is my longing for that pure, sweet, innocent love I felt for Denmark—my mourning for it because I lost it—that has caused me to isolate myself. I love Canada, my adopted home, but I love it in a way that cannot help but guard against pain, knowing that magic, like love, is to be treasured, yet wary that it is too fine to last.

The magic spell of pure love was broken, stolen from me when I had to leave Denmark. I would not, could not, ever love that way again. I had to move on, as my story will explain. My beloved Denmark will always be in my heart, safe and cherished forever—like everything else dear that I'd lost.

Tivoli – Copenhagen, Denmark

11
Soothing Pain

April. A gentle wind blew wispy clouds across the clear blue sky. The winter had brought particularly heavy snowfall, even for Canada. But now the spring burgeoned bravely, and the sun had begun to melt the icicles on the hedges. Tiny snowdrops began to peak through the snow. I could hardly wait for more early blossoms to emerge and brighten the last vestiges of winter with their joyful pastel palette. The fledglings in their nests had begun to chirp, and I smiled as their initially frail cheeps grew stronger and louder. Tiny rivulets had formed in the rock garden, and they began to flow, watering the newly emerging plants that had begun to grow. Even the soil seemed to have come alive, with small insects and crawlers moving around the rocks. It was wonderful to watch the delicate mist rise from the soil and fill the air with that fresh and fertile vapour that meant the earth had awakened from its wintry slumber. At last, spring had arrived!

My recital tour had wound down early that year, giving me time to assess it and also to start preparing for the upcoming one. The next tour would commence in September, and it would be more extensive than the last, taking me to several places in the United States: Michigan, Nebraska, Ohio, Colorado, California, and Tennessee, in that order.

It was exciting to prepare for each state where I was scheduled to appear during the tour. On previous trips I had noticed the fascinating differences among the states' people, nature, and history. I intuitively understood their different tastes. and I tailored the music to each audience. Their delight in my efforts and care always brought me such deep pleasure. The favourable response of the audience is a wave of love washing over the performer, bringing a particular type of indescribable nurturing. For performers with emotional wounds, the healing wrought is even deeper and more magical.

Once I completed the considerable yet delightful work of organising my repertoire, I turned my attention to the next step of tour preparation: choosing my wardrobe. I always enjoyed that part of the preparation, but with that particular tour I found that the process took me back to the precious days of my early childhood, when Mother used to look through various fashion magazines while I sat beside her, relishing the glimpses of glamour and sophistication. In those happier times, Mother had her dresses custom made, and mine as well. A nice elderly man made all the family's shoes; he always had a bag of raisins for me, and I would munch away while waiting for Mother to collect our purchases. In those days of my innocence, I could not have known how important and dear shoes really were—I had yet to learn, but the war would teach me most cruelly. While I planned my tour wardrobe I recalled Mother's beautiful rose-coloured dress and my own snow-white one with the silver stars—the dresses she and I had worn the Christmas Eve when Lars came home.

I coaxed my memory to remain on the happier images, visualising other early-childhood pleasures; because of the war, I did not have many, but that made the ones I did have all the sweeter, all the more deeply cherished. There were the days of practising my dance routines, for instance. Large armoires with mirrors covered one wall of my parents' bedroom. I used to dance in front of them, holding Mikus in my arms. My big cat was a wonderful dancer, in my opinion, even though most of the time he wiggled his way up to my shoulders, not content until his paws had batted my hair into a tangled mess.

On the days when Mother went to the esthetician, I would always go along. There were so many interesting things to watch and learn! At first I was content to just be a fascinated onlooker, but soon I longed to practise some of these exotic-looking procedures on myself, which I did as soon as Mother and I returned home. Father, however, was not amused—in fact, he'd seemed as perturbed as Mother had been when I used my toothbrush on big, furry Nero. I assured Father that my eyebrows and golden locks would grow back in no time, but he grounded me anyway.

I curbed my enthusiasm for grooming adventures after that, finding plenty of other delightful diversions to absorb my days. Mikus was always at my side, and the two of us spent a lot of time roaming around the house, frolicking in the garden, and playing the piano. Only I played, of course; Mikus just curled up beside me on the bench, purring in contented harmony with the chords. The time seemed to pass faster during that all-too-brief carefree time, and every day was full of joy.

Those happy days set a pattern for me throughout my life, not because of all that my family had materially but because of how our parents taught Lars and me to value life—to be thankful for the grace and love and peace that filled our home and connected us to one another. Those deeply imbedded values sustained me during the bleakest hours, and they are the reason why I never felt that we were poor, even during the coldest, darkest nights of the war—even when we had nothing to eat. Rather, I told myself that, for the time being, we simply had less than we'd had before. Whatever I had to eat or wear or do, I did so with dignity, grace, honour, and gratitude—I was proud to do so then, and I am proud to do so still. Valuing life is the noblest act of every human being.

★ ★ ★ ★ ★

The first days of spring in Canada always called to mind the first day of freedom in Denmark. No matter how many years filled the time between that day and the present, the recollection was crystal clear, filling my heart with bittersweet pain that soothed my soul after all the time I'd been numb, repressing my emotions because I had no time to feel and no time to cry. No sooner had the first springtime blossoms peeped above the Toronto soil than the images of that long-ago Danish spring would flash across my mind. The war was over, and I found myself in a new country, surrounded by people who were giddy with relief, yet still grieving their losses. The people seemed kind, and I felt glad to see them laugh joyfully, but I had forgotten how to laugh. Sometimes I was able to muster a hint of a smile, but that was all.

The details of that marvellous spring morning appear to me with the same clarity as the events of yesterday. Everybody in the barracks still slept, except for me. I dressed quickly, crept out of the barracks on tiptoe, and went toward the gate of the compound. It was open! No guards, no weapons. I hardly knew whether to jump up and down in exultation or weep with relief. There were not many people out on the street because of the early hour. I stood at the gate, just gazing in wordless wonder at the blue sky. Taking a deep breath, I watched the soft white clouds float like puffy sailboats on a tranquil sea of pure azure.

I am also free, clouds! Free just like you have always been. Is this what freedom looks like? Thank you, Angel, for freeing us from the war. The thoughts came rapid-fire and at random, and I acknowledged them and let them flow on. Briefly, I wondered why I had never thought of the clouds as free up to that point. I wished I could sing a happy song to celebrate the moment, but none came to mind. *Have I forgotten the happy songs I used to know?* After all those times I'd sung songs in my heart to sustain myself, in that instant all those words fled my memory, overshadowed by the brutal sounds of the war that was now over. I could neither explain nor understand it, but my mind reverberated with the sharp and bitter sounds of distress and pain, with the crushing roar of bombs and explosions, with the vicious crackle of ravenous flames. I could not escape the relentless echo of memory.

The words of the happy songs lay buried deep in my heart, and I would recover them when I was again able to feel joy. Until then, they would remain beneath the ashes of sorrow and grief, revered and cherished. I could still hear varied strains of music, because music is part of nature and it mixes emotions organically into a whole, unlike words, which categorise our emotions, organising them into compartments so that we can better understand them. The emotions of war cannot be understood.

Music, as ever, was my best source of expression. To the accompaniment of sounds that were appropriately mournful and triumphant all at once, I stepped outside the confines of the gate. Cautiously, I went toward the centre of the city. *I am truly free!*

My first steps in freedom were made in Aarhus, Denmark. The wide streets basked in the early morning sunshine of springtime. Many store windows were decorated with flowers. It was the city that would become my home for some years; it is the city I will never stop loving.

Now I was free to go anywhere I wanted; no danger lurked around the next corner; nobody would yell or push me away. But where would I go? I could not speak the language, and I did not know anybody. The gates—of the various compounds and of the war itself—had held me captive for so long that even now, when the war was over and there were no more gates to imprison us, there was still nowhere to go. The doors there were closed because we were strangers—foreigners, outsiders. I went farther and farther away from the compound, not wanting to look back, wishing it could just disappear. *If only the war could disappear forever—if only it had never happened at all!*

In the compound, I'd received a pair of heavy wooden-soled shoes to wear, and as I walked I heard their clatter. I stopped, not wanting to disturb those initial moments of freedom and peace. It was the first moment of truly quiet tranquillity that I'd experienced in a long time. For so long, even in the brief quiet moments, all we could do was wait for the next shower of bullets, the next bomb, the next explosion. This quiet was real. Lasting. It felt like a song from heaven, and it needed no words. It was pure and beautiful silence, filled with the music of the spheres. I heard an entire orchestra of peace resound in exultation, and I felt happy.

Passing another store, I stopped, catching my somewhat distorted reflection in the plate-glass window. It had been some time since I'd been able to really look at myself. The relief and gratitude of being alive, of having survived, filled my being, flooding through every cell in a warm, glad rush. I cherished the generosity of the people who had given me some clothing; it all was a bit large, but Mother assured me I would grow into it soon. I've already described the shoes as having thick wooden soles, and their tops were made of fish leather. Fitting better than the clothes, they looked rather nice. I was far too grateful to mind anything not fitting well; it had felt so good to exchange the three layers of torn dresses and paper-insulated boots. Thankful that what I'd had to wear sustained me, I wore all those items with dignity. Now I wore the new items with equivalent dignity and gratitude. Although I couldn't have articulated it as a child, I felt a mixture of pride and humility in having survived. What I felt, I felt keenly, and I continued to move on through the city.

After a while I felt tired, and I leaned against a building wall, watching the people walk by. No one noticed me, the forlorn little girl in ill-fitting clothing. But I understood that it was not apathy or avoidance on their part; rather, they needed to savour their day of freedom after the long, cruel occupation of their country, and they still needed to heal from all that they had endured, all that they had lost. Who could understand that better than I, a refugee child? I just felt so relieved to be in the midst of happy people who seemed good—people who valued life, which I could sense that the Danes did.

I would just live for and in the moment, I'd decided. The agony of the war was behind me now; I didn't have to be afraid. Child that I was, I could not possibly have known on that bright and promising morning that I would never escape my past experiences. I was free in the physical sense, but emotionally and psychologically, I would never truly be free. My memories would always haunt me, and the scars in my mind, heart, and soul would never be erased.

I knew that I could not describe how I felt; yet it seemed odd to me that I did not want to laugh and run and sing. I couldn't explain it, but I felt what I felt—and I couldn't deny it. That day when I walked through Aarhus was the first Sunday after the capitulation. Flowers were everywhere, and the church bells were ringing in celebration of Denmark's freedom. As I watched a happy and joyous group on their way to church, I wanted to join them. Some small children held onto their mothers; others were clad in black and appeared sad and somewhat lost in their thoughts.

Thinking of the little girl in the barracks who had turned away from my kindness, I resisted the urge to join the children. What if I approached them and they did not accept me? I turned slightly away. Rejection was something I could not have endured at that moment. I was a tormented and extremely sensitive little girl who had a lot of deep questions but nobody to answer them. Perhaps even then I knew, as I certainly do now, that there were no answers.

Although I did not wish to endure rejection, I had no expectations for anything more than what I had; I'd already received the greatest gift I could ever have wished for: my life. I knew that, and I felt that, and I honoured that. All I really wished was that I could share the suffering of this country and make it easier for them to bear the pain—even watching the other children walking to church, that was what I'd wished, not any selfish kind of friendship. But I was only a little girl myself, full of unresolved grief and traumatised emotions. My heart still seemed to bleed from all the injustice I'd had to suffer, but I kept it all inside so as not to burden others who were also grief-stricken. (Later on, knowing that pain all too well, I would not burden those who had not sustained trauma, either.)

All I could do was live each day the best I could, waiting to be accepted by the Danish people, hoping that I would have the chance to help the people and country I was gradually growing to love.

★ ★ ★ ★ ★

Time passed, and Denmark became the "Land of Smiles" for me. It was so nice to see people smile again; I had thought that smiles were buried beneath the ruins of my destroyed childhood. Denmark and the

Danish people helped restore my faith in goodness. Soon after the end of the war, the stores began to do regular business again, and storekeepers filled their shelves with merchandise. Flowers bloomed everywhere, spreading the fragrance of springtime as if they, too, were enjoying their newfound freedom.

I loved to walk through Aarhus, smelling the flowers and looking at the many happy, smiling faces. More than anything, I longed to be part of it all, to rejoice in the freedom and just be happy. Whenever I passed the big stores, I would stop to look in the windows, but all I could see was my reflection, which was hard for me to recognise as me: a small girl with a sad expression and ill-fitting clothing. It was impossible for me to shake the sadness; I tried in vain to force myself to smile. Even nature and music could no longer make me smile, though they had been able to while the war raged. The war was over, but I was still carrying the remnants of trauma and pain. As a child, I could not understand that it is harder to bear pain and grief in peacetime than in war. No matter what I did or where I went, the atrocities I had witnessed followed me, haunting me; my wounds would heal in time, but my scars would never disappear.

I was alive; I was grateful—I just wanted to learn how to live naturally again, how to feel safe and content, how to smile without having to tell my face what to do. I had felt and done all that as a young child, and I knew I would do so again. *Someday my fingers will dance across the piano keys again. I will play Chopin, and the chords will make my soul sing and my heart smile, and my face will beam with joy!* I promised myself. Throughout the war, I had kept going based on the belief that the war would end; that I would survive, and life would be happy again. The war had ended, and I had survived, but life was not happy again—at least not for me. I was too young to understand that war, and the trauma I had sustained because of it, had put my life on hold; I existed in a kind of warped time and space, and it would take time for me to learn how to live in it. Accepting freedom and normalcy was quite a challenge after so long a time of living every day as a fight for survival. Intuitively, I sensed that I had to allow myself the time and space I needed in order to adjust, although I was not consciously aware of sensing this. I believed that I would get through it and that life would be good again without actually realising that I believed. Looking back, though, I am certain that without that belief—without that faith—I would not have endured. It all was simply more than I could grasp at the age I was at that time.

I took things one day at a time, and I managed because I did not have a choice. Slowly, a semblance of a normal life began to take shape for my parents and me. The Danish Red Cross moved a group of us—thirty-seven in total, including my parents and me—to a four-bedroom bungalow in the suburbs. Mother, Father, and I would have a small corner to call our own. I looked forward to having a home again.

The Danish Red Cross extended their welcome in many ways, one of which included a piano for me to play wherever I stayed.

★ ★ ★ ★ ★

The days we spent living in the bungalow passed uneventfully, and soon we moved again. We went to an apartment near the sandy bay. The water was clear and warm, and some of the others went swimming. I could not take part, as I had never learned to swim. Father had begun to teach me at our farm the summer before we had to flee, but I did not take to the water as easily as I did to other sports. I actually almost drowned a couple of times, according to Father, but I'd felt safe enough with him there to keep trying. If we'd had another carefree summer, I'm sure I would have learned successfully. My terror during our Baltic crossing stemmed from the monstrous waves and explosion-tossed seas, not from my abbreviated childhood swimming lessons. I doubt that knowing how to swim would have precluded my fear that the waves would claim me; others who knew how to swim did not survive that treacherous crossing.

On stormy days, the seaweed washed up on the shore, and I had to avoid walking along the bay. The tangles of seaweed frightened me, leading to visions of the nights on the Baltic Sea. My memories kept tormenting me, and I had to take care or I would have nothing but sleepless nights and endless nightmares, both night and day. That was what freedom meant for me: taking one step forward and who knew how many back. I had yet to learn that anything could trigger my memories, and it was pointless to even try to stop them from flooding my mind. Tending my emotional wounds and healing my scars became a tedious and arduous process, with no solution in sight.

I didn't know what to do and was actually afraid to talk about what I felt inside. In the first place, I did not want to burden or hurt anybody; in the second place, my parents and everyone else around me were healing their own pain too. Besides, no one would find a solution for me. There was no solution. I just wanted to heal, to put the past behind me so that all the pain I'd been forced to endure did not destroy any more of my life than it already had. Nightmare after nightmare invaded my consciousness, and I began to despair; how would I ever find peace?

Soon after moving into the apartment near the bay, we all had to move again, that time to a refugee camp near Aalborg, in the north of Denmark. People of all ages occupied the barracks, and I was the youngest. I did not remain in the barracks for long. The Red Cross soon sent me to live on a farm, where my duties included helping the farmer's wife with the kitchen chores and washing the floors. Having not yet regained my strength, carrying the pails of water was quite difficult for me, sometimes ending in disastrous splashes, yet I never received a harsh word as a result.

The farmer and his wife had no children of their own, and I filled that void in their lives. After some weeks, they allowed me to make gravy for supper and gave me a special chair at the table. I kept hearing them use the term *ven*, which is Danish for *friend*. I misunderstood, thinking that was the name of the farmer's wife. From then on she was Ven to me—and a wonderful friend she was indeed!

★ ★ ★ ★ ★

Though I came to think of my hosts collectively as the Vens (Ven's husband I just thought of as "the farmer"), I never talked to them other than to answer their questions as best I could, given my limited knowledge of Danish. Working hard and without complaint, I only sought to please. I was scared that they would not like me and send me back to the camp. Fortunately, that never happened; on the contrary, the Vens loved having me around, and they let me play with the dogs and run through the meadows.

I had my own room. Any room in any house would have seemed like the palace quarters of a princess to me at that point, but this room was truly lovely. The window had beautiful curtains, and I would open them as soon as I got out of bed, loving how the morning sunshine filled the room with light and warmth. Best of all was the nice soft bed with its snow-white sheets, fluffy pillow, and warm blanket. Next to the bed was a night table, on top of which stood a lamp with a flowered design. In the drawer of the table I found a pencil and a notebook that Ven had put there just for me. I could hardly believe it when she told me those items were mine. *Something belongs to me now; these are mine, and I can keep them forever!* With a pang, I thought of my precious little stone, symbol of all that I'd lost. That was gone and could never be replaced, but now I had a pencil and notebook of my very own, and that made me feel special. It seemed that life was good, and I felt that I had everything!

At the time I could not fully comprehend precisely why that pencil and notebook were so significant to me, but as I look back, I can now understand. It was more than just my dear little stone, more than all that I'd lost. For such a long time I had lived in exigent circumstances, an innocent witness to horror and despair that would emotionally and psychologically cripple most adults, let alone a young child. On a daily basis I had observed people forced to remove boots from the dead, wearing them in order to stay alive themselves. This became as commonplace a sight during the war as observing people helping one another had been before the war. All those horrific scenes filled my mind, and my heart was still filled with pain from having watched so many suffer. I could not easily recall happier times; the pain persisted, and I just wished that my awful memories would cease tormenting me. The pencil and notebook became symbols of the goodness and happiness that would return to my life—of the normalcy I craved. I understood that intuitively, and I began to write poems in my free time.

At night, after supper and cleanup, I would get my notebook and read my poems aloud to the Vens. They were such a wonderful audience! I basked in their praise and beams of amazement at how quickly I'd picked up Danish, how wonderful it was that I could put thoughts on paper that made sense in a foreign language. One night I heard Ven tell her husband that she wondered why a child's poems should reflect such sadness, such absence of hope. I was relieved that she had not asked me; I could not have found the words to explain.

Some nights Ven would sit in my room until I fell asleep. One morning she said, "You tossed so in your sleep last night." As usual, I did not answer—I could not answer. And besides, only one who had lived through what I had would be able to understand. That night Ven sat beside me again. In the morning I awakened with a soft toy cuddled in my arms. Ven had taken it from the empty cradle in the nursery at the other end of the house. She never mentioned my tossing and turning in my sleep again. I realised that one does not necessarily need to understand in order to care; compassion and love are of the heart, and Ven's heart and mine had bonded. She might not be able to fix what was wrong, but she could still give me the love and attention I so desperately needed. And she did.

Soon after that, a powerful night-time thunderstorm shook the whole house. The wind was so fierce that it almost broke my window, and the dogs yanked the barn door open and ran inside for shelter. Ven rushed into my room. "Are you frightened, Lara?" I shook my head no. I had been through far worse than storms, which I considered to be merely part of nature. Visions of the thunderstorms during our trek through the wheat fields pricked my memory. Ven took me by the hand, determined that I should follow her. At first I was reluctant, but perhaps the memories would not be so hard to bear with Ven beside me. I quickly went back to my room to get my soft toy to cuddle, and then I went with Ven into the spacious living room.

A cup of hot chocolate was waiting on the table, just for me! Ven handed it to me; she smiled at me, and I smiled back. I had forgotten how good it felt to be well cared for and protected. Throughout the war, Mother and Father had all they could do to keep us alive. Out of necessity, I'd had to stop being a child, and yet I still was a child—it felt so wonderful to be taken care of like a child again. I wished my Danish were good enough to fully express all the gratitude I felt in my heart, but, looking at Ven's face, I knew she realised how grateful I was. We continued to smile at each other wordlessly, and I finished my hot chocolate.

I clutched my toy tightly, pressing its softness against my heart, while I sat next to Ven on the sofa. Ven's husband joined us, standing by the window and watching the sky. The storm intensified, and the lights went out. The thunder rumbled ominously, and the lightning continued to flash, long forks of sparkling energy piercing the dark sky.

With my head against Ven's shoulder, I fell asleep, my soft toy still cuddled in my arms. Though the storm intensified even further after I drifted off, I had my first night without nightmares, resting peacefully next to Ven, safe in the harbour of the love and care that she and her husband provided for me.

Bright morning sunshine filled every corner of my room when I woke up. I thought that I had dreamt about the storm, the hot chocolate, and everything that happened the night before. But it was not a dream: the Vens' hearts were filled with compassion for me, even though we were little more than strangers to one another. With tender care, they had brought me back to my room once I'd fallen asleep, covering me with the blanket and watching over me until, at last, the storm passed. They could not possibly have known how many storms I had already lived through, usually all by myself. Of course, they did know that I was a refugee, and so they realised that I had endured hardships; they simply understood that my greatest need at that time was love, and so they gave it to me. In turn, they received their own sense of closure and contentment by having a child upon whom they could bestow love, tenderness, and affection, filling the long-time void in their hearts created by the empty crib at the other end of the house.

★ ★ ★ ★ ★

Sadly, the day came when I had to leave the Vens' farm. I never met those two wonderful people again, but their compassion and benevolence changed my life forever. I began to believe in people again, and I no longer felt so forgotten. The Vens had shown me kindness without asking for anything in return. I felt a deep bond with and affection toward the Vens, in a way that I never felt before or since. Although the officer in northern Germany restored my faith through his kindness, he was a heroic figure to me. The Vens were "regular" people, and so their kindness made me believe that similar kindness would be possible again amongst new people I might meet.

Although no one ever told me the real names of the Vens, their significance in my life is inestimable. I never did understand why I never learned their names, and it grieved me. *I must be very unimportant if I do not deserve to know the names of those who showed me such kindness,* I silently concluded, but, not wishing to burden anyone by asking, I turned the pain inward, adding yet another unanswered question to the pile already crowding my heart. I resigned myself to the departure, because, once again, I had no choice. However, it is impossible to measure the extent of the pain and disappointment caused by the cruelly enforced departure.

A dusty vehicle waited at the fence as the Vens and I said goodbye. Pressing the soft toy into my arms, Ven kissed my forehead. I looked back at the house before taking my place inside the car. Ven was very sad, and her husband tried to comfort her. I thought of my lost little stone again, sensing that Ven felt the same way I had felt when I watched my stone sail through the air and land in the deep snow. It is deeply painful to lose that which has come to ease the pain of other losses. Nevertheless, both Ven and I had to go on.

The car was very dirty, and I just sat looking out the window, watching the farm and the Vens disappear from view. It was another goodbye, but something had changed deep inside me. I had begun to feel like a person, noticed and cared for; I'd had my own room and a routine to follow; I'd had chores entrusted to me, and I'd received praise for having done them well. I'd received care and compassion, and I'd received some things of my very own to keep forever: a pencil, a notebook, a soft toy. Because of these gifts from the Vens, I no longer missed my little stone from home quite so much. I still had the stone that my friend Ray had found for me in the refugee camp, and I treasured it, but it was different from the Vens' gifts. The Vens had restored my faith in human kindness, although I could not have articulated it as such at the time, and their gifts became symbolic of that. The pencil and notebook, even more than the toy, were to become instrumental in my life as I painstakingly rebuilt it.

While I'd been at the farm with the Vens, I had not visited my parents too often. In reality, the management of the refugee camp only needed me to entertain them with my playing. I was not aware of that, of course. I enjoyed playing as much as ever—the nicest part was the bouquet of flowers I received after my performance when I returned to the camp. The flowers were picked from the nearby meadow, and I took good care of them. I loved those flowers so much, delighting in every little bloom and leaf, feeling as if they had blossomed in the meadow just for me.

★ ★ ★ ★ ★

I started to feel somewhat impatient toward the people around me who seemed to be filled with complaints. I'd overhear remarks, such as, "The grass is always greener on the other side of the fence." I did not quite understand what that meant at the time, but I wondered, *Why don't they take care of the grass they are standing on, and then they can watch it become even greener?* Even now, understanding what the expression actually means, I think the conclusion I drew as a child offers far better, and more practical, advice. Positive is always better than negative! Quite simply, I was far too young to comprehend many of the stories I heard, but, nevertheless, I felt frustrated and oppressed by all the negativity that surrounded me. I did not think or feel as a child anymore—the brutal war had cruelly ended my childhood—and I realised, even while still a child in terms of age, that even worse than ending my childhood, the war had destroyed it. And all the traumatic experiences I'd endured and horrors I'd witnessed had transformed my whole existence. I could not subtract what I had lived through from the person I was. I would have to learn how to go on without ever being able to escape the torturous past.

★ ★ ★ ★ ★

My constant longing for a real home overshadowed every single day, especially after the time I spent with the Vens. I had encountered so many strangers whom I would never meet again whose kindness touched me forever. The impressions that they made upon me and left on my heart influenced me immeasurably, but I could not reconcile it all as a child. Left to sort it out all on my own, I was completely confused. No child can understand that people we meet for just a moment can change our lives forever—for good or ill—because we can live a lifetime in a moment; time can be stretched and compressed by significant events. This was true for me as a child during the war and the time that followed, regardless of my inability to comprehend it.

Because I understood nature so well, I came to think of life as being like the wind, which blows the good with the bad, leaving it up to each of us to sift through the windblown debris in order to find what we need. In short, I'd learned that I had no choice but to make the best of things, yet I still felt like I was just moving from moment to moment, with nowhere to go.

By that time I had read many books for children, but they all had happy endings and lovely pictures. My life—other than my earliest memories—had presented itself as quite the opposite, and so the words in these books seemed hollow. I would never move beyond the gruesome, vicious images of my wartime recollections. Instead of reading the books that I could not relate to, I turned to the pencil and notebook that the Vens had given me. I'd already written some poems and shared them with the Vens, and now I wrote even more. I poured all my feelings into my writing, but I didn't share any of it with anyone. Afraid that I might be punished, scorned, or simply laughed at, I kept my writing a secret.

I frequently thought about the Vens and the time I'd spent with them at their farm. That time was unforgettable, and I treasured it. The harvest would bring plenty, and I wished I were still there to help them with the reaping—and just to be with them. I imagined the sights of harvest-time: the whirlwind that would pick up the leaves and scatter them all over the yard; the mare harnessed behind the harrow that would break the ground or the wagon with the load of wheat, bringing it to the barn; the flock of birds that would pick at the grain.

Of course, the Vens' mare was not my Lolo and the birds were not my birds, but I'd grown to love them as if they were my own. I had begun to feel again and to let love grow again in my heart, and I'd been forced to leave it all behind. Again. *Why?!* It seemed so cruel to me, and I could not understand cruelty—whether in times of war or peace. Back at the camp, I would lean against the tall chestnut tree I'd found, consoling myself with the piano-chord sounds that it resonated whenever the wind rustled its branches. The chestnut understood, just as all nature's creations understood me, and I wordlessly shared with the tree my sorrow at having to leave behind the farm and the Vens, who had shown me such tenderness, lovingly managing to quiet my nightmares, at least some of the time.

It felt like ages since we'd left Latvia, but, in reality, not that much time had passed. It only felt that way because of how much I had gone through during that relatively short time. The war was over, but the days still seemed to pass like gusts of wind, tearing me apart. I persevered because I had no choice. Life was a gift, and I had survived the unimaginable. I still didn't understand how or why I had survived when so many others had not. But I was determined that I would prevail again, surmounting the injuries of injustice by looking forward to even the smallest achievement with deep satisfaction.

I survived, I would remind myself inwardly, and that was enough to get me through another day.

★ ★ ★ ★ ★

It was no coincidence that wherever I temporarily stayed, a piano would be waiting for me. Through my untiring practise, I earned acceptance and recognition among the people who would pave my future.

The fall had arrived, and the days became shorter. Preparations were underway for Mother, Father, and I to leave the refugee camp and move to Aarhus. Before we left, I was to be confirmed in the local Lutheran church, and all the arrangements for this had been set.

The confirmation was to take place on a Sunday, and the three of us were to leave on the following day. It had rained the entire week prior, and the Sunday of the confirmation proved no different. Transportation for the small group of youngsters and their families was provided for the long drive to the church. The ceremony was short, and all the children, girls and boys, gathered outside on the wet steps of the church to receive their bouquets of flowers.

I held my flowers, noticing the raindrops that hid themselves amongst the petals. Longing to cry, I nonetheless held back my tears, afraid to surrender to any emotion. I went back into the church and placed my flowers at the alter, along with a prayer and my gratitude for the Vens. The road ahead would be demanding, and I could not afford any indulgence that might weaken me. I stood stoically, thinking of the past with objective compassion far beyond my years. The memories were difficult to bear, as was the departure from the Vens. It was simply time to move on again.

My daily existence seemed to have turned into a sort of narrow dark alley from which I was determined to escape. I went back into the church and put my flowers on the altar. My heart was filled with conviction to work for my future, but I could not help but wonder, *Will I be given the chance? Is there enough left of me to make it?*

As always, I did not have the time to dwell on the answers to these questions. I had survived; now I had to go on. It was simple as that, yet it was not simple at all.

Monday, the day after the confirmation, dawned grey. Wordlessly, I followed my parents to the vehicle that would take us away from the camp and onward to Aarhus. I took my pencil, notebook, and toy along with me, holding the toy in my arms throughout the long drive. I let my face touch the soft toy, grateful for these gifts from the Vens, which had been so kindly given and which were now my very own, yet the greatest gift I'd received from the Vens was their unconditional love. The unqualified kindness of those two strangers made the rest of my journey much easier.

The time had come to leave again, but I had a little bit more to take along with me. I had some sense of security, albeit precarious; I had a few happy experiences, albeit mixed with doleful ones. Forced to grow up fast with so very little to soothe my pain, I did the best I could. Happiness and security had to come from within, I'd learned by means of my war-ravaged childhood. It seemed that I would have to carry that hard-won wisdom into peacetime, as well.

Only time would tell whether this departure would be for better or worse.

12
Courage

Summer in Toronto would soon transition to fall. I looked forward to seeing the splashes of vibrant autumn colours, which would turn my garden into an artist's palette. The birds nibbled at the scarlet berries on a nearby tree, fortifying themselves for the annual flight south.

The fall, as always, placed many demands on me. After I finished preparing the garden for its wintertime slumber prior to the new growth of spring, I would have to begin my preparations for the upcoming recital season. I looked forward to the process, as usual, even though sorting the references and organising the repertoire could become tedious. Yet those unavoidable tasks enabled the joy of performing, which I adored. The memorabilia I had to sift through as part of the process always brought back many memories, from which various feelings would arise.

Having withstood the gruelling tests of endurance enforced by the war and the time subsequent to it, I found no tasks overwhelming or particularly distasteful. I tried to remain positive and cheerful at all times, keeping in perspective what "bad" and "awful" really meant. However, sometimes, seemingly for no apparent reason, an everyday task would catapult me back to the years right after the war ended. They were not nightmares, not indelible harrowing images like the war-torn moments were, but they weren't always as pleasant as my time with the Vens had been.

The war had interrupted my school years, preventing me from attending a sound educational institution. Most of the time I'd been separated from my parents and, as a result, forced to rely on the gratuitous influence of strangers, who were not always kind and did not always have my best interest at heart—again, unlike the Vens. Because of all that, I always felt as if I were "missing" something, as if a deep and integral part of my life had been skipped. That made me feel helpless and inept at times, but I never shared those feelings with anyone.

While preparing items for the repertoire of the upcoming tour, I came across some items from the years just after the end of the war, and they called those feelings to mind. I sighed. It seemed like ages ago that my parents had decided to leave the refugee camp in Denmark. We would be the first to take such a big step, and it was a huge risk. The other refugees in the camp treated us with contemptuous laughter, content to stay behind, forever complaining of their losses but never trying to improve their lives. My parents were brave, and they taught me by example how to live with courage and conviction. We could not replace what we'd lost, but we still could do our best to make the rest of our lives as good as possible. As an adult, I came to see that the contempt of those who stayed behind was nothing more than sheer jealousy: they resented the fact that they did not have the confidence and strength to seek a life beyond the stifling, unproductive existence at the camp. They envied my parents' courage and fortitude, plain and simple.

Even all these years later, I still smile at the thought of my parents' fearlessness in making this bold move. We did not discuss it; I accepted the plans they announced to me, obeying unequivocally as all children were expected to do at that time. Mother and Father were two valiant people who had lost all that was dear to them in life except each other and me. Possessing nothing but great courage and abiding faith in themselves, each other, and the goodness of life, they stepped into the unknown—without money, without having yet acquired adequate knowledge of the language of our new land. Their dreams and positive outlook overpowered any doubt, inspiring me to be equally brave and confident. We three left the camp together, and we never looked back.

★ ★ ★ ★ ★

With the help of a minister, we settled in Aarhus, the second-largest city in Denmark. We had a lovely room in the attic of the YMCA. It had a small window facing the street, a table, and makeshift beds. That was more than enough—it was more than plenty! At last, I lived in a real house with my parents! I felt so happy—beyond happy, really. I could not imagine ever wanting more than what we had in that attic room.

The days were full of new and exciting activities. I tried to be helpful, offering to be a server in the YMCA dining room. This proved to be a challenging experience, as I had to carry trays that were quite heavy; nevertheless, I felt fit for such duties, especially after my well-performed chores at the Vens' farm.

Trays laden with dishes and hot food are quite different from pails of water! One day while carrying a full-course dinner, my arms gave out, and all the food ended up on the floor, including spilt gravy that made a slippery mess. Petrified that I would get into trouble, which might jeopardise our dear little attic room, I hid behind the door. The grown-up waitresses joined me, and because they could not stop giggling, I joined in. Our giggles grew louder, becoming contagious, until all the patrons had broken out in laughter, watching some of us trip and fall into the sticky mess as we crept out from our hiding place. The colour of the clothing of all those who landed in the mess quite involuntarily changed drastically, but, otherwise, it was a relatively quick cleanup, with everyone helping and no harm done at all, much to my relief.

One of the waitresses, Ruth, was especially kind, and she always tried to help me carry the heaviest trays. As the years went by, she became a dear friend of the family. She invited me to her parents' home in the small town of Hunborg, where they also had a cooperative store, complete with an enormous garden and a strawberry patch. Those were wonderful and relaxed days, the first that I'd known since the war. That friendship grew stronger, much to my delight.

By that time, I had begun to feel content. Unexpectedly, the time came to move again. That relocation was particularly disruptive, as I had come to feel that those days were behind me, part of the painful past, not the present or the future. I felt as if the arm of the law had descended, effectively ending my happy days forever. It became evident that the relocation meant separation from my parents. *I'm not ready to face the unknown all alone!* my heart cried inwardly, but no one ever heard the words. The separation hurt so much that my wounds ripped wide open again; they had only just begun to heal, and the delicate new seams of their repairs could not withstand new pain. Slowly, I was drained of hope and confidence. I felt bereft in a way that I had not experienced before, even during the war and our wretched flight.

Where will they take me this time?

At the time I did not know that a prominent Danish gentleman had arranged for me to live with a well-known pianist, Augusta Haugsted, in her and her husband's residence in a large apartment building. After having heard of my fate, this kindly man had reached out to assist me in so many ways. He brought me presents and treats, and he took me to the symphony and to recitals. Even now I can recall sitting beside him at a performance of Mahler's *Fourth Symphony.* The magnificent performance brought tears to my eyes then, just as recalling it does now.

★ ★ ★ ★ ★

At the beginning, it was difficult for me to understand what the Haugsteds expected of me, given that my knowledge of Danish was not that extensive. Better at reading and writing the language than engaging in conversation, I could communicate at a basic level but was far from fluent. The Haugsteds were kind and patient, and, eventually, I understood what I was supposed to do.

My hosts had quite a large apartment, including a good-sized room in their attic, complete with a piano that had been delivered the day before I arrived. This was to be my place for as long as I stayed with them. I fell in love with the piano, longing to feel my fingers fly across the keys, but even more inviting was the bed, which looked like a white cloud because of all its goosedown comforters.

This is my bed! I thought with utter glee, jumping on it and delighting in its bounce. I remained so engaged for a few brief, joyful moments— and then, *crash!* Without any warning, I went right through the bottom of the bed, with my feet stuck between the boards. The mountainous pile of wood, mattress, and comforters had to be removed to fix the disaster I'd wrought with my boisterous joy, but the Haugsteds did not seem to mind. Perhaps they understood that I could not resist the urge to simply play like a child; bouncing on the bed made me like a child again, free to play without any cares. It felt so good!

After that, I settled down and adjusted to my new routine quickly.

The Haugsteds were very well known and influential people in Denmark. In exchange for my piano instruction, I was to cook for them and dust the furniture. I accepted my duties, performing them cheerfully, always eager to please. It was so lovely to be there, and I felt like I had a real home, even though I missed being with Father and Mother. I often stood at my attic window, looking down to the street and wondering if the people I watched were as happy as I was.

The longer I stayed with the Haugsteds, the more I enjoyed being there. The only problem was the wintertime, when my room was ice-cold because the central heating system did not reach the attic. Mother knitted gloves for me to wear to keep my hands warm; they had no fingertips, so I could practise without my hands getting cold.

Practising the piano went well once Mother resolved the problem of my frozen fingers. Cooking dinner, however, was quite a different story. The task was completely new to me, and it was not my hostess's forte, either. I would go to the store as instructed, bring the purchase home, and then the two of us would look at it and try to decide what the best approach for cooking the item would be. Nevertheless, whatever I was able to manage to prepare was always perfect and much appreciated by my hosts. Fortunately for me, they were not picky eaters, and they were usually hungry, which always supersedes mastery of the culinary arts! Suffice it to say that dinner was always a delightful surprise to all three of us.

One day I was asked to put a chicken in the huge oven down at the bakery. Hours passed, and we became engrossed in our activities; likewise, the bakers had gotten busy with their own workload, and we all forgot the poor chicken in the oven. Late in the evening, the Haugsteds were hungry, and suddenly they remembered the chicken waiting for them in the oven at the bakery. Delighted that their hunger would be appeased momentarily, they sent me to pick up dinner.

Almost spilling it on the steep stairs upon my return, I was quite relieved to put the pot on the counter. Augusta removed the lid to serve her husband, but there was no sign of the chicken! It all had dissolved into a kind of soft mass, leaving hardly any bones visible. She and I served dinner, but my hosts did not utter a word about the outcome. Without trying to, I had invented a new recipe for "chicken surprise."

The best part of that whole episode was that I'd had time to learn my assigned piece by memory during the many hours that the chicken had been in the bakery oven. My hosts praised me for my musical accomplishment, eager to finish the meal. Augusta and I quickly returned to my practising, and her husband went back to his elaborate library to resume his own work.

★ ★ ★ ★ ★

All was not laughter and gleeful moments, however. I was a sensitive child, and my wounds had not yet healed. Many times, afraid that the Haugsteds might not want me anymore, I would go into a far corner to weep. Mr. Haugsted had a knack for finding me on those occasions, and he would take me into the library, close the door, dry my face, and give me a cookie that he had found in his pocket, seemingly by magic. We would sit together on the leather sofa, and he would sing the children's song about the spider that crawled up the waterspout. This simple song was to become my motto, as I learned that the rain can never fall in anyone's life for so long that the sun will not shine again.

My hosts were the dearest and most understanding people, and my affection for them only deepened over time. The library was a favourite spot for me, and not just because of Mr. Haugsted's magically appearing cookies. He allowed me to go to the library to read whichever books I wanted, whenever I wanted. I would enter the library and just gaze all around the room, marvelling at how it seemed to have no walls: every inch of wall was covered by tall bookshelves, just as Father's library in our home in Latvia had been. Many mornings Mr. Haugsted would find me on the sofa, with the book I'd fallen asleep reading open across my chest. He would gently rouse me from sleep with a pat on the shoulder, and he never reprimanded me. I think he sensed how much comfort the library brought me, even though I never told him why.

I have so many fond memories of my time with the Haugsteds, some indeed unforgettable. After a time, I began taking part in recitals, and the bouquets of flowers that I frequently received always delighted me. Most of the time, my parents were in the audience, which was best of all. During one such recital, I played a movement of Tchaikovsky's *First Concerto,* along with the school orchestra. This performance was very well received, resulting in a massive bouquet of roses for me. I can still recall their incredible fragrance as I cradled them in my arms, the pleasure of praise filling my being.

That night it was bitter cold. My parents returned to the Haugsteds' home with me after the recital. The attic was so chilly that all three of us sat huddled together on my bed, covering ourselves with the goosedown comforters to keep warm. I went a floor down to fill the bathtub with water in order to put the roses in for the night, hoping that they would last forever. After an hour or so, commotion filled the whole apartment building. I had forgotten to turn the water off, which resulted in a flood on the two floors below.

Needless to say, this broke the magic of the evening. I was frightened into speechlessness when I faced my hosts, but Mr. Haugsted just smiled. "Don't worry, Lara! This also happened a few times after the concerts of our son-in-law." He did not need to say anything else. The Haugsteds' son-in-law was none other than Denmark's most-beloved performer, Aksel Schiotz, who had sung beautiful Danish folksongs throughout the occupation. This remarkable tenor had helped all of Denmark overcome those awful times by filling the air with love and hope, helping his countrymen to muster their courage and restoring their faith that better times lay ahead.

The ill-fated chicken and flood notwithstanding, my time with the Haugsteds was filled with joy. I no longer felt immersed in malevolence, and my nightmares had begun to plague me a bit less. And then, without warning, tragedy struck their household. Doctors diagnosed Aksel Schiotz with a brain tumor, and they admitted him to a hospital in Sweden for the surgery. I felt the Haugsteds' pain and did everything I could to help them bear it, keeping vigil with them through the long hours of the surgery. It touched me deeply that they wished me to be near them to lend support and empathy. They must have appreciated my demeanour, discerning that I had endured tragedy and emerged from it scarred but not destroyed, and they reached out to me so that I could help them deal with their own pain. I was honoured to be considered in that manner, and I felt as if I were part of their family. The telephone calls to Sweden went back and forth all night long, while I sat between the two of them, frequently reaching out to hold their hands. Inwardly, I prayed to my Christmas angel: *Please help the Haugsteds, Angel. Please let Mr. Schiotz get well.* The surgery was most successful, and Mr. Schiotz came through it all quite well, although he would have a long recovery.

As things turned out, I met Aksel Schiotz many years later. I had already been living in Canada for a number of years when, at a concert at the Massey Hall in Toronto, I found myself sitting next to Mr. and Mrs. Schiotz and their twin daughters in the upper gallery. The Royal Conservatory of Music of Toronto had invited him to fill the position of Professor in Residence. It was a wonderful surprise, and I had the great joy and privilege of receiving them at my home, where we talked endlessly about Denmark and the wonderful days I'd spent with the dear Haugsteds.

I had countless fond memories to share with the Schiotzes, and to recall in solitude as well. Augusta Haugsted was a very well-known pianist and teacher, and she always took me along to recitals as part of my education. Many receptions were held at the Haugsteds' home, and so I met many other renowned musicians and overheard quite a number of inspiring conversations. I had plenty of time to practise, even with my requisite household chores, and my teacher was so impressed with my progress that she trusted me to teach some of her students when she went on her tours. As a result, I no longer felt inept, but because many of the students I was to teach were older than I, I did feel a bit intimidated. It proved to be a marvellous experience, as it taught me to believe in myself, to always do my best, and to take pride in my accomplishments without being arrogant.

In addition to being an outstanding musician, Augusta Haugsted had a vibrant personality. On her seventy-fifth birthday, her family presented her with a bicycle as a gift. She used that bicycle to commute all over the city. It was so heart-warming to watch the tiny lady with platinum-white hair don her slacks, hop on her bicycle, and then pedal through the busy streets of Aarhus. She inspired me in many others way too. For instance, Augusta always wore a red velvet gown when she was teaching, and that image of her was to be a lasting example for me once I became a full-fledged teacher. I would recall Augusta standing at the piano, regal in red, and attempt to mirror her dignity, strength, and grace, as well as her patience with and devotion to her students.

I cannot overemphasise how much my time with the Haugsteds meant to me, or how much Augusta taught me. Yet another example of her sterling character was the way in which she treated me while entertaining at home. After dinner, the Haugsteds' guests always gathered in the beautiful living room, where paintings by the great masters covered the walls. Two Hornung and Muller grand pianos filled one part of the room, and Augusta often asked me to play for the guests. I felt honoured that she asked me to play for them when she herself was a world-renowned pianist. That was yet another example of what a great teacher she was: her students were far more important to her than her own ego.

I could go on and on about the Haugsteds, but, to put it simply, everything had changed for me because of their benevolence. My confidence and self-esteem skyrocketed, and yet I retained humility— that was all the result of Augusta's teaching me by example. In other words, I felt confident that I could cook, play the piano, and teach others to play, yet I remained humble and grateful for my gifts, and I did not overlook my own shortcomings. I often recalled the flood that had resulted from my neglecting to turn off the water in the tub, and so I did not get "too big for my breeches," as the saying goes! However, I felt secure enough in the person I was becoming to acknowledge my triumphs even as I apologised for my mistakes. Without even realising it, I was learning to become a well-grounded person. We all are a mixture of talents and shortcomings, and it is how we deal with unpleasantness that measures our character, as no one can get through life without making mistakes or encountering hardships—these are what allow us to grow and to become stronger, wiser, and kinder. At the time, I merely reassured myself that the day would come when I would no longer have to remind myself to turn off the water in the tub. The wisdom we gain in childhood is often the best kind!

Perhaps the greatest gift the Haugsteds gave me was making me feel needed and accepted. They showed me through their words—and, even more important, through their actions—that they wanted me to be part of their lives, lending them joy when they were happy and support when they were sorrowful. In short, I felt loved, respected, and trusted—and I carried that with me throughout my life, forever reciprocating their love, respect, and trust.

Nevertheless, my time with the Haugsteds proved to be short-lived. Augusta had entrusted me with much responsibility as a result of my achievements, and that yielded a great honour: the following season, I was accepted at the studio of virtuoso Georg Vasarhelyi, who came to Aarhus from Copenhagen every other week to teach local pianists and three students at the Conservatory. That meant that I was to be one of three, and my accomplishment thrilled and excited me, yet I did not want to leave the Haugsteds. It was not that I was afraid of relocating—after all, I had long since grown accustomed to moving about—but I was sad to say goodbye to the people who had taught me so much and been so kind to me. In addition, as I grew older, the anticipation of new circumstances began to bother me. Seeking to manage my feelings of uncertainty, I wanted to know what to expect so that I could plan how to deal with it.

Focusing on the once-in-a-lifetime opportunity of studying with Georg Vasarhelyi, I relegated my trepidation to the back of my mind and, as always, maintained a positive attitude. My life would be filled with the music I loved so deeply, and my gratitude knew no bounds.

★ ★ ★ ★ ★

The Danish Red Cross moved me to Riiskov, a suburb of Aarhus My entire education was based on scholarship and recognition, and I always worked very hard and aimed to please. I still fondly recall the many hours I spent under the supervision of Thoger Rasmussen, the director of the Conservatory, who taught me how to master the art of the accompanist. After our sessions, I was lucky enough to enjoy the delicious meals prepared by Mrs. Rasmussen.

I must be the luckiest girl on earth! I would think to myself. *Somehow, someone is always there to help me.* In truth, I missed my parents and often felt extremely lonely, but I never lost sight of my good fortune in receiving such wonderful opportunities.

The Danish Red Cross had many exceptional volunteers and donors; indeed, it seemed some of them practically lived just to help me. I was frequently invited to perform in the homes of many influential people, and so those in positions of authority heard me play.

On one such occasion a person who chose to remain anonymous offered me a scholarship at the Academy of Music, in addition to my attending the Conservatory, and so I was also able to study under Denmark's most celebrated pianist and composer, Niels Viggo Bentzon. Because of my benefactor, I had a studio at the Academy where I could practise. Although I did learn a great deal, my recollections of those lessons still cause me much amusement. My teacher talked in such a loud voice, and he had a penchant for feeding me prunes while I played. Fortunately for me, they were pitted! As I've mentioned, we musicians have a logic all our own, but the reason for the prunes still escapes me.

One principal teacher loved to come in during my practise sessions to bring me a plate of delicious pastry and a glass of milk. I much preferred this treat to the prunes, I can assure you! My time at the Academy was wonderful. Many years after I left Denmark, I remained in touch with several teachers from the Academy. Along with our correspondence, they would send me scores of Niels Viggo Bentzon's compositions, as well as newly released theoretical volumes and pieces crafted especially for me. These were such a delight to play! My solfège teacher sent me a small crocheted cross she had made, also especially for me. The attached note read: "To my little friend with the tears in her eyes." I keep all these treasures in a special place, and they have become symbols of the many kindnesses that fill my heart with eternal gratitude for all my friends in Denmark.

I lived in Riiskov for quite some time, at the villa of the Olsens. These were two of the most loving people in the world, and I called them "Auntie" Anna and "Uncle" Marius. I had a room downstairs, and their little dog, Svips, came into my room every morning to wake me up. Svips was better than any alarm clock! Little Missy, the black-and-white kitten, slept on my windowsill, jumping onto my bed while I was asleep. Her purring comforted me through the night. Missy made the loss of my beloved Mikus a little easier to bear, and I suppose her commandeering my bed would make me more tolerant of Mauser's antics later on in my life. I have always had a soft spot for animals, and I always shall.

It was so nice to be with the Olsens, and uncertainty no longer troubled me. The only thing that was missing from my life now was my parents; I was rarely able to see them because my time was so limited. In order to meet all my scholastic demands, I had to attend several schools, and I spent much time practising too. Mother and Father understood and only wanted what was best for me, but we still missed each another.

The scholarships did not cover the books that I needed for my courses, so I had to take care of providing those myself. After the war, books could no longer be taken out of the library. I spent countless hours at the library trying to memorise the music I needed to learn, and then I would race home to practise. As a result, I developed a photographic memory.

As I could not afford to buy textbooks, I would sit in the reference section of the library and copy them by hand, page by page. I shared these copies with my classmates, and I was glad to start making friends my own age. It was important for me to start meeting other youngsters, especially ones who did not know that I was a refugee. I spoke Danish well enough by that point, which made me feel happy and proud. Aarhus had an outstanding ballet school in addition to the music schools, and I was hired to play for the classes. I also started to paint on porcelain, selling the pieces so that I could pay for my books.

I began to feel accepted and liked for what I was able to do, for what I accomplished. I no longer felt that the people around me were kind to me in acknowledgment of what I had suffered, and that was a huge blessing. I began to feel like others were treating me as an equal, which helped make the pain of the past fade. My wish had come true: life was good again, and normalcy had returned.

★ ★ ★ ★ ★

Meanwhile, Mother worked at the YMCA, and Father worked at a crane factory. He was not yet a full-time employee, but with the help of the owner of the factory, Father and Mother both earned ample benefits.

I still lived in Riiskov, at the Olsen's beautiful villa overlooking the bay. Taking thecommuter train to the city on school days, I enjoyed the lovely ride along the coastline. On one side was the sandy beach, on the other a big park. In the sunlit clearings, deer playfully entertained the visitors. Ferns and wildflowers covered the clean wooded grounds. The trees were tall and dense, home to many birds that filled the park with song, whether remaining in their nests or flying through the park.

Those were very busy but peaceful days for me. My only despair was that when I got off the train I had just enough time to get to school. My parents lived quite close to the station, but I had no time to stop for even the briefest visit. I so longed to Mother and Father, yet there was not even the faintest hope of changing my schedule.

I never did understand why I could not live with my parents in the city; no one explained the reason, and I did not ask. I felt sad that I had no time to be with my parents, but I tried hard not to dwell on it. Auntie and Uncle were such loving people that I never felt neglected. Sensing that I missed my parents, even though I never complained, the Olsens gave me a birthday party. I was still in the process of making friends at that point, and so I did not have anybody to invite, other than Mother and Father, of course. To fill the guest list, the Olsens invited their own friends. It was such a joyous evening! All too soon the party ended, and all the guests went home. Mother and Father had to leave as well, but it was so wonderful to share that special evening with them—that was the best gift the Olsens could have given me.

In truth, I had everything I could possibly need and want in Riiskov, with the exception of my parents. At times, when I saw children walking along hand-in-hand with their parents, I felt like an orphan. Nevertheless, I was grateful for the Olsens, whom I grew to love dearly. My time with them was unforgettable in many ways.

I still remember the day that time stood still. All the smiles vanished, and the Danish flag seemed soaked with tears of sorrow. The war was long over by then, but its horrors returned afresh on that fateful day.

A mine had somehow detached itself and travelled into Danish waters, where it lay in wait for victims. One June day catastrophe struck the beautiful *Copenhagen,* with 350 passengers onboard, 48 of whom would never return home. As during the war, a single second changed so many lives.

The *Copenhagen* had a daily domestic route from Aalborg to Copenhagen, which I had taken numerous times, enjoying the fresh waterborne breeze on the sunlit deck. When we learned of the tragedy, I felt that horror echo through the entire land, bouncing off the coastline, while the waters of the Kattegat were filled with sorrow. That same horror echoed through my own heart, filling me with indescribable pain.

There is no known scale to measure pain, so I can only relate that the tragedy affected me very deeply, and in a way that I still cannot adequately put into words. I felt so close to Denmark; I thought of the water, the harbour, the people, even the ship itself, as my own. Once again, "my" people were drowning in the pain and sorrow of tragedy caused by the tools of war. *When will this stop?!* I asked inwardly, knowing there was no answer.

The country I called home was in mourning. Yet I prayed that it was the last act of the doomed villain, a spasm of its skeleton, and that it would breathe no more. *Please, Angel, keep all innocent people safe and at peace,* I prayed. I already felt like a veteran of grief, but even that could not lessen my grief. All I could do was express my condolences to the people of Denmark, lend them my support, and join them in their prayers.

★ ★ ★ ★ ★

Father made me a bicycle from some old parts that he had found at the factory site. Some nights I missed my parents so much that I could not bear their absence any longer. I would sit at my window, look out into the vast darkness, and wish I were with them. One night this wish deepened into longing, becoming so overwhelming that I went outside, hopped on the bicycle, and headed toward the city.

The only way was through the park. All was very still, with the exception of the faint call of an owl. I rode fast, rushing past the trees and bushes, barely even noticing them. The dark shadows did not bother me; I had lived through far scarier things than a dark night-time park. If anything, the dark and the shadows comforted me; I knew them so well. My only wish that night was to see Mother and Father.

It took a good half hour to reach their building. Finally, I was at the tall iron gate, but it was locked! I saw a dim light in the attic window. I knocked and knocked on the iron beams, banging until my knuckles began to bleed, not even caring that I might damage my hands and fingers—all in vain! Nobody could hear me. It felt like an iron wall separated me from my own parents. It began to rain, and I went across the street to take shelter beneath an overhang. All the while, I kept looking at the window, so close but yet so far from them. Loneliness overcame me, and I felt forgotten. The rain soaked my clothes, giving rise to painful memories. I looked at the window again, and the light went off. I started the long walk back to Riiskov, too tired to pedal.

I purposely took a long time returning to the villa, imagining that I was not alone on the dark trail. The trees cast long shadows, and as I walked I pretended the shadows were my parents. I trailed behind them, just as I had throughout our harrowing flight.

During the war, I had learned how to overcome my heartache by making up stories in my head; it made me feel even better to write them down in my notebook from the Vens. I knew that nobody would be interested in reading them, but I wrote them down anyway. After all, it was my story. I filled the notebook with it, and it cleansed the pain in my heart and soul. I wished I were back at the villa in Riiskov so that I could write in my notebook, but the walk would take a while. Perhaps the rain would cleanse me in the meantime.

★ ★ ★ ★ ★

The persistent rain caressed me gently, very calming and soothing. I stepped in the puddles, letting the clean, cool rainwater cleanse me as I'd hoped it would. Every now and then I stopped to watch the raindrops make small ripples in the puddles. Standing still and breathing in the fresh, rain-kissed air, I simply relished my deep connection with nature and thought about the many times that the connection had helped me escape from death, move on, and survive. I felt surrounded by the connection, protected by it just as I always had been, and I was able to manage my emotions again. As ever, nature helped me find my place in the circle of life.

I reflected that I knew how to deal with physical pain—far too well, perhaps—but emotional pain was not so easy to manage. In fact, it was much harder. This was partly because it had no end and partly because just when I thought I'd moved past it, it would flare up again, leading me to despair that I'd never move on—that I was trapped and a prisoner of the memories that would never cease haunting me. *Is the biggest villain my own sorrow?* I wondered, overwhelmed by misery and feeling as if I would never get over the failed visit that night. The pain saturated my body with every step I took, but I just kept walking.

Finally, I reached the Olsensvilla in Riiskov. The garden gate was open, and I stepped onto the walkway beneath the cascading white rose bush that covered the whole arbour. It blocked my way to the garden, but the fragrance of the roses was so intoxicating that I did not even feel the sharp thorns scratching my face. The fragrance welcomed me back, reminding me that life is a gift and we each have our place in the world. For a moment I felt absolute peace, and my pain was easier to bear: the garden had waited for me, just as my animal friends always for me—just as my music always waited for me. Everything would be all right.

I hesitated to leave the garden to go inside the house. The raindrops had settled on the grass, and when dawn came they would mix with the dew. I sat down, surrounded by all the flowers I had helped Auntie and Uncle plant. It felt good to be in my own microcosm, and I fully enjoyed the serenity. I came to see that violence is not the only thing that can kill a person; yes, bullets and bombs, and the hatred and ignorance that precipitate their use, are inevitably destructive, but so is loneliness—in a vastly different way, of course. Never again would I allow being alone to separate me from the deepest part of myself, or from my connections to nature and the whole of life. I might have to be alone, but I did not have to feel lonely. Only those who do not value life can feel lonely.

My perspective widened that night, and I realised that the malevolence and egomania of tyranny had made the Baltic countries so open to attack. Those nations, built by people of good character and strong spirit, had remained undefended because those people had never imagined the depth of tyranny's evil—never believed that they would be invaded and occupied. Yet the power of tyranny stems from the sterility of its leaders' souls, the utterly insidious hatred toward altruism and goodness, and that nullifies any recognition of causing harm or pain.

The assassins who had perpetrated the atrocities of war were destroyed, just as all villains inevitably have been. Villains always pave the path to their own destruction, losing their power and becoming useless because they are leeches that live at the expense of others. At the root of all malice lies the absence of humanity and compassion; such individuals continue to inflict torment and harm on others without realising that they are really fighting any traces of goodness within themselves, which strives, usually in vain, to kill the evil that they glorify. Such evil is the worst kind of virus, but the assassins, in their vanity and misguided efforts, seek only to extol and perpetuate it. As proven many times in history, the defeated villains die in agony. This also proved to be true of the horrific events that I survived.

In my own small way, I had defeated the assassins, and I acknowledged that as I sat in the Olsens' garden. I'd been but a little girl, yet the perpetrators of evil had not been able to break me or make me stop valuing and loving life. During the moment of that spark of insight, I let go of my resentment. I had survived. Now all I wanted was to live the rest of my life in peace.

13
Lone Walk

Throughout my early childhood in Latvia, I'd always felt deep affection and love for each of the four seasons. Each displayed its own characteristic changes, bringing unique rewards to the country. Latvia and Canada shared similar seasons , which made my eventual transition pleasant and comfortable in many ways. Although I came to love living in Canada and eventually made it my new home, the relocation was filled with all sorts of struggles. I had to readjust to the severe winter climate after having become accustomed to Denmark's milder winters, as I've described. Many of these struggles were so overpowering that my body almost gave up, and I would wish I'd never left Denmark.

Nonetheless, when I had to follow my parents to Canada, and I was committed to achieving a positive outcome. The decision to relocate had affected many people; any revocation of it would certainly do likewise, perhaps even more so. Thus, I remained in my new country; I was determined to face all the hurdles, overcome all the obstacles, and be happy in my new life in Toronto.

Although the transition was challenging at times, I refused to allow any heartache or disappointment—whether from the past or in the present—to discourage me or "keep me down" for long. Life is a precious gift, and I reminded myself of that fact as often as necessary. I believe that valuing life is key to self-esteem and self-reliance; I live my life to honour the gift of life. I had observed how, by not valuing life, the assassins had destroyed everything they touched. And those who did not stand up to the assassins—the living dead, as I thought of them—did not value life any more than the assassins did; they seemed to have no ability to discern the difference between good and evil.

I knew the difference, and I always had, even as a child—the assassins had not broken my spirit or poisoned my heart. I had survived the inconceivably gruelling times. My childhood had been destroyed, but I had survived and still had the gift of my life. It was time to pick up the pieces; it was time to move on. I might never fulfill the dreams of my early childhood, but I had new dreams, new opportunities, new gifts—all of which I appreciated—but I never forgot that life itself is the greatest gift of all. I could, and would, make the most of what I did have; I would not bemoan what I had lost. My parents' fearlessness in leaving the refugee camp inspired me. I was their daughter, after all—not the daughter of those who had stayed and ended up wallowing in self-pity instead of rebuilding their lives.

My scars covered deep psychological and emotional wounds that lasted long after my physical wounds had healed. I had learned to stop seeking justification for why we'd endured what the war had forced us to. That night in the Olsens' garden had been more than just a turning point in my life: it had been an epiphany. I simply did not want to encounter any new pain that could damage my already battered heart. I was strong and resilient; I was thankful for what I had, and I knew what mattered; I kept things in perspective and always maintained a positive attitude. However, I was not superhuman. I knew that moving to Canada meant starting all over again—from scratch—in a new place, with new people. I felt all alone, but I had to stay strong so that I could find a way to steel my resolve and not anticipate disappointment. I told myself: *Disappointment might come my way, but then again, it might not. I've withstood far worse. I will face and deal with whatever I have to, and I will overcome whatever I must. It is time to move on.*

Sometimes I still felt that the largest part of my past was grief and ashes. But I never lost sight of all the joy and blessings in my life. No one could possibly feel good as a result of always looking back—or forward—even if every memory were happy and every dream were sublime. Life happens in the moment, and so we each must live for the day, grateful for our happy memories and wonderful dreams, and willing to accept the unchangeable past. I knew that was true. Refusing to keep looking back, I started to truly live for and in the moment, acknowledging that no past moment, good or bad, could ever be resurrected or relived.

Grief was a part of me; it always would be, and I lived with it the best way I could. The ashes had buried the good along with the bad, but time moved on, and it always would. I was determined to continue my lone walk, scattering the ashes as far as I feasibly could.

My joy in, and respect for, the seasons helped me do so. I acknowledged the four seasons, as I did all of nature. Each season presented its own variety of activities, changes, and delights, and embracing them helped ease my losses and my pain. The past was behind me, and the time had come to plan for the rest of my life. In nature, no organism dwells in the past; they all simply follow their encoded wisdom to know what is right for them in every season and at every time. We humans would do well to follow suit.

Eventually, with significant inward encouragement, I simply resigned myself to accept the inevitable: *It is pointless to think any longer about what I lost, no matter how much it was. Rather, I will focus on all that I gained as a result of enduring all the danger, horror, suffering, and pain that I did and surviving. I did survive! And now I will master the remainder of my life.*

And, with that, I was ready to make the move to Canada. I was nervous and a bit unsettled, yes, but, nonetheless, ready and positively motivated too.

★ ★ ★ ★ ★

Moving to Canada made me think of the Vens, the dear farmer and his wife in Denmark. Although no one ever told me their names, I loved them with all my heart and never stopped being grateful for their genuine loving care. I had no way to contact them to thank them; the only way I had to show my gratitude was to help those in need in Canada, my new home. This I did as often as I could, within my means. The Vens, seeking to cope with their own loss and soothe their own pain, had helped me, showing me that every human being has the power to help another. No matter how bad a situation might be, if people just helped one another, they could, and would, overcome it all—together. And togetherness is the key aspect of that. Nothing is nobler than helping another in need of help.

The Vens had restored my hope and faith in my fellow humans, and because of them I knew how far kindness could reach. I had been far more damaged and tormented than they could have guessed, but not so much that their compassion could not positively change my whole attitude and outlook. Indeed, they restored my faith that people would be kind again and life would be good again. In order to honour my cherished Vens, their care, and their sterling faculty of believing in humanity, I have never turned my back on anyone in need; rather, I promised to reach out to others as much as I could, and I have kept that promise throughout my life.

The beginning of April always inspired me, evoking the end of the occupation in Denmark. I loved watching all the changes in my garden in Toronto. The flowers seemed to compete with one another, each variety proud to show off its signature colour and fragrance. My daily route followed Toronto's Don Valley. As I drove along, it seemed as if an artist had awakened early, picked up his palette—choosing different colours every day—and then, with bold strokes, swiftly repainted the whole valley just for me to enjoy. Vast stretches of daffodils lined the roadside in a burst of gold, seamlessly meeting the patches of countless blue snowdrops. As in a master's landscape, the gorgeous colours blended in complementary splendour as the blooms basked in the warm, bright spring sunshine.

The road seemed a part of heaven, undisturbed and wholesome and serene. I often stopped near a remote ledge, parking my car and allowing some pleasant events of the past to course through my mind as I tried to intertwine them with the present. That was the best I could do in regard to the past that I would never understand, not in any of the several languages I had become comfortable speaking. I'd never understood the agenda of the vicious aggressors—the assassins—and I never shall understand it. I had no intention of even trying to understand, as that would allow the assassins to steal even more of my life. I did intend to keep making the most of my life, savouring every drop, and I always shall do that.

Alone on the ledge, I could look up to heaven and then all around me, grateful for nature and life and all that is. Spring, quite simply, reignited my hopes and dreams and faith. I breathed in the new air and reaffirmed my commitment to living as fully as possible.

★ ★ ★ ★ ★

The preparation for the upcoming tour season went well, giving me more leisure time. As I recollected some memorable moments, it seemed to me that my life was like a chain, each moment one of its links. Sometimes the journey had felt like a tight-rope act, with me engaged in terrifyingly painstaking steps across what seemed like a thread. At other times it felt as if I were the hapless prey caught in the gossamer web of the spider lying in wait. But then I reminded myself that the spider was a creature of nature—innately a predator, yes, but also a survivor, the hero of my motto, waiting for the rain to stop and the sun to re-emerge.

I encouraged myself to remain mindful of all that I'd learned and all that I knew. It had been such a lonely haul, and I could not deny that. Circumstances had made me an outcast of sorts, and I had lost my basic trust in people. Yes, the kindness of the officer and the Vens and the Haugsteds and the Olsens had inspired me and rekindled my faith in goodness, but I felt this in a way that resided deep within me. My faith infused my beliefs, and I strove to show my gratitude by being kind to others in acknowledgment of the kindness I'd received. But I could not be more than human. In other words, I still had doubts and weak moments, and there were times when I momentarily lost sight of all that goodness, sinking into despair and misery, mistrusting those around me. I must say that I was often wise to do so. We each experience intuition for a reason; mine had enabled me to survive extreme circumstances, and so I trusted it more than anything, or anyone, else. I had to learn to balance trusting others and trusting myself, assessing whether the many suggestions and bits of advice I received were worthwhile, and if so, whether I would be able to implement them. I then had to learn how to respond to what was, or was not, acceptable. This is not easy for anyone, least of all a refugee child. At the time I was learning to accomplish all this I was really too young to draw logical conclusions or make informed decisions, and yet I had no choice but to do so.

Because of the circumstances of my scholarships, I was alone in my day-to-day life. The people who took me in and cared for me were wonderful beyond what mere words can describe, but they were not my parents. And I could not burden my parents with the concern that I was not happy; they had been through far too much already, and I had long since become accustomed to resolving things on my own. Almost automatically, I had come to be able to make the best of things, no matter how painful they might be. There was no set example for me to follow. All the people around me sought to rebuild their lives too, and they each had their own views as to how best to accomplish that. To escape from conflicting views would have increased my confusion and isolated me even further.

I already felt like an outcast, with no place to truly call my own. My real home was my music, but that home lies within. As a child or young person it is difficult, if not impossible, to accept and embrace this kind of inner truth—no matter how much we might know that it's true. The young long to "fit in," and only the wisdom of aging shows us this is folly (and many never realise that). Regardless of how much I thought about it, or how hard I tried to move past it, the end result was that I often felt lost and unwanted—as if I did not belong anywhere, and never would. Eventually, of course, I did recognise that my true, eternal home *was* my music, but it took some time and experience to recognise and embrace this inner truth.

★ ★ ★ ★ ★

I came to love my adopted country of Canada, but I had my share of trials and tribulations when I arrived. I found it as difficult to find acceptance among my colleagues in Canada as I had among my schoolmates in Denmark. The emotional impact I'd felt as a refugee child resurrected itself, and I quite unexpectedly found myself reliving those experiences. I had long since accepted that the indelible images of the war would always haunt me, but I had not anticipated feeling like a child and an outsider again in the midst of my colleagues—that is, fellow musicians, professionals, and adults. Nevertheless, I took it all in stride. Not everyone achieves inner security, self-esteem, or self-reliance just by reaching a certain chronological age. I respected the needs of those colleagues who made it clear that I would have to "prove myself." In truth, I did not need them to welcome me with open arms—I had learned how to be resilient, and I would thrive and succeed because I had made up my mind to do so. However, a warm welcome would have been so nice! *Stop being so thin skinned!* I chided myself. *Everyone has not endured extreme circumstances that help them keep things in perspective. The music world is competitive, and all these people have had to learn the hard way how to look after themselves. They do the best they can, and it is not for me to judge them.*

That was true, of course, and it helped—but I still believe that kindness is always the best we each can do, and it doesn't take too much to accomplish. I have not yet become bitter from not receiving kindness—I never intend to, for life is too precious to waste even a moment on bitterness. I made the conscious choice to be tolerant and compassionate toward others, not in spite of the hardships I'd had to endure but because of them. Nonetheless, I still felt disappointment whenever I encountered intolerance and lack of compassion; and yet, I realised I would simply have to get used to it. If I had to start from the beginning with my new colleagues, so be it. I had come to Canada with qualifications upon which I would find a way to further develop my skills and talents. I was under a great deal of pressure to do so, and the noticeable lack of camaraderie and collegial rapport perturbed me.

My experiences had taught me how to survive, but in order to do so I'd had to learn how to suppress my emotions and to overcome seemingly insurmountable odds; developing the ability to learn how to do all that comes at a steep price. I was far too sensitive to ever be able to completely relinquish all capacity to feel. Instead, I'd learned to channel all my sensitivity and depth of feeling into my music. This I would still do; and so, although I remained determined to ensure that my relocation to Canada had a positive outcome, I decided to continue my lone walk. I would remain within the safety of my invisible shell of protection, although I did not think of it in those terms at the time.

★ ★ ★ ★ ★

Memory and time helped me to adjust to Canada. My fond recollections of Denmark, the Danish people, and all my cherished friends there sustained me. Perhaps it was sheer longing for them that called up my frequent fond memories. I only knew it helped, and so I didn't question why.

In particular I would recall the day of the capitulation, when I had walked from the refugee camp to the core of the city. Travelling aimlessly, I'd eventually reached the city square in Aarhus. Directly across from the beautiful and elegant Hotel Royale was the enormous cathedral. The doors were open, and the parishioners began going inside for the service. I waited until they all had gone inside. The door remained half-open. Afraid that my wooden-soled shoes would disturb the solemnity, I slipped them off and moved inside in my stocking feet, carrying my shoes, which were far too valuable a commodity to risk losing.

Seeking a secluded spot, I spied an empty pew at the far back of the cathedral, which the multicoloured light from the magnificent stained-glass windows did not reach. Settling myself in this darkest corner where I would escape all attention, I focused on the minister. I could not understand the Danish words, but the minister's voice was so soothing that I felt myself absorbed by its tranquillity. The congregation joined in a song that I had never heard before. It was a lovely song, and I joined in, picking up the melody and humming along.

The cathedral was beautiful, a truly holy place. I felt the air, infused with the strains of the psalm, become sublime in the truest sense. The presence of heaven filled the space. For a brief moment I was suspended in time, feeling no pain from my as yet unhealed injuries and no loneliness of spirit. I had found a refuge where I was accepted unconditionally. Nobody actually knew that I was there, and yet I felt important—I felt that it was *my* service as well as the congregation's.

The service ended, and everybody exited the cathedral. I did not want to leave and return to the refugee camp; I so longed to have a real home to go to. Mother and Father would likely be looking for me, but they would not mind when I explained about where I'd been. I remained sitting in the back pew in the farthest dark corner. The beautiful sounds of the psalms continued to resonate in my mind. My connection to music bridged the space between heaven and earth for me. I gazed up at the high ceiling, admiring the splendour of the sun's rays as they streamed brilliant reflections through the rainbow-hued windows. It all was so glorious that I felt special just to be a part of it.

Utterly at peace, I closed my eyes. I felt so warm and safe that I slipped into a dream. A gentle touch on my shoulder woke me up, and I looked into the kindly face of the minister. Having noticed me sitting in the dark corner, he'd come to look for me. I could not understand his words, but I instinctively trusted his soft voice and calm demeanour. He made me feel welcome, for the first time in a long time. The minister took me by the hand, and we walked out of the cathedral into the sunlit street. A slight breeze blew my hair in my face, and the minister smiled at me. It felt so good that somebody wanted to spend time with me.

The two of us walked along, the minister keeping my smaller hand in his. Behind the Aarhus Theatre was a small store that sold ice cream and cookies. We went inside, and the minister bought me a cookie and an ice-cream cone—the very first ice-cream cone I ever had in my life! It was so marvellous to look at; it contained all the colours of the rainbow. I just held it in my hand and admired it, scarcely believing that something that lovely was there for me to eat. The minister looked on, smiling, and then he encouraged me to start, using charades to show me how to eat the cone. I twitched a bit when I saw that the ice cream was beginning to melt, but I soon got the hang of it. It was delicious, and I had such fun licking the ice cream round in circles. Then I ate the cone like another treat! I decided to hold onto the cookie, which I would share with Mother and Father back at the camp. Throughout the years since then, I've often recalled that experience, actually tasting that delicious treat all over again and remembering the face of the gentle man in the black robe.

★ ★ ★ ★ ★

Not all my experiences in Denmark were joyous and peaceful. I often wondered why some people were so nice while others were not. Some of the children I met rejected me harshly, and that hurt me deeply. I was not looking for pity or asking for anything; all I wanted was to be understood and accepted for the person I was, just as I was. This was the way that I understood and accepted others, and so it seemed fair to me that I should receive the same in returned. After all, I was a child just like the other children—I wished to play and run and laugh just like they did. I did not understand why they could not sense this, even though I do understand now as I look back. Of course, that does not minimise the pain I felt or make the recollections less hurtful.

I could not run very fast in my wooden-soled shoes, which were cumbersome in the best of circumstances. They were downright awkward to manoeuvre in because they felt so heavy on my legs, which had not yet healed from injuries sustained during the war and our flight. My legs still hurt a lot, in fact, but none of the other children knew this. I would not tell the reason for my painful movements to anybody, and so I was caught in a dilemma with no resolution: I longed to be accepted just as I was, but I resisted letting anyone see the "real" me. My resistance stemmed from fear—the fear of trusting and then being hurt—and that fear was far stronger than the longing. As had already become my habit, I redirected that longing for connection into my love of music and nature, and that love became my strongest "relationship."

I could not separate what I had experienced from the person I became as a result of those experiences—I still can't, and I will never be able to, as that is impossible for anyone to accomplish. Our past is part of who we are, and the rest of our lives consists of what we each do to accept and embrace that truth, or to reject and deny it. Few people truly succeed in accomplishing the latter. Needless to say, as difficult as this is to bear as an adult, it was even more so for me as a child. Although I was not actually conscious of any of what I now describe, per se, I did know what I felt on an intuitive level, and I also knew that I could not deny how I felt.

On top of all that, I distrusted others to an extreme degree. All children need time to accept one another, but I had lost the time from my childhood that would have helped me become accustomed to this truth. As a result, their warming up to me over time seemed to me to be "fake," and I would put up my wall of defence to keep them from hurting me. I had lost my basic sense of trust, and I preferred the known safety of being alone to the unknown risk of misplaced trust. The other children's interactions with one another seemed a parody to me. It took a very long time for me to able to process their individual demeanours and characters in order to find any true friends among the potential foes.

My relationships with the Danish children my own age were vastly different from the wonderful experiences I'd had with the Vens, Haugsteds, Olsens, and other kind and caring adults. I suppose I just felt more comfortable with adults, as my childhood had been cut short so cruelly and my earliest friendships so horribly destroyed. Perhaps I was protecting myself from even thinking about that last part. In addition, adults had the ability to empathise with what they surmised I must have endured, whereas other children could not. All this became part of me, however, and it helped me become the person I was destined to be. This did not make my interactions with other children any easier, even though I sensed it all to a certain extent at a subconscious level. There was no way around any of it, and so I simply avoided any tendency to trust unfamiliar faces, as I did not really understand their intensions—were they honest and sincere, or presumptuous and shallow? In the end, I decided that I simply preferred being ignored to being rejected—which, to me, meant being betrayed and hurt all over again.

The unfair judgments of other children abounded, as predictable as the change of seasons or the tides. At first, my clothing was not the latest fashion; later, it was simply envy of my success at school and talent for music. I came to see that jealousy and envy were symptomatic of deeper emotional and psychological issues, and so I ignored them, refusing to respond to any judgments or premature prejudice on the part of my schoolmates, whether in sports, academic subjects, music, or otherwise. That helped me further develop my resilience, self-esteem, and self-reliance. Solitude—isolation, some might say—trained me to increase my already strong sense of discipline and focus. Rather than seek social acceptance, I simply strove to do my best in all my pursuits, which simultaneously made it easier to bear inevitable disappointments and gave me more time for productive work in school and piano practise.

I came to realise that encountering resistance from my colleagues in Canada brought up all the painful memories of my interaction with other children in Denmark. On the one hand, I had not expected to have to endure such behaviour from colleagues and fellow musicians— from adults, to put it bluntly. On the other hand, I recognised that not everyone outgrows insecurity. Envy and jealousy exist in people of all ages and from all walks of life, and those of us who eschew these traits tend to harbour the hope that those who possess them will come to eschew them too. It is better to hope in vain than become bitter, but experience has taught me to temper that hope with a realistic level of expectation.

In particular, my colleagues in Toronto reminded me of my childhood introduction to table tennis. As the first girl to join the table-tennis team, I had certain benefits, but disappointment inevitably followed. I received special treatment and equipment, and because men taught me how to play I became very skilled in the sport's demands for both speed and accuracy. I enjoyed it immensely. Later, more girls joined the team, but I always managed to surpass their efforts, winning every game and remaining champion for several years. The only title I did not win was the national one; I was not permitted to take part in that game because of my displaced-person (DP) status. That was perfectly understandable, of course, but to a child it made no sense at all. I was quite unable to reason out all the laws and regulations involved; quite simply, the decision hurt! I felt that just when life was beginning to improve, I had to face a senseless punishment, and it was not easy to accept.

One young boy on the team had a physical disability, making it a challenge for him to meet the demands of the game. Some teammates made this even more difficult for him. I wished that his taunters would not waste their time with pointless discrimination and meanness and would instead focus on their own performance, developing better skills—not to mention better sportsmanship. They never seemed to notice that this boy did not have time for their nonsense—he just did his best to get through the day. If they did notice, they did not care. It was the total absence of empathy and kindness that I found distressing, both as a member of that team during my growing-up years in Denmark and again as a professional musician in Canada. I came to realise that this is just what compassionate and empathetic people must "learn to live with," but it was hard-won wisdom, indeed.

Throughout my years in Denmark, I experienced frequent inner turmoil; so many people around me had contradicting values and attitudes. People in those years certainly had many difficulties to deal with and overcome, but I could not understand how discrimination was able to infiltrate their consciousness or character after all that we had endured during the war. This was the time when we should have been celebrating freedom together, without prejudice or mean-spirited behaviour dividing us.

In spite of myself, I often felt hurt when I was overlooked and avoided: I wanted a chance to prove myself, even though I mistrusted the acceptance I sought. *Why don't the others understand I am not a refugee by choice? I wish I were still in Latvia, growing up where I belong! I wish to be there far more than they wish for me to go back. I was merely a pawn for the savage aggressors. Latvia was no different from Denmark.* Most of us cannot move past our own pain to reach out to others; those children were just human. Yet it still hurt.

At the table-tennis tournaments, I always stayed in the cloak room during the presentation of the trophy. My ragtag clothing—whether hand-me-downs or homemade—made me feel very awkward. I did not want to walk to the podium, past my teammates clad in their fine clothing. I could never hope to have the fancy stuff to wear that they had, and I was afraid they would jeer and laugh at me. The truth is, I would gladly have lost the match if doing so would have made my teammates happy—and granted me unconditional acceptance. But that was not to be. My devoted trainer would always come to the cloak room to give me my trophy and a pair of new tennis shoes.

★ ★ ★ ★ ★

In spite of my busy academic and practise schedules, I took part in all the tournaments across the country, maintaining my status as the reigning champion from year to year. Eventually, my success was taken for granted, and some well-wishers donated their sterling silverware to be recast as my trophy.

The joy of the game faded for me, especially because my teammates kept their distance from me. At that time, I believed that they simply did not accept me, having not yet come to recognise that I guarded myself to avoid being hurt. So many people surrounded me, but I felt lonelier than ever. Every week my picture was on the front page of the local newspaper, which had earned me a nickname: "Smiling Lara." No one guessed that my smile was just to fulfill an obligation. Only my face was smiling; my heart was still in tatters, and yet nobody heard the grief inside me. I had worked so hard to learn to smile again, and I just kept smiling whenever I needed to, determined to never again lose that ability, no matter the cost.

During the games, I would forget that I was a refugee; momentarily, I was able to simply feel like a child playing in a field scattered with objects that I'd appropriately learned how to either make the best of or avoid. The greatest reward of all was not any trophy but the tennis shoes! I could walk to school in them instead of the wooden-soled shoes. Prior to winning, I'd had no choice but to play barefoot, and the wounds on my feet caused by the sharp slivers that dug into them had only just begun to heal. The wounds in my heart would take longer to heal, but no one could see them, so I did not feel embarrassed or vulnerable because of them.

Time went by, and my teammates' attitude toward me drastically changed. They wanted to be close to me, and they frequently invited me to their homes. It seemed that they just wanted to be a part of my life, and for me to be a part of theirs. I knew that I had not changed, and I was wary of their changed demeanours, but I began to realise that they had gone through the healing process they'd needed to undergo as a result of the occupation of their country. They had suffered, and it took time to get over the ordeal. Although my trust issues persisted, I had always understood that at a deeper level. I bore my own scars, and so I empathised with their need to heal theirs. What I could not understand was why they had taken out their pain on me; after all, I'd never hurt anybody. I never did understand it, but it was similar to the little girl in the barracks in northern Germany, who also had rejected my kindness—perhaps she, too, had taken her pain out on me. Recognising that I would never understand people who took out their pain on others, I chose not to let any of that overshadow my joy in the good things that came my way. I'd learned to feel good when anything in my life began to change for the better. It had been so difficult to have my childhood wrested from me—to be so young and feel so abandoned and alone. I didn't want to lose any of the good that I had now.

Gradually, the Danish authorities began to establish various kinds of support for the refugees. As this effort progressed, my teammates realised that times had changed, and they made every effort to make me feel welcome. The team prospered, and we teammates reached out to one another in friendship. Many of the bonds we forged then grew even stronger, and some have lasted a lifetime. Those lifelong friendships are the most important "trophies" I have ever received—even more than the tennis shoes, though those were essential when I needed them.

★ ★ ★ ★ ★

Many years had elapsed since those table-tennis tournaments. I became truly free, and I lived in Canada, where I was an established professional musician and teacher. I often enjoyed looking through my boxes filled with memorabilia—photographs, gifts, letters, mementos, etc. Having travelled a great distance and survived such difficult times, I treasured my memories of Denmark all the more. Although I hadn't consciously been aware of it at the time, I had gone through my healing along with the Danish people; it had become a "joint effort" of sorts, and so my love for them would always be special and dear to my heart.

How could I have ever dreamt that I would be fortunate enough to meet people willing to sacrifice their time and means to help me? But they had been willing, and their kindness had saved me. I dared to dream, even though my dreams would be shattered many times in Canada. Eventually, I started to wonder if it was meant for me to remain in solitude. *Can it be that a short-lived happiness is only a shield to delay the impact of another sorrow?* I asked myself. I never forgot how Denmark and the Danish people had given me a chance to improve my life, or how their empathy had set me on the course that proved to be my true destiny.

How well I remembered my first recital in Copenhagen! It was a short programme providing musical accompaniment for an art exhibition, and I was twelve years old at the time—too young, thankfully, to get nervous facing the audience! The only problem was that I did not have appropriate shoes for the event, and so I borrowed a pair from a friend. (Yes, once again my dilemma concerned my shoes. No wonder I pay such close attention to wardrobe selection for my tours!) The exceptional review expressed admiration for my ability, at such a young age, to interpret the Romantic period, and then it further described how I had played my selections so passionately that tears ran down my face. I loved the pieces to be sure, but I would not have shed tears for their beauty. The truth be told, one thing alone caused my tears: the unbearable pain of having to wear shoes that were way too small! Neither the audience nor the reviewer ever could have guessed.

The Christmas I'd spent at a Danish farm was another pleasant memory that I recalled quite often. I eagerly accepted the invitation from a friend to spend a few days at a small farm a little south of Aarhus. A massive snowfall, uncharacteristic for Denmark, had almost buried the house, and we two girls had to make our way through banks of the cold, white fluff as we walked from the station; it was not far, but it took hours to get there. We had so much fun tripping and falling and rolling around in the snow! By the time we finally arrived, we were covered in white powder from head to toe. Had we not had so much fun, I'm certain the walk would have conjured up awful memories of wartime treks through the snow.

We changed out of our wet clothes, and soon it was time for dinner: the traditional twelve cabbage dishes, a pork roast, and potatoes which only Danish women can prepare that skilfully. A bowl of rice pudding with chopped almonds was the dessert; traditionally, somewhere in the bowl was a single whole almond, and whoever found it received a marzipan pig. Imagine my astonished delight when I found the perfect whole almond in my serving of pudding! The adorable little marzipan pig ended up in my hands, my real smile as big as the one the confectioner had crafted on the face of the edible little creature.

The largest room of the house had been cleared of all the furniture in order to make room for the huge spruce tree that stood decorated for Christmas, complete with lit candles and Danish flag streamers. After dinner we all danced around the tree and sang carols. The hostess had baked cookies, and everyone had a small gift waiting under the tree. (Mine remains among my treasured memorabilia; I've kept it all these years.)

After carolling, my friend and I went upstairs to retire. It was a clear winter's night, and the moon hid behind the snow-filled clouds that continually cascaded a wealth of white. The snow fell in a soft steady rush, until mountains of white powder dwarfed the farmhouse. Our window faced the yard, which had become one of those mountainous white drifts, beneath which parts of the barn were still visible. We were snowed in! Again, the camaraderie kept me from sinking into painful memories. Instead, it seemed to me that peace had descended across the whole earth. *It is so special!* I marvelled. *But will it last? Can it last?*

I have stayed in contact with many of my friends in Denmark, and I remember their generosity so well. The kindly minister, the Vens, the Haugsteds, the Olsens, and many others—including the anonymous benefactor, whom I never met but who touched my heart eternally, as all kind people I've encountered have done.

★ ★ ★ ★ ★

An acquaintance of my parents owned several buildings in Aarhus, and he used a unique approach to arrange for us to move into a small apartment. I'd finished my studies, left the Olsens, and was living with my parents again. A benefactor I'd never met generously moved his grand piano into the apartment for me to use for the duration of my stay in Denmark. This was courtesy of the kindness of the owner of Hornung and Muller piano store, who had allowed me to practise on the fabulous concert instruments in his store for some time. The first music books I owned after our flight were gifts from this generous man. The ink of his inscription has faded, but my gratitude never shall—it only grows stronger each time I practise or perform Chopin's *Preludes* and *Nocturnes*.

I set up a studio in the apartment, and I taught several students there. Some of these, sent to me by the Conservatory, also had a programme: for each pianist, a couple of string players and a vocalist came to practise ensemble. This must have gone well for me, because I was sent to accompany the soloists of the Danish Royal Opera during their rehearsals in Aarhus. I was very excited to play for them! After the sessions they invited me to the café next to the opera house and gave me a large box of the favourite Danish treat: chocolate frogs. That was almost as exciting as the rehearsals, but not quite.

By that time, I had several students, one of whom, Torben, always came to his lessons with his mother. He and his parents became close family friends. The day arrived when I had to tell them of my move to Canada. I saw that Torben was crying. My grief was boundless; I was torn up inside, but nobody could see it. No one could possibly have known that my horrific childhood experiences had left me unable to show emotion. I alone knew how difficult it was to say goodbye.

★ ★ ★ ★ ★

Torben's parents continued to correspond with me for many years after I moved to Canada. Suddenly I stopped hearing from them. A while later I received a letter arrived from Torben, informing me that his parents were deceased, as were mine. Thus, we renewed our contact, much to my delight, although his parents' deaths saddened me. I developed a wonderful friendship with Torben and his lovely wife, Lene; we exchanged both letters and visits. Whenever I visited them, I had a glorious time, playing the piano and driving around the countryside; staying at their summer house tucked away on a cozy island, where warm, bubbly waves caressed the beautiful coast and clouds cast their reflection in the bay. I so enjoyed walking barefoot on the pebbles near the shoreline and picking the wildflowers that swayed in the soft breeze from the fjord.

Torben and Lene

I had many friends throughout Denmark, and I remember one visit spent in a suburb of Copenhagen. As I walked along the alley of fruit trees that led from my friends' yard to a meadow, I smiled at the laden branches that almost reached the lawn. My friends' dog decided to accompany me. Engaging in carefree mischief as only dogs can do, he rolled happily in the thistle, only to have his fur covered with the tiny thorns. He'd loved his fun but hated having to stand still for the thorns to be removed! It reminded me of our dogs at the farm. I'd learned how to smile at the happy memories and not always be overwhelmed by sadness.

These memories kept the friendships strong, bridging the ocean between Canada and my beloved Denmark like a magical rainbow, visible only to my friends and me.

I never kept a diary as such; I wrote down my feelings in my notebook, sometimes as random thoughts and sometimes as poetry. Somehow I needed to keep the memories in my heart, where they were safe—it was difficult for me to reveal my emotions. I still harboured a basic sense of distrust. Even though I treasured every kindness shown me, I continued to find it difficult to trust new people. I'd suffered so many disappointments, and I simply did not want to be hurt all over again. Consequently, I was not ready to share my recollections. As time passed, I wanted to share my story with my friends, hoping that it would not burden or depress them. I regretted that my story, by its very nature, would cause others to feel sorrow, but the time inevitably came when I had to share the story of my lone walk.

Epilogue

Boxes holding very special contents filled the shelves of my home in Toronto. The memories they represented were even more precious than the contents themselves: countless pictures, gifts, mementos, and letters, all of which reminded me of my hard work and resilience, of my dreams and plans for the life I imagined I would have in Denmark. I cherished those dreams, never having imagined that it all would end so abruptly.

It was cruel, indeed, for me to watch my dreams vanish, time after time. There was no guarantee of success, no matter how much effort I put forth. I began to feel as if I were on top of the world one day, happily surveying my achievements, only to find that it all had disappeared the next day, bringing me crashing back to earth. *Is this to be my lot in life?* I wondered. From the time I was six years old, it seemed that I had to endure losing everything dearest to me; what I did keep, I never got to keep as close as I wished or for as long as I wished. It took tremendous effort not to sink into despair.

When desperate feelings loomed, I turned to my cherished keepsakes in order to rekindle the happiness I'd felt during kinder times. The memories of the friendships I'd enjoyed in Denmark meant so much to me that I never shared them with anyone I knew in Canada.

As I ran my fingers lovingly across the surfaces of the treasures that symbolised relationships and moments I valued more than the objects themselves, a lump formed in my throat. I swallowed hard, long accustomed to holding back my tears. *Am I afraid that if I share my recollections I'll lose part of myself? Or am I afraid that others, even my current friends, will think of my story as meaningless? Am I afraid of abandonment or rejection?* I well knew the pain of loss and abandonment—the pain and panic from feeling that what most mattered to me had been taken from me against my will, without a thought or care for my feelings. *Am I willing to face that again? Am I strong enough?*

I had deeply appreciated the new life I'd been able to build in Denmark after the war; I also came to appreciate receiving the opportunity to build a new life in Canada, but the latter did take time, as leaving Denmark had devastated me. Upon leaving for Canada, through sheer force of will I had stabilised myself, inwardly promising to improve my life through my own efforts. I had willed myself to ensure a positive outcome, in spite of my grief over leaving—and then later, in the face of disappointment about my colleagues.

It was time, at last, to confront the feelings that continued to present themselves—and that I continued to deny or repress. I had trusted my friends in Denmark enough to share my story. I had to take the next step and tell my story to the world, starting with those I trusted in Toronto.

★ ★ ★ ★ ★

Some friends in Denmark had accepted me unconditionally, and they were ready and willing to go to great lengths to help me. Most important of all was their moral support, and the bond between us had grown stronger as the years went by.

Most of my friends in Aarhus were from the faculties of music and law, as a result of some mutual assignments. Ours had become a close circle, with all of us helping one another to reach our respective goals. One of those friends had taught me to paint on porcelain, a skill I pursued until I was good enough to sell my wares, earning money to buy my books for school. Another friend helped me improve my Danish, and so on. I cannot possibly enumerate here all the things we did to help one another, but that is what it means to be a true friend.

One friend among us scarcely kept himself afloat financially, and we all gave him moral support. I wished I could do more. One Christmas I figured out how to accomplish my goal of helping my dear friend, who had so little materially yet gave so much of his kindness and spirit. Knowing how much Christmas meant to him, I decorated a tiny spruce with candles and streamers, went to where he lived, and knocked on the door. The rest of our little group was waiting "in the wings" for my cue.

"Jens!" I called from the door when he did not answer my knock. I peered through the window to see him sitting at the window in his dark room. I turned the knob, and the door opened. The rest of the group dashed in, and I followed. We immediately started to sing carols, much to Jens's surprised delight! He loved the little tree I made for him, but best of all, he did not spend another Christmas alone in his unheated room.

That Christmas was a turning point for me: I had assimilated fully, and I had a close circle of friends who unconditionally accepted me. I was so happy that I could not even imagine those newfound good feelings would ever end. After all, hadn't I been through enough? It wasn't fair that I would have to endure further heartache. Yet my happiness with those friends was not meant to last—not in Denmark, anyway.

I had to move again. Words were not sufficient to express my feelings. If I'd set them to music, they would have sounded like a dirge. It felt like I was leaving my siblings behind—like I was losing Lars all over again.

Nevertheless, the law prevailed, and the time came for my parents and me to prepare to emigrate. This became an urgent decision, because refugees with no resources would have to leave the country on the last International Refugee Organization ship or face more serious issues. I was still young at the time, and, although I understood the reasons and knew my parents had no choice, I could not quite accept our imminent departure from Denmark, which I thought of as "my country," or from all the friends I felt so close to, especially after how much time and effort it had taken me to make friends there in the first place. Plus, I would have to sacrifice all my dreams, all that I'd worked so hard to achieve in Conservatory, and follow my parents to Canada. I would have to leave my students, too, and that hurt me deeply. I felt that I had betrayed them somehow, through no fault of my own. Knowing how deep the pain of betrayal could go, that hurt me terribly. The pain seemed much harder to bear than I was prepared for, and yet I was used to putting the needs of others before my own. This was no exception: I would do what I had to do, just as I always had done.

Mother's face remained etched with the suffering she'd endured as a result of having lost Lars. I could not stay behind in Denmark, knowing Mother and Father would be heartbroken to leave without me. It was time for me to cope with another goodbye, and I found no way to express my sorrow. Almost immediately, I went into denial, realising but refusing to accept that I would have to start all over again. I could not consciously face the reality of having to assiduously rebuild my life in another country yet again—this time on another continent, all the way across the Atlantic. Denial was better than full-blown panic and grief, so I remained in denial for as long as I possibly could. I could not find any immediate solution to the problem, and I had no time to search for one in any dialectic process of reasoning. Eventually, I had to emerge from denial, and the unanswerable questions remained: *Why is this happening to me? Why must I always be forced out of the place I love?*

As a small child, I had noticed people reacting in many different ways to the same circumstances. I came to the conclusion that when everything seems like it is falling apart and looking hopeless, that is the time to think positively—otherwise, the situation will just get worse. Suddenly I reminded myself of this wisdom. After all, it had kept me going throughout my childhood, during circumstances far more dire than the one I now faced. My positive attitude had become second nature to me, my one and only reliable resource—and it was what had enabled me to survive. I might have lost sight of it in my new heartache, but I had not forgotten. Quite simply, I had to think of Mother and Father, not myself. Thinking of myself would only lead to a more negative outlook. Besides, I had the resilience to begin again, but I knew my parents did not. Thus, it was evident that nothing would change the situation; I had to leave Denmark.

How I would adjust to Canada was to be an entirely different matter.

★ ★ ★ ★ ★

As the date of our departure from Denmark neared, I thought more and more of the wonderful days in Riiskov and the tender care I'd received from the Olsens. I recalled helping plant trees that had now reached maturity and cast long shadows. I could smell the intoxicating fragrance of the rose bush that had filled my room with its heady scent. I also remembered the night I'd sat in the garden after riding my bicycle to visit my parents and the wisdom I gained from my sadness.

I would have to leave all that behind, and my heartache was too raw for me to be able to see that I was only leaving the place and the people— not the memories, not the bond we shared, not the love. Memories persist—for good or ill—and true bonds and real love are eternal. Filled with dismay, I lamented that my existence was meaningless; I had no choice but to leave and put my own life on hold. I was not bitter, just sad. Eventually, I simply accepted what I had to do, just as I'd done so many times before, giving priority to the needs of others. Holding tight to my tenuous dreams and cherished keepsakes, I hoped for the best in Canada. Sometimes I wondered if the decisions that others made for me wound up causing them great disappointment because I did not measure up to their expectations. Ironically, I did what I had to do because I had no choice. I put others' needs ahead of my own, but all I ever wanted was to follow my own dream, which rarely matched anyone else's.

The moment came when I stood at the waterfront in Copenhagen. It was the third harbour of my exodus. Was my story to be the saga of the three harbours? Everyday activities continued throughout the city, and no one seemed to notice the drama at the dock. I took my last look at the verdigris patina of the copper rooftops glittering in the warm summer sun.

Anna Salen lay at anchor, prepared for a long voyage. It was a cargo ship, without any frills or fancies. The walk to the ship was not difficult—no slippery narrow plank from the dock to the deck as in Riga. I felt as if my life had become a stone, making a few ripples when thrown in the water and then sinking to the dark depths, never to surface again, just as my dear little stone had sunk in the depths of snowbank all those years ago in northern Germany. *Why is it so difficult?* I'd been forced to learn far too young that where there is love, there is also grief—it seems that the greater the grief we each have to bear, the greater our capacity for love.

How will I bear the pain of leaving? When will I stop hurting? I could not afford to take the necessary time to grieve; the future was so uncertain, filled with unforeseen demands. I had to save my strength so that I would be able to pick up the pieces of my interrupted life and start all over again.

Just as during the war and our flight, I had no time to cry.

★ ★ ★ ★ ★

Some refugees could not face the departure from Europe, and their grief culminated in suicide. Such a course of action I could never have abided, as nothing is more precious or of greater value than life itself. Love of country can flourish anywhere, but a life taken is gone forever.

In the distance, I saw a flock of seagulls circling the statue of the Little Mermaid. She reminded me of my Christmas angel from long ago. Many times I had watched the water try to reach her fins. I almost thought I heard the Mermaid whisper, "Safe journey, Lara! Come back to us. Denmark will always be here." But it was my own heart whispering through unshed tears. The only sounds I actually heard were the cries of the gulls and the cargo ship shifting in the water.

The Little Mermaid

Will there ever be a place I can call my own and not have to leave?

The anchor was raised, and *Anna Salen* set sail. I stayed on deck until I could no longer see the flag swaying from the city hall in Copenhagen. The coastline disappeared from view, and I felt as if yet another part of my life had vanished. The waves tossed the cargo ship like a toy boat, tiny and insignificant in the endlessness of the open sea.

I had developed a deep dislike and distrust of water, and I cringed involuntarily. I thought about how I was leaving Europe behind me, perhaps forever. What would the future hold for the only countries I knew? The liberation of Europe had triumphed at a high price. The question remained: Who would have to take the fall and for how long? Many issues had yet to be resolved, but at least the war was over—for some, anyway.

The Baltic countries were the gateway to the East and West, and the children of these nations learned several languages early on. Having spent my early years in Latvia and then much time in Denmark, I had acquired quite a few languages. As a result, I was placed at the radio to work as a translator during the voyage to Canada. A violent storm whipped up, and the captain urged everybody to stay off the deck. The sleeping quarters were equipped with hammocks, and those passengers already overcome by seasickness, through no fault of their own, had turned the meagre space into a disgusting mess.

★ ★ ★ ★ ★

The passengers were from all walks of life: scholars, performers, athletes, writers, doctors, and so on. The ones able to stand on their feet were joyful and provided entertainment by means of whatever talents they possessed. The largest common room was empty, with the exception of a scratched and battered piano that had obviously seen better days. The poor instrument must have sailed through many storms, as it appeared quite accustomed to the rolling sea. Those of us not overwhelmed by illness gathered in that room, soon turning it into a quite a revue, complete with singing, dancing, poetry recitations, and joke telling. Nobody noticed that the storm was worsening. Eventually, my turn came, and I approached the piano. I must say its sea legs were more impressive than mine! I had chosen to play an "Impromptu" by Franz Schubert. That proved to be quite a challenging adventure! When the passage called for the high register, the piano rolled to one side of the room; when I had to play on the lower, it rolled to the opposite corner. The piano and the bench hadn't exactly synchronised their movements, and I sometimes ended up in the middle of the floor all by myself, with the piano at one end of the room and the bench at the other! We were all relieved when the storm abated—no one more than I.

On calm days, I played table tennis on deck. When the waves had been high, the deck was slippery. More than once my attempt at a fast move resulted in my unintentionally skidding to the opposite corner. Quite frequently, the weather changed abruptly—not unusual on the open sea. The vessel would be sailing on calm waters one moment and then cutting through mountainous waves the next. I began to find myself severely affected by seasickness as the storm intensified. The voyage continued without a translator at the radio controls. The latter part of the voyage I did not even recall, having been admitted to the sickbay. The transatlantic voyage, combined with the terror of our journey across the Baltic Sea, served to make me utterly aquaphobic—something I would have to overcome years later.

At the beginning of July, *Anna Salen* dropped anchor in the harbour in Halifax. *Yet another sea voyage? Another harbour? Another journey by train now that we've landed? Is my life about anything but flights and treks and goodbyes?*

I had learned to accept the changes that were unavoidable, trying to adjust as best I could, but it was not always easy. In fact, it was usually hard. Very hard. I longed to feel secure, to feel that I had a real home and a place where I belonged, to feel that my dreams and goals were alive and well and attainable. But I could not help asking myself, *How? Where? When?*

The train ride, cutting through vast fields, dense forests, and small towns, seemed to last forever. This train was comfortable, but travelling by train in and of itself was hauntingly familiar. I forced myself not to think of the metallic serpents that had terrified me all through our flight from Latvia to northern Germany and ultimately to Denmark. Days passed, and finally the train reached its destination: the small town of Sarnia, Ontario, comfortably settled in the tranquillity of the countryside.

★ ★ ★ ★ ★

Days came and went. Our guarantor received us, offering a place to stay. Lacking knowledge of both the language and references, we had no hope of finding work. Within a few weeks of arriving, my parents and I moved to a neglected building near the foundry. On windy days the fumes infiltrated the walls, making it unbearable to stay inside. Our meagre savings dwindled quickly, and we faced hunger again.

More time passed, and the townspeople learned about the newcomers. They extended a welcome with such kindness! Just like in Denmark, the YMCA became a haven for the three of us. Soon enough, my practising would start at five the morning and continue until whenever I decided to stop.

Fall arrived, bringing cooler temperatures and brisker winds, making the fair distance from our home to the YMCA seem longer. Winter came early that year, and it seemed as if the snow would never stop. The climate in Canada was noticeably different from that of Denmark; it was more like Latvia, but I was unaccustomed to it by that point. I had no heavy winter coat or boots, and that proved a bit of a challenge. I loved the walk—it was so peaceful, with the snow so pure and white—but I was frozen! Large snowflakes fell on my fingers, and I watched them dissolve, just as the happiness of my early childhood had disintegrated. The snow always triggered my painful memories, and as I walked I would begin to tremble from both the cold and the haunting recollections of the long and fearsome winter years before. Indelible images of the past would intrude upon my consciousness for the rest of my life, unbidden and unpredictable, and I had to learn how to deal with it. I'd almost forgotten how white snow was; my frolicking in that one big snowstorm during the visit to my friend's farm notwithstanding, my memories of that awful winter of flight always showed the snow running crimson with the blood of massacres.

★ ★ ★ ★ ★

Night settled over the little hamlet of Sarnia as I walked aimlessly down the street. The lights had been turned on in the houses, and the heavy snowfall continued. Some people engaged in a cheerful conversation passed me, but I could not understand a word they were saying, which made me feel lost and alone. *I have become confident speaking other languages; when will I be able to communicate with people here in Canada, where I must make a new life for myself?* I lamented. Eventually, I did learn the language, but it took time, just as it had in Denmark. The younger we are, the easier it is to adjust and adapt. I had to give myself time, but I resisted. I longed to find my place in the world—finally!—and I didn't want it to take any more time or effort than it already had. That was folly, of course. It took as long as it took, and life forced me to be patient.

In the meantime, while I railed against the unfairness I had no choice but to accept, I continued to turn to music to fill the emptiness inside me. Music was everything to me—the only dream that did not disappear, the only joy that never faded away. Practising continued to go well, which buoyed my spirits. In addition, I was invited to perform at a country club, which helped me regain my confidence. After a few months, I received other opportunities, including radio performances. I made many trips along the winding Ontario road that took me to the radio station, where I performed live on a programme transmitted all across the province. That was exciting, but after spending a year in Sarnia, it was time to move on.

I decided to move to Toronto, and I was fortunate enough to be able to study with an exceptional teacher, Alberto Guerrero, who was known as the "musician's musician." Although Toronto was also in Ontario, relocating to a new city all by myself without any means of support proved to be quite challenging. Before long, I faced many difficulties. Discovering that a charitable association needed a typist, I applied for the position. I did not have typing skills, per se, but I reasoned that my technique and long years of playing the piano would enable me to type well enough to do the job competently. Once again, my musical talent helped me survive. I secured the position, which paid me enough to meet my rent of seven dollars per week for a small room a in house, although I barely had time to sleep there.

The only place where I could practise was the local Latvian Lutheran church, and the only time when I could practise was after ten at night, once the office staff had finished their work and gone home. A piano was located on the second floor, and I was given a key to lock up after myself. The light switch was at the very far end of a long dim hallway. All sorts of noises came from every inch of the old wooden floor, which creaked endlessly, frequently raising goose bumps along my spine and arms. But I had no choice: it was the only way I could practise, and so I made the best of it.

One night when the noises were unusually creepy, my heart almost stopped. Fear superseded discipline, and I ended my practise abruptly, grabbing the few books I had brought with me and running downstairs into the sanctuary. The light switch in the sanctuary was so well hidden that I couldn't even find it. In my haste, I had not switched off the upstairs lights, and so a faint beam filtered down the stairs, providing just enough light for me to make my way without falling flat on my face.

I walked tentatively, tripping a few times over uneven parts of the floor, and finally reaching the small steps of the platform for the organ. The church was known for having the best pipe organ in the city, and the desire to play overwhelmed my earlier trepidation about the weird noises. Finding the power switch, I flipped it, and a dim light illuminated the stand and three manuals. I pulled out a few stops and began to play from the *Well-Tempered Clavier,* a book of preludes and fugues by J. S. Bach. My legs were long enough to reach the pedals, but I was barely able to press them because I had no strength. I had little money for food, and so I subsisted on three cookies a day. As a result, I was constantly almost as hungry and weak—the latter caused by both lack of food and lack of sleep—as I had been during the war. Yet I still had my music, and I was not about to pass up an opportunity to play

Bach undisturbed on a renowned instrument! Calling upon my energy reserves, I mustered every ounce of my strength to press the pedals. The sublime sound of the organ resounded through the sanctuary, nourishing me as music alone had the power to do. Suddenly I was no longer hungry or exhausted but simply at one with my instrument. I still wonder if I inadvertently scared the life out of anyone who might have happened to pass the church at that hour of night. Perhaps the late-night resonance emanating from the darkened church even lent credibility to the existence of ghosts! Regardless, playing Bach far into the night remains an unforgettable memory—I can still hear the chords of that magnificent organ even now.

As a rule, my practise ended around four in the morning. I could not spare the ten cents for public transportation, so I walked the six kilometres back to my small rented room. After a brief nap, I washed and dressed, and then I headed downtown to work.

★ ★ ★ ★ ★

The bitter-cold winter presented problems in addition to insufficient sleep and food, as I still did not have boots or a proper winter coat. I found the underground concourse very welcoming, and at least I was able to keep warm during my multiple long walks each day.

Come spring, my current room would no longer be available. I found a small attic room in a building farther north of the city, but that created more challenges because I still could not afford the transportation fare. I continued to make the best of things, eventually deciding that I had to find an alternative means of practising—the lack of sleep was taking too much of a toll. Purchasing a piano by means of a long-term loan would leave me even less money for food, but I had no choice. After scheduling the delivery, I eagerly awaited my piano. The day finally arrived; the doorbell rang, and I jumped off my bed, all set to rush downstairs. Unfortunately, hunger had taken its toll, and I fainted before I could even emerge from my little attic room.

I recovered rather quickly and was able to accept the delivery of the piano, on which I practised many hours a day in order to prepare for my first recital in Toronto. All proceeds would go to support the Latvian soldiers. I kept Lars in my heart always; every note I played during practise and the recital was for my brother. My schedule was gruelling, but I had to catch up after all the time I'd been unable to practise; it took time for me to arrange the delivery of my piano, and in the interim I'd been too exhausted to continue practising at the church. Nevertheless, I was determined to be ready for the recital—and for the music to be perfect in honour of the soldiers who had sacrificed so much, my beloved brother most of all.

A couple of weeks before the recital, neighbours called the police, claiming that a menace had been keeping them up all night, resulting in illness and sleepwalking. Needless to say, said "menace" was none other than I, practising far into the wee hours, night after night. Seeking to incur no ill will from the neighbours—and also not wanting to lose the only affordable room I'd been able to find—I decided to resume practising at the church. It was a last resort, but I would be able to play my own piano again once I could resume a normal practise schedule.

I had to walk many kilometres every day—my lodgings were much farther from the church than my first ones had been—but I didn't mind it too much. After the first day or so, I actually found myself enjoying the time I spent walking, which calmed me. The nicest time was sunrise: I could restore myself by enjoying the peace and quiet, as I had precious little sleep or food to replenish my energy reserves. The only sounds were those of nature—the early birds chirping or the wind blowing. Pastel shades of pink and lavender limned the sky as the first rays of the sun emerged to brighten the morning. A lone stray city cat or dog might run from a narrow alley, frightened, and then hide in a doorway. Occasionally, one or two people might be out in the street, but for the most part, I felt as if the city at sunrise belonged to the "critters" and me.

Eventually, I would reach the church, which was still dark even after dawn. The creepy noises always waited for me, and sometimes I had company. Every now and then, a little mouse would sneak out of its hole and just sit there, looking at me. "Did you come to listen, or complain?" I asked aloud one morning. It continued to observe me with what I can only describe as defiance—after all, it had set up housekeeping in the church long before I'd begun practising! No matter: after sharing the grain bin in the barn with dozens of mice, the appearance of this one caused me nothing more than amusement. I simply played a very loud chord, watched the little thing dart right back into the tiny hole in the wall, and then laughed out loud.

Those creepy noises that caused me such alarm were just little mice! From then on, I never felt alone or afraid within the massive dark walls of the old church. My practising went quite well after that, and I was suitably prepared for the recital several days later. The recital itself went splendidly, and I began to feel that my life in Toronto was truly underway.

★ ★ ★ ★ ★

The years passed, and more solo recitals and ensemble engagements followed. I spent so many wonderful hours practising with outstanding musicians from Canada, the United States, and Europe. As the youngest Latvian concert pianist at that time, I felt duly honoured to have the opportunity to perform with world-renowned musicians.

One local recital was particularly memorable, and it proved to be a turning point in my life. I'd gone to the hall an hour early in order to familiarise myself with the acoustics, as was my personal custom. The hall was rather cold, and I moved quickly toward the stage. I'd expected it to be empty, and so I was surprised to see a young boy sitting in the front row. I stopped, and we exchanged greetings and introductions. Arthur, too, was a musician, and he'd been waiting in the hall for a while. We engaged in a delightful conversation, discovering that we even had the same teacher, Alberto Guerrero, whom we both adored.

It was a wonderful recital, and that preliminary conversation was the first of many. As the years went by, Arthur Ozolins and I became good friends—almost like siblings—and that was important to both us, as we each needed someone with whom we could share our joys and sorrows.

When our beloved teacher passed away, we stood together at the far back of the chapel, crying. It was more than just another goodbye; it was devastating. How could I say goodbye to the person who had become my mentor? I found myself rocked by emotional upheaval all over again. Aside from that, I didn't know if I could ever trust a new teacher, and I still sought to master my artistry as a pianist. I could not have gotten through that difficult time without Arthur.

I knew too well that no one would ever replace Lars, but Arthur did become a surrogate younger brother to me. Our relationship was very special to both of us, and our bond grew stronger with each passing year.

Over time, he earned his place among the world's outstanding pianists. Latvia still faced unsettled times then, and Arthur was going to perform there. I felt very uncomfortable about that. I went to the box that contained my greatest treasures. Reaching in, my fingers found what I sought: a tiny gold cross. I gave it to Arthur to wear as a talisman.

For some years after that, Arthur and I worked together at my home. The highlight of our collaboration was when I joined him at his sixtieth birthday recital at the Glenn Gould Studio Recital Hall. That was thrilling, and we each felt an even deeper connection, as Glenn Gould was another student of our beloved mentor, the late Alberto Guerrero.

Me with Arthur after the recital

Here in Canada I feel blessed with the friends around me. I am received with such kindness. In one very special place, I practically run from one floor up to the other, where beautiful pianos seem to be waiting for me. I almost hear them "sing" to me, and in my heart I sing a song of gratitude to my friends for their unconditional love and their emotional intelligence toward me. It helps to heal the wounds from losing my three pianos in the inferno. I have now replaced them and keep admiring their ability to help me move on. The wounds have healed, leaving scars that my three pianos, as well as the two kittens, have to contend with.

I still wonder if the piano in the attic and the grand piano in the lovely home in northern Germany where the convoy stopped for the night during our flight are missing me. I sometimes see them in my dreams, and I hope my Angel will keep them, as well as my little stone, safe. My only true friends at that time, they were instrumental to my survival and the survival of the faith and optimism I never lost—and never will.

★ ★ ★ ★ ★

It does not matter where we come from or what struggles we have endured in life; all that matters is who we each become. If we move forward in benevolence toward others, that truly is the best, and most, we can do with our lives. I have always felt that it is wrong to become bitter or malevolent after having survived horror or tragedy; if we do so, we have lowered ourselves to the level of the villains who persecuted us. All we will accomplish is losing the battle for freedom, losing the fight to value life. If we surrender to evil, we have joined those who relish tyranny, and we will help them destroy everything good and valuable.

We must cherish the simple things and always place life itself as the thing we esteem above all else. Life is a treasure of inestimable value, and if we forget that, we will lose our way.

I have always found peace sitting at the window in winter and watching my garden slumber. Bright sunshine has continually filled my home, which I share with my three pianos and my two cats, Pinky and Mauser. During Canadian winters, it can snow most of the day for days on end. The large snowflakes seem to glimmer individually in the sunset, making the whole sea of snow shimmer an iridescent white. Strong gusts of wind blow the snow into high drifts. I still love to go outside, find the highest heap, and roll around in it, making a snow angel or burying my face in the soft white powder. After all my years in my adopted country, its snow has come to smell of freedom!

My garden in winter

I sat at my window, watching the snowfall. It had simmered down considerably, but a lacing of white still threaded the sky. The setting sun slipped behind the trees, making the snow stand out even more against the darkening sky. The first stars began to twinkle, almost shyly. Stepping outside, I chose the brightest star to wish upon, just as I had during my childhood. I closed my eyes, made my wish, and then mentally whisked that star across the ocean. With one star, I blessed my homeland of Latvia, my beloved Denmark, and my adopted country of Canada. With that same star, I blessed the souls of my late parents and brother, all eternally beloved, as well as all my dear friends who have departed this earth. Again with that one little star, I blessed the dreams I would never realise and the dreams I had been able to achieve; I blessed the past, the present, and the future—I blessed all life.

Enjoying the radiance of the celestial view and the sacred silence, I breathed in the cold but did not feel any chill. The snowflakes landed on my hands in a gentle brush of frostiness. My hands were so cold that the flakes did not melt on my skin, and my breath created a smoky vapour that quickly disintegrated into the frigid air. The horizon darkened, showing just the barest tinge of gold at the rim where the sun had departed; evening had come.

At long last, the magic of winter had returned for me. The moon began to rise, casting its silvery-white beams to light my way as I walked back to the house. *What a wonderful winter's night! I have learned how to release my grief and celebrate my joy—everything in its time and place, and now I can look forward to spring.*

It had been a long journey, much of it harrowing. As a child, I'd never had time to cry, or to process any of my emotions, but now I did. More of my journey still lies ahead, but I feel safe exploring my emotions now. I will take each step at my own pace, with time enough to laugh and cry and feel. I can live as I chose, and it feels so good!

My garden in summer

Acknowledgments

As I described in the preface, I owe my humble thanks to the people who helped me to survive the exodus from my homeland, as well as to those friends who have encouraged and helped me over the years and who continue to do so. I thank all of them for reaching out to me with their emotional intelligence.

I would especially like to thank my friend and mentor for the unqualified moral support shared over the years.

Most of all, thanks to my wonderful writer/editor, Lisa Drucker, who walked so lovingly along with me as I relived my ordeal and who helped make my dream come true by capturing my thoughts and recollections so vividly in this memoir.

—VL

CPSIA information can be obtained at www.ICGtesting.com
Printed in the USA
LVOW08s1015260716

497749LV00001B/66/P